THE ASHBURNER SCHOONERS

FRONTISPIECE: The William Ashburner, *photographed in 1891 drying her sails, probably at Cardiff's West Bute Dock. She was the pride of the Ashburner fleet, and her magnificence is emphasised by comparison with the smaller three-masted schooner alongside.*

THE ASHBURNER SCHOONERS

The story of the first shipbuilders
of Barrow-in-Furness

by Tim Latham

Published by Ready Rhino Publications
1991

Dedicated to the memory of my father,
Richard James Latham, 1920–1990.

© Tim Latham 1991 All rights reserved. No reproduction permitted without prior permission of the publisher.

First published 1991 by Ready Rhino Publications,
17, Wallingford Road, Urmston, Manchester, M31 1QN.

British Library Cataloguing in Publication Data
Latham, Tim
   The Ashburner Schooners : the story of the first
shipbuilders of Barrow-in-Furness.
   1. Cumbria. Barrow-in-Furness. Shipbuilding
industries, history
   I. Title
338.476238200942781

ISBN 0-9516792-0-1

Front Cover Picture
The *James Postlethwaite* was the longest survivor of the schooners built at Barrow. She was wrecked at Youghal in 1954, shortly after appearing in the film "Moby Dick". She is seen here in the 1920's, when she still retained her original rig as a three-masted topsail schooner. [Terry Belt]
Back Cover Picture
The two-masted schooner *J.& M. Garratt* was the last wooden sailing vessel built at Barrow. She was owned at Connah's Quay and is seen here at Torquay in the 1930's. [Craig/Farr Collection]

Designed, typeset and printed by MRM Associates Ltd.
322 Oxford Road, Reading, Berkshire.

CONTENTS

		PAGE
	PREFACE	8
1	THE EARLY HISTORY OF FURNESS SHIPPING	11
	The Furness district/The Ashburners' first ships	
2	BARROW AND ITS FIRST SHIPYARD	19
	Barrow village/The first Barrow shipyard	
3	THE RISE OF BARROW	27
	Town and port/Ashburners' Hindpool shipyard	
4	SHIPBUILDING AT HINDPOOL	37
	Rawlinson & Reay/Furness Ship Building Co./Graving Dock Shipyard	
5	WILLIAM ASHBURNER & SON – SHIPBUILDERS	41
	Construction details/Building the *Mary Ashburner*/The final schooners	
6	OWNERS & SAILORS	58
	The Schoonermen/Ships' shares and shareholders	
7	TRADES	63
	Foreign trade/The short sea trade/The coasting trade	
8	THOMAS ASHBURNER & CO. – SHIPOWNERS	77
	Schooner management/The Ashburner fleet	
9	SHIPOWNERS & SHIPBUILDERS OF FURNESS	86
	The Barrow fleets/The Duddon fleets/Ulverston and Millom shipbuilders	
10	YACHTS AND SMALL BOATS	95
	Pilot boats/Yachts	
11	THE ASHBURNER SCHOONERS IN WALES	101
	Dee River ports/Schooner auctions/Welsh schooners lost/Connah's Quay auxiliary schooners	
12	THE IRISH AUXILIARIES	110
	Loss of the *James & Agnes*/Arklow between the Wars/The last years of the Ashburner schooners	
13	FIGHTING AND SURVIVING	119
	Q-23, the *Result* at War/The last survivor	
14	MEMORIES OF THE LAST DAYS OF SAIL	126
	Jim Brauders/Alan D. Maunder	
	Glossary	131
	General Index	133
	Index of Ships	135

ILLUSTRATIONS

PLATES

		PAGE
	William Ashburner drying sails at Cardiff, 1891.	Frontispiece
1A	Bow view of *Lady of the Lake*.	16
1B	The first Windermere steamers, at Bowness *c.* 1855.	17
2A	*Tom Roper*	23
2B	*Lord Muncaster*	25
3A	Barrow's Buccleuch Dock in the 1880's.	29
3B	Hindpool waterfront in the 1890's.	30
3C	Ashburner shipyard, 1990.	33
3D	*Margaret Ann* at Kippford.	34
5A	Round stern of the *Isabella*.	42
5B	Counter stern of the *William Ashburner*.	43
5C	*Mary Ashburner*	53
5D	*Isabella* under sail, entering Newlyn Harbour, 1930's.	54
5E	*M.E. Johnson*	56
5F	*James Postlethwaite* at Dover, 1922.	56
7A	*Catherine Latham*	69
8A	The wreck of the *Twin Brothers*, 1909.	81
8B	*Result* at Connah's Quay, pre-1909.	83
10A	Roa Island, 1905.	95
10B	Half-model of the cutter *Rose*.	96
10C	*Rose* hauled out, 1909.	97
10D	*Rose* under sail.	98
10E	*Rose* dressed overall for a regatta.	99
11A	*J. & M. Garratt* at Bridgwater, April 1935.	106
11B	*Isabella* beached at Par (bow view), 1935.	108
11C	*Useful* at Ellesmere Port, 1937.	109
12A	*James Postlethwaite* off Seven Heads, Co. Cork, 1931.	111
12B	*M.E. Johnson* at Newlyn, April 1936.	112
12C	*M.E. Johnson* at Narrow Quay, Bristol Docks, Sept. 1947.	113
12D	*William Ashburner* at Dover, 1920's.	114
12E	*William Ashburner* wrecked at Beachley, March 1950	115
12F	*James Postlethwaite* at Bridgwater, Sept. 1948.	117
13A	*Result* in the film "Outcast of the Islands", 1950.	121
13B	*Result* as a ketch, at Exeter in 1967.	123
13C	Foredeck of the *Result*.	124
14A	*William Ashburner* at Penzance Dock, Aug. 1935.	127
14B	*William Ashburner* at Avonmouth Dock, 1948.	129

FIG. NO.

1	Furness ports and industries	13
2	Ashburners' Barrow Channel Shipyard	21
3	Ashburners' Hindpool Shipyard	33
4	Hindpool in the 1880's	38
5	Half midships section of *Elizabeth Latham*	46
6	Half midships section of *William Ashburner*	47
7	Builders' draft of the *Mary Ashburner*	51
8	Dee River ports	102

LIST OF ABBREVIATIONS
AS USED IN FOOTNOTE REFERENCES

Ash.Hist.	Notes on the Ashburner family history, by John Ashburner.
BRL	Barrow Reference Library
BSR	*Barrow Shipping Register* at CRO
B.Herald	*The Barrow Herald* (newspaper 1863–1914)
B.Times	*The Barrow Times* (newspaper 1868–85)
Charn.Hist.	Notes on the Charnley family history, by Keith Thompson.
CRO	Cumbria Record Office, Barrow-in-Furness
CSR	*Chester Shipping Register*, at Clwyd Record Office.
Disb.Book	Capt. Robert Latham's disbursement books for the schooners *Mary Ashburner*, *Margaret Banister* and *James Postlethwaite*. Transcripts by Dr. Dennis Chapman are at the Merseyside Maritime Museum and the NMM.
F.& I.R.	J.D. Marshall, *Furness and the Industrial Revolution* (1958)
F.P.& P.	Joseph Richardson, *Furness Past & Present* (1880)
Furn.Folk	William White, *Furness Folk and Facts* (1930)
GLL	Lloyd's Library at the Guildhall Library, London
LRO	Lancashire Record Office, Preston
LSR	*Lancaster Shipping Register* at LRO
Mer.Sch.	Basil Greenhill, *The Merchant Schooners* (4th ed.1988)
NMM	National Maritime Museum, Greenwich
Obit.(R.A.)	Richard Ashburner's obituary in *The Barrow Guardian*, 4th March 1922, p9.
Obit.(W.A.)	William Ashburner's obituary in *The Barrow Times*, 12th November 1881, p8.
Reay.Hist.	Notes on the Reay family history, by Keith Thompson.
Surv.Rep.	*Lloyd's Survey Report* at NMM.
Ulv.Adv.	*Soulby's Ulverston Advertiser* (newspaper 1848–1913)
Ulv.Mirror	*The Ulverston Mirror* (newspaper 1860–85)
Wreck.Ret.	B.o.T. Wreck Returns at Public Record Office, Kew.

Photographic Acknowledgements

Photographs are acknowledged as follows: Ashburner family, 10B; Terry Belt, 8B; Dr. Dennis Chapman, 10C, 10D, 10E; Dick Charnley, 2A; David Clement Collection, 8A, 13A, 13B, 13C; Clwyd Record Office, 5E; Craig/Farr Collection, 5B, 11A, 11B, 12B, 12C, 12E, 12F, 14A, 14B; Dorothy Latham, 7A; Muriel Latham, 5C; Keith Lewis, 11C; Alan Lockett, 3A, 3B; National Maritime Museum, Greenwich, Frontispiece, 5A, 5D, 5F, 12A, 12D; Sea Breezes, 3D; Keith Thompson, 2B; Windermere Nautical Trust, 1A, 1B.

PREFACE

It is January 1991 and the VSEL shipyard at Barrow-in-Furness is preparing to launch the most technologically advanced ship ever built in Britain. When *H.M.S. Vanguard*, the first Trident submarine, is lowered on the yard's shiplift into the Devonshire Dock she will touch the water first at almost the same place as Barrow's first ever ship, launched 139 years before her. That ship, the schooner *Jane Roper*, had a wooden hull and was powered by sail, and she had been built by William Ashburner. She was followed by a further twenty three schooners built by Ashburner and his sons, of such high quality that Barrow's first shipbuilders were amongst the most celebrated of British builders of small sailing ships. This book is the story of those ships and the family that built them, from their early years and the launch of Lake Windermere's first passenger steamers in the 1840's, through until the last schooner ceased trading in 1967.

Schooners formed the majority of the sailing vessels at ports on the West coast of Britain, and in the 19th Century there were many hundreds of them, built at scores of shipyards. The Ashburners were undoubtedly amongst the leading schooner-builders and their shipyard became one of the most sophisticated of its type. Their later schooners were amongst the very few that were built from drawings rather than from a model carved from a block of wood, and this expertise in design was matched by the quality of materials and workmanship used in construction. A consequence of this was that many of their ships had long lives, and in the dying days of the sailing ships some of their later schooners were amongst the last survivors. The Ashburners launched their final schooner in 1884, but six of the last seven that they built were still sailing during the Second World War. The story of these ships therefore perfectly mirrors the history of the merchant schooners in general, more so than the products of any other single shipyard. The coastal schooners' heyday was in the second half of the 19th Century, and in these years the Ashburner schooners were built and traded all around the coast, and in some cases to Europe and beyond. Many ships were lost and after the turning point of the First World War there was a steady decline as the railways and steamships took their livelihoods. The surviving schooners earned a precarious existence in an ever decreasing number of ports until the last were confined largely to the Irish Sea and Bristol Channel. They were amongst the last working sailing ships in British waters and they eked out a living in a few remaining trades, sometimes supplementing their owners' income by an occasional film appearance, often unemployable and laid-up. Gradually they were lost by wreck or deterioration or conversion to yachts and houseboats.

The Ashburners were more than just shipbuilders, since many of the schooners built by William Ashburner were owned and managed by his eldest son. Thomas Ashburner's fleet was small in comparison to some of the other Furness fleets, but by combining shipowning with shipbuilding the family ensured that their story gives an even more complete view of the history of the merchant schooners of the North West. The final schooner to join Ashburner's fleet was the *Result*, a steel vessel built in Ireland to designs by his brother. She was acclaimed as one of the finest small sailing vessels ever built, and today, preserved at the Ulster Folk and Transport Museum, is one of the few survivors from the days of sail.

The Ashburners' story reflects not only the rise and decline of the merchant schooners, but also that of their home town. From the small village at which William Ashburner arrived in the 1840's, Barrow rose in forty years to become a town of nearly 50,000 people and a port that was second only to Liverpool in the North West. The iron ore which had given birth to the town also supported a vast number of sailing ships. The Barrow fleet of James Fisher and the Millom fleet of William Postlethwaite were the largest in the country, and there were many other schooners sailing out of Furness ports. The history of the Furness sailing ships has been recorded only in a fragmentary way, and not in the detail accorded to other prominent schooner-owning areas such as Portmadoc, Devon and Anglesey. Unlike these areas, Barrow's maritime history did not end with the passing of the sailing ships, for the town's steel shipbuilding industry ensured that it would have a maritime tradition that continues to this day. The story of the battleships, liners and submarines produced by Vickers has formed the major part of Barrow's recorded history of shipbuilding, and indeed the new museum of the Furness Maritime Trust will largely concentrate on this theme. However, the story of the Furness sailing ships deserves to be told, not least because their strength and quality of design ensured that very many of the schooners that survived into the age of photography were launched from shipyards at Barrow, Millom or Ulverston, or were first owned in these ports. Although it has only been possible to briefly describe the Ashburners' rival builders and owners, it has been my aim to at least outline the story of the Furness sailing ships and the development of Barrow as a town and a port.

Barrow has suffered the misfortune of having many records of the history of its sailing ships destroyed, dispersed or gathered into inaccessible private collections. Those that remain are housed in archives located all around Britain and Ireland. To have had to undertake all the necessary research myself would have been an overwhelming task, and this book has therefore only been made possible by the efforts and co-operation of a great many people. To all of them I wish to express my gratitude, not just for providing information, but also for their often needed encouragement and enthusiasm, and also in several cases for their hospitality as I travelled about the country.

My most valued 'informants' are Cumbrians. Trevor Morgan of Seascale, historian of the Hodbarrow schooners, provided much research material on Furness schooners. From Barrow, Alan Lockett's special interest in the yachts and pilot boats of Morecambe Bay helped with this aspect of the Ashburners' history. Carrie Garnett of the Furness Maritime Trust, together with Sue Benson at the Cumbria Record Office, collected material on the history of the Hindpool shipyards. She also interrupted a hectic schedule preparing for the opening of the new museum to show me around the site of the Ashburner yard.

It was particularly fortunate that several descendants of Barrow's maritime community had thoroughly investigated their family histories. John Ashburner has done a marvellous job of tracing his family's origins, and in this respect I would also like to thank Elizabeth Ashburner and Kathleen Mellor for providing further details. Keith Thompson has done a similarly thorough investigation into the history of his own ancestors, the Reay and Charnley families. Capt. John A. Smith D.S.C., Dorothy Latham of Barrow and Dick Charnley of Roa Island also allowed me access to family documents. My parents, Richard and Muriel Latham, researched the careers of my own ancestors who commanded Ashburner schooners. Much of the searching through archive records held in the North of England was done by them, and I extend my thanks to Aidan Jones at the Cumbria Record Office, Barrow, and to the staffs of the Barrow Reference Library, Clwyd Record Office and Lancashire Record Office who gave assistance.

Miriam Critchlow of the Manx Museum provided the material on the Ashburners' activities in the Isle of Man, and the Irish history of the schooners came from Jim Rees of the Arklow Maritime Park Project. He interviewed Jim Brauders and directed me towards another seaman who had sailed in the *William Ashburner*, Alan Maunder. Mr. Maunder's memories of life aboard this ship originally appeared in "Ships Monthly", and I am indebted to the editor for giving permission to reproduce it here. Harry Sinnott of Limerick gave details of his father's ownership of the same vessel.

In the search for photographs I was greatly helped by Terry Belt, who loaned me his own remarkable collection and directed me to many others. For further photographs and information I thank Robin Craig and David Clement. Unlike the museums they charged no fees for reproducing photographs, and their munificent attitude greatly helps in spreading maritime history to a wider audience. Derek Blackhurst advised on the history of James Fisher's fleet, and hopefully his own research on this subject will be published in the near future. My final thanks go to Dr. Basil Greenhill, whose excellent book, "The Merchant Schooners", provided my first insight into the world of the coasting schooners. His early help and continuing interest was a great encouragement during the writing of this book.

Steel shipbuilding still continues at Barrow, but the days of the sailing ships are now over and there is little left to remember them. The Furness Maritime Trust are planning to open a new museum in the town, only a few hundred metres from where the remains of the Ashburner building slips can still be seen. Displayed at the museum will be Richard Ashburner's last and most beautiful boat, the yacht *White Rose*. Together with the *Result* she bears testimony that Barrow's first shipbuilders were as much at the forefront of their craft as their successors are today.

TIM LATHAM
Berkshire, January 1991

1 THE EARLY HISTORY OF FURNESS SHIPPING

The Furness District

The Furness district is a peninsula on the Northern coast of Morecambe Bay, bounded to the West by the Duddon estuary and with its landward approach obstructed by Coniston Water, Lake Windermere and the high fells that border them. In the 18th Century this geography made Furness as isolated as anywhere in England. The main overland routes to Furness required hazardous journeys across the sands at low tide, from Lancaster across Morecambe Bay or from the North across the Duddon estuary. The alternative was along a difficult pack horse trail to Ulverston from Kendal. Neither was suitable for the transport of significant quantities of goods, so what little trade there was went by sea.

The industrial history of Furness is founded on its large deposits of iron ore, located chiefly in the area around Dalton. This ore, high grade haematite, had been exploited by man from prehistoric times, but with the arrival of the Industrial Revolution the scale of this exploitation began to increase. Mining and the local manufacture of pig iron generated the area's first substantial exports and led to a vast increase in maritime trade. Ultimately it changed the character of its shipping, from small vessels trading mainly within Morecambe Bay to the large coasting and deepwater vessels of the Victorian era.

Shipping and the early iron industry

The Industrial Revolution can be said to have reached Furness in 1711, when the first blast furnaces were built there. They were at Cunsey, near Lake Windermere, and at Backbarrow on the River Leven. Both were sited close to sources of charcoal and limestone, but the third ingredient for iron manufacture, the ore itself, had to be brought by sea and river from the mines at Dalton. To support this trade, the Backbarrow Co. had a small fleet of sailing vessels based at Greenodd, a port on the Leven estuary. In 1713 there were seven vessels, none longer than 50 feet, named the *Wherry*, *Good Speed*, *Nightingale*, *Whiteside*, *Three Friends*, *Rose* and *Dogger Spink*[1]. They would have brought ore and charcoal to the furnaces, and also carried away their pig iron. This was refined into bar iron at forges elsewhere around Morecambe Bay, or sent to market in its raw state. The coastal position of Furness benefitted its iron trade, for transport of large quantities of goods was far easier by sea than by any overland route. As the trade grew, Furness ore and iron began to be exported, first to ports on the Severn and Bristol Channel, then to the Mersey, for ironworks in Cheshire, and sometimes to more distant ports. However, it seems that most Furness vessels were small and largely confined themselves to transporting their cargo to Lancaster, where it was transferred to larger ships for the onward journey. In 1772 there were about 50 vessels owned in Ulverston, but none were larger than 30 tons.[2]

The Backbarrow and Cunsey companies were joined by others. In 1736 two new furnaces were built, one at Duddon Bridge and the other at Nibthwaite on the River Crake. From them grew the Duddon and Newland companies, and after the Backbarrow Co. acquired the Cunsey furnace in 1750 these were the only three iron manufacturers in Furness. All the furnaces were sited near supplies of charcoal, and received their ore by sea.

The supply of charcoal became a problem as the iron industry developed. There were no reliable sources of coking coal in the area, but the high quality of the local haematite meant that the charcoal process could still compete with the coke processes being introduced

---

1. Henry Peck, 'A History of Local Sailing Ships', *Proc. Barrow Naturalists' Field Club* (1951) p32.
2. *F.& I.R.*, p86.

elsewhere. The Furness companies preferred to tackle the problem by building furnaces in areas where there was a plentiful supply of charcoal. The Highlands of Scotland were the first choice, and the Backbarrow Co. established a furnace at Invergarry, Invernessshire. This was unsuccessful, and had closed by 1736. In 1752 the Newland Co. opened the successful Lorn furnace at Bonawe, Argyllshire. This continued in operation until 1874 and was supplied exclusively with Furness haematite. One small vessel that brought the ore to it in its first year was the *Flying Spark*, a 14 ton sloop previously employed carrying ore from Ulverston to the Duddon.[3] In about 1775 the Duddon Co. too opened a furnace in Argyllshire, on the shores of Loch Fyne. There was a regular shipping connection between Furness and Scotland, though it seems that this was still mostly in the form of small sloops and flats, often crewed by just a single man.

In 1818 the Newland Co. acquired the Backbarrow furnace, and ten years later took over the Duddon Co. to become sole owner of all the Furness ironworks. However, the company also owned mines, and its profits were earned largely by the export of ore rather than iron. It managed a significant shipping trade, and its goods were shipped from several different places around the Furness coastline.

The Morecambe Bay ports

Lancaster was the major Morecambe Bay port during the 18th Century, and it alone was graced with a Customs House. It acted as a transhipment point for cargoes brought from the smaller harbours around the bay, and during the second half of the Century became extensively involved in overseas trade, especially with the West Indies. After London, Liverpool and Bristol it was the fourth largest slave trading port, and it was also the first port to which cotton was imported. The main harbour was at Glasson Dock, at the mouth of the River Lune, and this was also the location for the port's shipbuilding industry. John Brockbank's yard operated from 1791 to 1820, building ships primarily for the West Indies trade – the brig *Barbadoes Packet* was one such vessel, built in 1802. Five years later he also launched one of the earliest three-masted schooners to be built in Britain, and she too was later sailing in the West Indies trade. Later Matthew Simpson established a shipyard at Glasson Dock that was to build several schooners for Furness owners.

The other harbours around Morecambe Bay were classed for official purposes as part of the Port of Lancaster and came under the jurisdiction of its Customs House. They were involved mainly in coastal trade and the most important were Greenodd and Ulverston [See FIG. 1]. Greenodd and Penny Bridge were ports on the River Crake, where its estuary joins that of the River Leven. Their principal export from the mid-18th Century had been slates, quarried at Coniston and brought by river from Coniston Water. Another product originating from Coniston was copper ore, though this trade remained fairly insubstantial until the mines were greatly developed in the following Century. No doubt these industries used gunpowder manufactured at Backbarrow, and some of this too was exported, and the sulphur and saltpetre needed by the works formed some of the incoming cargoes. Other imports were guano fertiliser and coal. With the expansion of the iron industry, ore and pig iron eventually became the most important exports, and it was only in 1781 that Greenodd acquired its first quay, built by the Newland Co. Previously the ships had been loaded from the shore, and this must have limited the size of vessels that could be received.

Ulverston lies only a few miles from Greenodd and shipped many of the same cargoes. However, its importance was as the principal market town and commercial centre of Furness, and its merchants were able to give it a greater variety of trade. Agricultural products, mainly oats, malt and barley, were shipped to the industrial towns of South Lancashire, and manufactured goods were received from them. However, like all the other Furness ports, iron ore became its most important export. The town itself was a mile or so from the foreshore, so in 1793 work started on the construction of a canal. It was completed in three years and

---

3. F. Barnes, *Barrow and District* (1981) p82.

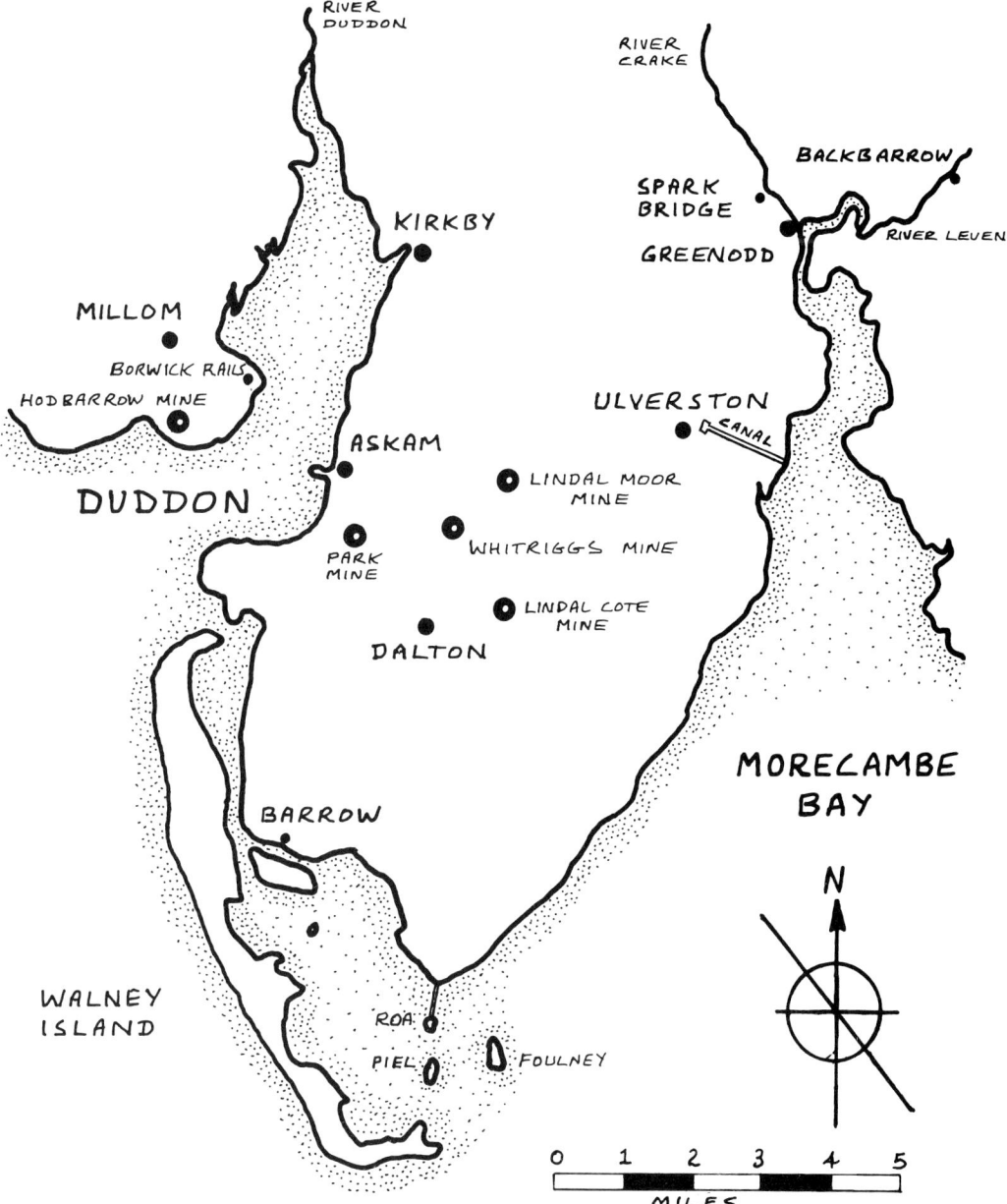

FIG. 1 *Furness, its principal ports and iron mines.*

benefitted not only Ulverston's trade, but also its shipbuilding industry.

There were many other places where cargoes were shipped. Kirkby Ireleth, on the Duddon Estuary, exported slates in large quantity. Small sailing ships did not need all the facilities of a developed harbour, and could be put ashore at any place with some shelter and a foreshore free from obstruction. There were ore-loading places all along the Furness peninsula, from Ulverston round to Kirkby Ireleth. These 'mine floors' were places where iron ore was stockpiled during the summer months, whilst the cart tracks from the mines were passable. Principal amongst them was the small hamlet of Barrow, which ultimately would become the major port of Furness.

Early shipbuilding

The sailing vessels owned in Furness were small and were built locally, at places such as Penny Bridge, Arnside and Piel. The limited records of early shipbuilding in the area suggest that a start was made on a warship at Piel Island in 1668, but that this was never completed. At Cark, ships ranging from 50 to 200 tons were built in the years up to 1750. These vessels were destined for the West Indies and Baltic trades, for the ships' owner, James Stockdale, owned a cotton mill at Cark and a plantation in the West Indies. His vessels made only one voyage each year and were beached during the winter.[4] There were some significant shipyards on the River Crake, at Penny Bridge and nearby Spark Bridge. They produced large brigantines and barquentines and, in 1800, their largest ship, the *Kitty*, of 323 tons and 20 guns.[5]

At the start of the 19th Century it was Ulverston that was home to the major shipbuilding industry in Furness. Its earliest shipyards were at Salt Cote, an area of marsh to the South of the town, and were operated by Ephraim Swainson, and by Joseph Hart and Christopher Ashburner. Hart and Ashburner were partners, and after the opening of the Ulverston Canal in December, 1796 they moved to a new yard on its banks. They built vessels of up to 350 tons, including the armed West Indiamen *Hope* and *Argo*. On her maiden voyage, to Jamaica, the *Argo* was attacked and sunk by a French privateer near Madeira. In 1811 Ashburner and Hart returned to Salt Cote to build the *Ulverstone*, at 354 tons the largest ship ever built in the town, too large to be able to pass through the locks of the canal. Eventually the partnership was dissolved, Hart continuing at the old yard and Ashburner moving to a new yard at the head of the canal.[6]

From about 1820 another yard was launching sloops and small schooners into the canal basin. Run by George Shaw Petty and William Postlethwaite, this yard was noteworthy because it provided the training for several of the most prominent Furness shipbuilders, including one William Ashburner.

The Ashburners' First Ships

Ashburner is a common surname in Furness and it seems that Christopher Ashburner, the Salt Cote shipbuilder, was unrelated to those of the same name who followed him in this profession. Thomas Ashburner was a farmer at Gameswell, near Ulverston, and was occasionally described as a sawyer, which could indicate that he too was sometimes involved in shipbuilding. He fathered ten children and five of his eight sons are known to have been shipwrights. The eldest, William and Richard, were destined to achieve most in the local shipbuilding industry. William was born in 1809 and Richard two years later. Both were apprenticed to the Petty & Postlethwaite shipyard, as possibly also were the younger sons, John, Robert and Thomas.[7]

William Ashburner in the Isle of Man

The Bath shipyard at Douglas, Isle of Man, had been opened in 1826 by James Aiken, a Liverpool shipowner. It was the first Manx yard to launch large ships, and in its first year a 206 ton brig, the *Columbine*, had been launched. The import duty imposed on timber was lower there than on the mainland and shipbuilding had flourished. A number of barques and brigs of up to 300 tons had subsequently been built and by 1831 the number of people employed by the yard had risen from twenty to about eighty. The newly-arrived manager was John Winram, son of the foreman of the Petty & Postlethwaite shipyard at Ulverston. With him

---

4. Peck, *op.cit.*
5. Alan Lockett, *Northwestern Ships & Seamen* (1982) p84.
6. *Furn.Folk*, p32.
7. *Ash.Hist.* Younger brothers were Giles, Stephen and James, who died at sea in 1847. There were two sisters, Jane and Mary.

had come William Ashburner, who had served his apprenticeship there. He was engaged as foreman, a position which earned him the wage of 1 1s per week.[8] Winram's younger brother, James, also later arrived at the yard from Ulverston, as did at least one other of the Ashburner brothers, John.

After the arrival of these Ulverston shipbuilders the Bath yard was very productive, and the vessels built ranged from large full-rigged ships for the China trade down to trawlers for the Manx fishing fleet. Details are known of twenty four vessels built in the years 1831–45 inclusive.[9] The sailing vessels comprised six full-rigged ships, four barques, six schooners, four trawlers and a wherry, with another of unspecified type. There was also a steam yacht and a paddle steamer. Several of these ships earned themselves a reputation for speed, and undoubtedly the yard placed a high priority on the quality of the ships that it produced. It must have been the Bath Yard, rather than Ulverston, that gave the foundation for William Ashburner's later achievements at his own shipyard at Barrow.

Some of the schooners were built for the West Indies coasting trade, and others were bought by Liverpool companies for the fruit trade. One such craft was the *Fenella*, a wherry of 100 tons. She was launched in 1838 and was owned by James Aiken himself. Fruit schooners had to be fast, and on a trial run soon after her launch the *Fenella* was claimed to have achieved a speed of 11 knots an hour.[10] A larger ship that achieved distinction was the *Parkfield*, a 500 ton East Indiaman launched in 1833. Four years after her launch it was reported that she had travelled 13,300 miles in 78 days, on a passage from Liverpool to Bombay, and that her previous return voyage from India had been the shortest on record.[11] Similar performances were expected of the *Dumfries*, another clipper launched for the tea trade in 1837. The *Mencius*, launched in 1848 after William Ashburner's departure from the yard, made a 118 day passage from Liverpool to Shanghai, also claimed as a record.[12]

The Bath yard produced not only sailing ships, but at least one wooden paddle steamer as well. This was the 433 ton *King Orry*, launched in 1842 – the only locally-built vessel ever to sail for the Isle of Man Steam Packet Company, and their last wooden steamer. It has also been claimed that William Ashburner built the first Douglas lifeboat, for Sir William Hillary, founder of the Lifeboat Institution and himself a Manxman.[13] Since a lifeboat built at another Douglas yard was operating before 1830, perhaps Ashburner's boat was only the first to be built specifically for that purpose.

Two years after arriving in the Isle of Man William Ashburner had married a local girl, Elizabeth Kaighin. They had three sons, Thomas being born in 1834 and Richard and William born two and four years later, all at Douglas. The Bath yard seems to have reached its peak in about 1839, when 120 men were employed there. In 1847 William Ashburner decided to return to Furness, but the Bath yard continued in operation and in 1851 John Winram was still manager and employed 47 men and 4 women.[14] He died two years later and the yard was closed down.

Richard Ashburner and the Windermere Steamships

After his brother's departure to the Isle of Man Richard Ashburner started a shipyard at Greenodd. This became the most productive of the several yards on the River Crake, turning out small fishing boats and coasters. Four of these coasters were registered at Lancaster, the

---

8. *Obit.(R.A.)*
9. From a summary of newspaper reports provided by Miriam Critchlow.
10. *Manx Sun*, 13th July and 10th Aug. 1838. A wherry was a type of fore-and-aft schooner rig, common to several Irish Sea ports.
11. *Isle of Man Advertiser*, 28th March 1837, reporting from the Bombay Gazette.
12. *Manx Sun*, 6th June 1849, quoting from a letter received from Shanghai, and spelling the ship's name as *Menseus*. She beat the iron clipper *Panic* by 18 days.
13. *Obit.(R.A.)*
14. *1851 Census*. John Winram was 44 years old and his 24 year old son, also named John, was also described as a Ship Builder.

first being *Jane*, a 41ft. sloop of 25 tons launched in 1846. The following years saw the launch of the schooners *William* and *Margaret*. They were both relatively short-lived, the *William* being lost in 1859 and the *Margaret* in November 1860, off the Pembrokeshire coast.[15] The largest vessel built by Richard Ashburner, and the last, was a 113 ton schooner launched in September 1849. The *Ann Rennison* was owned by two millers from Cark, Edward Hall and Joseph Allenby, and was commanded by Capt. Isaac Stones of Ulverston. She survived only until October 1852 when she was lost on a voyage from Ulverston to Bristol with iron ore. She had endured stormy weather all the way down the coast, losing some of her sails off Holyhead and finally foundering at Shearweather Sands in Swansea Bay, without loss of life.[16]

Richard Ashburner's most notable feat in these early years was connected not with sea-going trading vessels, but rather with two passenger steamers built for the calmer waters of Lake Windermere. The idea for these steamers was conceived by John Barraclough Fell, one of the engineers who pioneered the construction of the Furness Railway. He had long dreamed of introducing pleasure steamers onto the lake and, together with John Wakefield of Kendal, he formed the Windermere Steam Packet Company for this purpose. Their commission to build their first steamer was given to Richard Ashburner. The vessel was designed by his brother in the Isle of Man, who possibly used the experience gained from the Bath yard's *King Orry*, built only a few years earlier.[17]

The new steamer was not constructed at Richard's Greenodd yard, but instead at Newby Bridge, at the foot of Lake Windermere itself, where the River Leven begins its journey down to the sea. The river is shallow here and for this reason early plans for a propeller-driven boat were abandoned in favour of a shallow-drafted paddle steamer. Her draught was 16 inches and her other dimensions were 75 feet length and 11 feet 6 inches beam, and she displaced 49

PLATE 1A: Bow view of Lady of the Lake, *Windermere's first passenger steamer. Built by Richard Ashburner at Newby Bridge in 1845, she had a working life of nearly twenty years.*

PLATE 1B: Lady of the Lake *and the burnt-out hull of the* Lord of the Isles, *at Bowness c. 1855.*

tons. She had fine lines and her paddle boxes were designed to be as small as possible to avoid spoiling these looks.[18]

The boat's appearance owed much to the coastal schooners. She had a square counter stern, two masts and a long bowsprit, and was rigged as a fore-and-aft schooner. Between the masts was a single tall funnel, painted black with a broad white band. This served her two steam engines, which gave her 20 horsepower and a maximum speed of 9 knots. Painted black, she had gilded moulding on her hull and on her bows carried a striking female figurehead. This represented the "Lady of the Lake", the name she was to be given by her owners.

She was launched with great ceremony at Newby Bridge on Saturday, 31st May 1845. As she moved off her slip she was christened with a bottle of champagne, broken on her hull by Mr. Fell's wife. The Directors of the Windermere Steam Packet Company later presided over a celebratory dinner to which Richard Ashburner and his workforce of about fifty men were invited.

After her launch the *Lady of the Lake* did not immediately go into service, since she still had to be fitted-out. She had been launched as a bare hull, so first her masts and rigging were put in place. The interior was extravagantly decorated, her saloon in pink and white and with carpets and mirrors. She was completed, ready to sail, in eight weeks, and on the 26th July she took her first excursion on the lake. Richard Ashburner attended and Mr. Fell presented him with a silver table snuff box in recognition of his work.[19]

The *Lady of the Lake* [PLATE 1A] was the first passenger steamer to ever sail on an English

---

15. *LSR*
16. *Ulv. Adv.*, 4th Nov. 1852. The crew landed at Porthcawl after taking to their small boat. Their rail fares home were paid for by the Fisherman's Society, to which Capt. Stones belonged.
17. *Obit.(R.A.)*
18. George H. Pattinson, *The Great Age of Steam on Windermere* (1981) pp13-16.
19. This is still owned by the Ashburner family and bears the inscription "Presented to Mr. Richard Ashburner by the Windermere Steam Packet Company as an acknowledgement of the satisfactory manner in which he fulfilled his contract for building the *Lady of the Lake* steam yacht, Lake Windermere, July 1 MD CCCXLV".

lake. She had a carrying capacity of 200 passengers and regular public services commenced immediately, twice a day during the summer and then once a day over the winter period. In her first season she carried 5,000 passengers, an achievement that encouraged the Company to order, in October 1845, another paddle steamer from Richard Ashburner. Like her predecessor, this vessel was designed by William Ashburner and was of almost identical size. After being constructed on the lake shore, the *Lord of the Isles* was launched at Newby Bridge on the 29th April, 1846, almost exactly a year after her sister ship.[20]

A possible indictment of Richard Ashburner's skill as a shipbuilder is that, four years after her launch, the *Lady of the Lake* had to be extensively repaired. Her bottom had rotted, and there was conjecture that this was because unseasoned timber had been used in her construction. The following year the *Lord of the Isles* suffered even greater misfortune. Her short career ended one night in August 1850 when she caught fire at her berth at Bowness Steamer Pier, sustaining irreparable damage. Arson was suspected but never proved. At this time there was fierce rivalry between the Windermere Steam Packet Company and the Iron Steam Boat Company, which operated the iron steamer *Fire Fly*. The *Lady of the Lake* [PLATE 1B] continued her career at least until 1863, and had stopped running by 1865. She was probably broken up in a boatyard on the Lake shore at Old Fallbarrow.

In January 1850 Richard Ashburner sold his Greenodd shipyard to Samuel Schollick, an Ulverston shipbuilder, and moved to join his brother in Barrow. Only one more large ship was ever built at the yard, the schooner *Edward and Margaret* launched in 1857.

---

20. Pattinson, *op.cit.*

2 BARROW AND ITS FIRST SHIPYARD

Barrow Village

At the beginning of the 19th Century Barrow was so small that it hardly merited even being called a village, consisting as it did of only eleven houses. They were sited on the mainland side of Barrow Channel directly opposite Barrow Island. It was one of several places from which ore was shipped, the only other industry being farming. Its great advantage as a port was that it was sheltered from the worst of the weather by Walney Island, and though the channel to it was marred by shoals and sandbanks, it was no worse in this respect than the other ore loading points nearby.

The Newland Co. had first recognised the potential of Barrow as a port and had built the first quay there, in 1782. The same company had also built the quay at Greenodd in the previous year. They opted to develop Barrow as their principal outlet, later extending its shipping facilities by building a wooden jetty out into Barrow Channel. At the turn of the Century their ore shipments amounted to about 3,000 tons per annum, representing cargoes for perhaps only thirty ships. The Newland Co. evolved to become Harrison, Ainslie & Co., and was at that time the leading iron mining company in the area. They continued to prefer Barrow as their shipping point, in part due to disatisfaction with the tariffs charged by the Ulverston Canal Co.[21]

As the ore shipments slowly increased three more wooden jetties were built by rival iron merchants, the last of these by H.W. Schneider in 1842. By this time Barrow was beginning to challenge Ulverston as the principal port of Furness. In 1844 half of the Furness district's iron ore was shipped from Barrow, amounting to about fifty thousand tons. The village was still an isolated and ugly collection of houses and huts, populated by only 39 people, with another 13 in neighbouring Hindpool. The iron ore came from the mines at Lindal and Whitriggs, an average distance of about six miles from the ore loading quays. It was transported in heavily-built horse-drawn carts, hired from local farmers and carrying between 10 and 14 cwt. each. The ore jetties were each about 100 yards long and were equipped with tramways on which rode three-ton waggons. Ore was tipped from the carts into these waggons, then pushed by three or four men down the jetty and tipped into the holds of the waiting ships. If all went smoothly it was possible to load a 100 ton schooner in the duration of one tide. Most of the ore then went to the Bristol market or directly to the furnaces of South Wales.[22]

The idea of building a railway to bring the iron ore to Barrow had been considered as early as 1825, when the quantity of ore began to exceed that which could be carried by the available carts. This would have been an extension of the tracks on the jetty and would have used horse-drawn waggons. Although this idea was abandoned, the iron companies later paid for a survey of the district, as did the leading local landowners. It was their initiative that lead to the formation of the Furness Railway Company in 1843, and it was largely their money that financed it. The Earl of Burlington (later to become the Duke of Devonshire) and the Duke of Buccleuch contributed substantial sums, and of the five main iron companies in the area only Harrison, Ainslie & Co. bought shares. Barrow was selected ahead of the other local ports as the site for the railhead and the company's headquarters. The first thirteen miles of their rail network was opened in 1846, connecting the mines at Dalton and Burlington's slate quarries at Kirkby Ireleth to the quays at Barrow and Rampside. Schneider's wooden jetty, the easternmost of the four, was demolished to make way for the railway company's steamboat pier.

---

21. *F.& I.R.*, p93
22. Francis Leach, *Barrow-in-Furness, its Rise and Progress* (1872)

The First Barrow Shipyard

Although it still consisted only of 28 houses, the basis for Barrow's future industrial expansion was now in place. In 1847 William Ashburner arrived there with his family and moved into a house on Fisher-street, near to a large farm. His reasons for locating his shipyard at Barrow are open to speculation. Ulverston, his birthplace, was already well provided with shipyards, and nearby was his brother's yard at Greenodd. The opening of the railway had dramatically affected the fortunes of the two main ports. The iron companies were forced by the terms of their leases to use the railway facilities, and as a consequence Barrow's trade was expanding rapidly. In 1848 1,413 vessels visited the port, and in the following year this increased by a further 500.[23] Meanwhile Ulverston's trade was in steady decline, its canal accommodating less than a quarter of these numbers. Barrow's shipping had expanded to the point where there was certainly a need to improve the harbour facilities, and the provision of a repair yard would have been paramount amongst these. Perhaps William Ashburner realised the potential of the port's expansion, but it seems likely that Harrison, Ainslie & Co. had persuaded him to open the shipyard. His brother was already associated with them, and he himself later gained much of their shipbuilding business. That the iron company had an interest in developing Barrow harbour is shown by the fact that Montague Ainslie was one of its first Harbour Commisioners, appointed in 1848.[24]

The new shipyard was known as the Barrow Patent Slip. It was located on the mainland side of Barrow Channel, a few hundred yards West of the village and its three ore-loading jetties [FIG. 2]. A patent slip extended out into the channel, and alongside this there was space only for a single building slip. The shipyard bordered on the estate of Hindpool farm. Farming and ore shipping were Barrow's only industries, so shipbuilding was the first manufacturing industry. At first, however, the yard was used only for repair work. The capital required for its construction seems to have been raised, at least in part, by selling shares. In the summer of 1849 there was a notice in Soulby's Ulverston Advertiser, appearing for several months, offering for sale at £20 a paid-up share in the Barrow Patent Slip that had originally cost £60. Perhaps the yard was unprofitable in these early years, for soon after Richard Ashburner closed down his own shipyard and moved to join his brother at Barrow.

The 1851 Census gives the first record of the people working at the shipyard. William Ashburner was described as a carpenter employing thirteen men. Four of these men, three carpenters and an apprentice, were lodging at his home. Since they were all described as having been born in Cumberland, it is likely that they had been recruited from the shipyards of Maryport or Whitehaven rather than those of the Morecambe Bay ports. Elsewhere in the village, either as householders or lodgers, there were other carpenters, sawyers, several blacksmiths and a sailmaker and his apprentice. Richard Ashburner was unmarried and lived with his housekeeper. Another brother, Thomas, was also described as a carpenter and was undoubtedly working at the shipyard. He lived with his wife and two children.

Two other brothers, John and Robert, had been working at the Naval Dockyard at Woolwich, John Ashburner having arrived there from the Isle of Man. Robert seems to have moved to Barrow in the year after William. Only his wife and children were at home at the time of the Census, and Barrow's other three Master Mariners were also away at sea. One of these men was Robert Reay who, like Robert Ashburner, had trained initially as a shipwright before turning to a seafaring career. Five years hence he would start up Barrow's second shipyard.

The Census showed that Barrow had expanded somewhat in the four years since the Ashburners' arrival, having 75 houses and a population of 448. The professions of househol-

---

23. *F.& I.R.*, p187
24. *ibid.*, p197
25. Map compiled from 1856 plan of Barrow Channel (*F.& I.R.*, p230) and 1847 Ordnance Survey.
26. *F.& I.R.*, p194
27. *LSR*

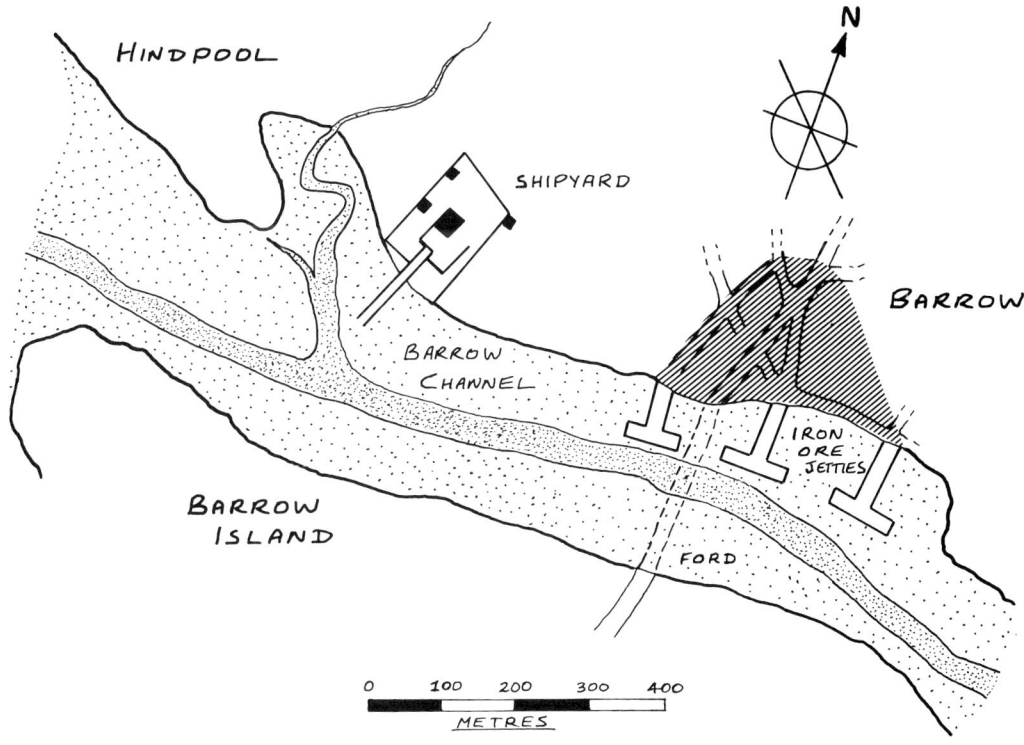

FIG. 2   William Ashburner's first shipyard, Barrow Channel, 1847.[25]

ders elsewhere in the village illustrated the course upon which Barrow was set. There were four ore agents and the Harbour Commissioners had appointed a harbourmaster. Barrow Island remained aloof from the frantic industrial activity on the opposite side of the channel. It was occupied by the Michaelson family, their servants, gardeners and a tenant farmer.

Four schooners for Harrison, Ainslie & Co.

Harrison, Ainslie & Co. in 1849 was still the biggest ore firm in Furness, producing 55,000 tons from three mines, at Whitriggs, Lindal Moor and Pennington. The company's principals were Benson Harrison, Montague Ainslie and Thomas Roper, an "astute and hard-dealing general manager" who had succeeded his father, Richard Roper, in 1840.[26] Although the company still operated four charcoal furnaces, these consumed only a small fraction of its ore output. The company's business was primarily in mining and ore shipping. They operated a small fleet of sloops and schooners, amongst which was Richard Ashburner's *Margaret*. In January 1852 one of their sloops, the 35 ton *Earl of Glasgow*, was sold by the three principals to the Ashburner brothers. They presumably bought her for repair, for she was resold to a Fleetwood fisherman after only five months.[27]

However, at this time the Ashburners would have had more important business with the iron company, for they and their thirteen employees would have been in the late stages of constructing a schooner. On the 15th September 1852 a crowd of people assembled at the shipyard to enjoy what was to become a frequent spectacle for the people of Barrow – the launch of a ship. The weather was fine, and a visiting band of German musicians contributed to the carnival atmosphere of the occasion. On her slipway stood a square-sterned two-masted schooner of 105 tons. Like the ships in the channel she was decorated with flags, and as she slid into the water she was christened with the name of Thomas Roper's wife, the *Jane Roper*.[28] The new schooner was surveyed for Lloyd's by the local tidesurveyor, Joseph Taylor of Roa Island. Her square stern was unusual for a Furness-built vessel, and possibly this was a legacy of William's experience on the Isle of Man. In other respects her construction was entirely typical, and she set a pattern that the Ashburners were to follow with all their succeeding schooners. Her heavy frames and beams were of oak, and her planking was elm, morra, greenheart and oak, with deck planking of yellow pine.[29] Her first master was to be Capt. Robert Stones of Ulverston. He was a certificated master and the ship was destined for the coasting and foreign trade. Although the ship had nominally been built for Harrison, Ainslie & Co., the ownership of her shares was widespread [See TABLE 1]. Of the men who had built

TABLE 1: INITIAL SHAREHOLDERS IN THE FIRST ASHBURNER SCHOONERS[30]

			SHARES		
			Jane Roper 1852	Tom Roper 1857	Lord Muncaster 1859
Henry Bond	Master Mariner	Barrow	8	–	8
Richard Kendall	Ironmonger	Ulverston	4	4	4
Robert Kendall	Manager – Iron Ore Mines	Lindal	4	4	–
William G. Ainslie	Clerk	Ulverston	4	2	–
James Davis	Iron Master	Ulverston	4	–	–
Thomas Roper	Iron Master	Newland	2	2	–
James Roper	Gentleman	Liverpool	–	4	–
T.G. Bissett	Accountant	Barrow	–	4	–
Samuel Radnall	Mercantile Clerk	Ulverston	–	3	–
Thomas Harrison	Labourer	Barrow	–	2	2
Thomas Harrison	Farmer	Biggins Hall, Cumberland	–	2	2
Alexander Kelly jun.	Clerk	Ulverston	–	–	4
Joseph Hellen	Rope Maker	Ulverston	8	4	4
Matthew Todd	Blacksmith	Barrow	4	4	–
John Benson	Sailmaker	Barrow	4	–	–
Robert Stones	Master Mariner	Ulverston	4	4	–
James Stones	Master Mariner	Ulverston	4	–	–
Isaac Stones	Master Mariner	Ulverston	4	–	–
James Brewer	Master Mariner	Ulverston	–	2	–
Robert Charnley	Master Mariner	Barrow	–	–	4
Richard Charnley	Master Mariner	Barrow	–	–	4
William Storey	Master Mariner	Ulverston	–	–	4
William Harris	Master Mariner	Ulverston	–	–	2
William Stones	Grocer	Ulverston	4	4	–
Adam Woodburn	Miller	Bardsea	–	2	2
John Slater	Butcher	Barrow	–	2	2
James Mason	Draper	Ulverston	–	2	–
James Tyson	Innkeeper	Barrow	2	2	4
Joseph Walton	Farmer	Walney Island	2	2	–
Thomas Greenwood	Farmer	Walney Island	2	4	4
Robert Greenwood	Gentleman	Walney Island	–	2	–
Thomas Thompson	Gentleman	Kirkby Ireleth	–	2	–
Robert Woodend	Gentleman	Kirkby Ireleth	–	1	–
Elizabeth Townson	Spinster	Bardsea	–	–	4
James Ashburner	Gentleman	Bardsea	–	–	4
Richard Ashburner	Gentleman	Barrow	–	–	2
John Richardson Crayg	Gentleman	Walney Island	–	–	2
William Hawkrigg	Farmer	High Seathwaite	–	–	2

PLATE 2A: Tom Roper, *date and artist unknown.*

her, only the blacksmith, ropemaker and sailmaker invested in her future.

The shipyard continued to be largely occupied by repair work and it was five more years before the next new ship was built. She was the *Tom Roper*, slightly larger than her sister ship but also a square-sterned two-masted schooner [PLATE 2A]. She had been built to Lloyd's Special Survey and was given Lloyd's highest classification for materials, 12 years A1. Not only was her frame of English oak, but her outside planking was largely oak and teak. She was launched in July 1857 and her first master was to be the same Capt. Stones that had earlier been in charge of the *Jane Roper*.[31]

This second launch for the Ashburners was soon followed by others at Hindpool. William Gradwell had established a Steam Saw Mill there and was importing timber from abroad. He launched what was described as a small boat in August 1857. That this was probably a

---

28. Launch described in *William Fisher's Manuscript diary and Commonplace book 1811–59*, Lancaster University Press.
29. *Surv.Rep.(Jane Roper)* LIV 11640 Box 582.
30. The table is compiled from the list of shareholders in the three ships at the date of their first registration in *LSR*. The occupations and residence of the shareholders are as listed there. Some assumptions about family relationships and the exact nature of their occupations have been made in grouping together those who were possibly involved with Harrison, Ainslie & Co.
  The 1851 Mannex Directory (*History, Topography, and Directory, of Westmoreland*, republished by Michael Moon, 1978) states that James Davis of the Furness iron & steel works was resident at Tytup Hall, between Ulverston and Dalton. Samuel Radnall was a book-keeper at the Furness iron works. Thomas Bissett was manager of the goods department at Barrow Railway Station. He was listed as the managing owner of the *Tom Roper* in the *Mercantile Navy List*, 1871.
  Mannex describes Matthew Todd as a blacksmith and shipsmith resident at Barrow, and James Tyson was landlord of the Burlington Arms at Barrow. The two Ashburners mentioned were unrelated to the shipbuilding family.
31. *Surv.Rep.(Tom Roper)* LIV 14679 Box 14.

pleasure yacht can be inferred from the Ulverston Mirror's report, which expressed the hope that "this beautiful new boat . . . will be a stimulus to incite others to improvements in boat construction before the next Barrow regatta".[32] Boatbuilding was only an occasional occupation for Gradwell. His main business was as a timber merchant and builder, and eventually he would build many of Barrow's principal buildings and much of its housing. A month after Gradwell's launch the patent slip at Barrow's second shipyard was nearing completion. Alongside the slip a two-masted schooner, the *Gummershow*, had been built and was ready for launching. The yard's proprietor was Joseph Rawlinson and the ship had been designed by one of his partners, Robert Reay. When the patent slip eventually came into service they were able to compete with the Ashburners for repair work. Since Rawlinson was himself a rival ore merchant, the new yard's shipbuilding activities would not have attracted any attention from Harrison, Ainslie & Co.

The iron company's fleet in 1857 comprised nine schooners and three sloops. Its ore output had risen to 200,000 tons, virtually all of which was exported by sea, amounting to half the total ore shipped from Barrow in that year. Barrow's ore exports were being taken principally to South Wales (about half), the rest going to Staffordshire, via the Mersey ports, Cleveland and the West Riding of Yorkshire. This was far too much to be carried by the still few local schooners, and many Welsh-owned schooners became involved in the trade. In 1859 the Anglesey schooner *Heir Apparent* visited Barrow five times to load ore for South Wales ports. On three of these occasions she purchased repairs or materials from the Ashburners, including a new gaff charged at 10s 2d. Matthew Todd, the Ashburners' blacksmith, also carried out repairs for her.[33]

The third Ashburner schooner, also built for Harrison, Ainslie & Co., was the *Lord Muncaster*, launched in March 1859 [PLATE 2B]. Although she too had been built to Special Survey, her materials were of a lower quality than her predecessors and she was only classed 9A1. The emphasis in her design was on speed rather than strength, for her hull was longer than that of the *Tom Roper*, but narrower and shallower.[34] She was ultimately to earn herself a reputation as one of the fastest of Barrow's two-masted schooners. Her name derived from Lord Muncaster, of Muncaster Castle in Cumberland, who owned the company's Gilbrow mine at Pennington.

The fourth schooner for the iron company was the fifth from the yard, the *Mary & May*, launched in April 1862. Of 97 gross tons, a similar size to the *Lord Muncaster*, she was destined for the same iron ore trade, under the first command of Capt. John Thomas.

Later schooners from the Barrow Channel shipyard

William and Richard Ashburner had bought shares in several sloops and small schooners during their first ten years at Barrow, principally amongst those managed by Thomas Fisher, a Dalton ore merchant. They did not however retain any shares in their own earliest vessels, presumably because they were investing their income into the shipyard. It was only with their fourth schooner, the *Mary Jane*, that some of the shares were kept within the family. She had been built for Capt. Robert Ashburner. He was then commanding the schooner *Isabella Fisher* in the coasting trade, but in his twelve years since arriving at Barrow from the Woolwich dockyard he had become an experienced deepwater captain. His new ship was 180 tons burthen and was designed for the same coasting and foreign trades as her predecessors, and Robert was to be both her managing owner and master. His daughter's name was given to the ship, and when she was launched, on the 20th August 1860, it was the fourteen-year old Miss Ashburner who performed the ceremony.[35] Robert was the principal shareholder in the new vessel, and his brothers and William's two eldest sons also retained shares.[36]

The Ashburner yard was now less confined to repair work. From the time that the *Mary Jane* was started there was always to be at least one new ship under construction, and after the launch of the *Mary & May* two new ships went onto the stocks. These were completed in the following year and were launched together on the 4th July 1863. They were both schooners, though of markedly different design. The *Elizabeth Barrow* was the second to enter the water. She was built in the tradition of William Ashburner's first five ships, and was of similar size,

PLATE 2B: Lord Muncaster *by J.S. (probably Joseph Semple), undated. Built for the Spanish ore trade in 1859, this fast schooner made a record passage from Cardiff to Lisbon in 1863, under the command of Capt. Robert Charnley.*

with a cargo capacity of 180 tons. Like them she had a certificated master, Capt. James Pernie of Ulverston, and had been principally designed for the Spanish ore trade. All the previous ships were trading, during the summer at least, to Spain, Portugal and Gibraltar.

The first schooner to enter the water had been the *Furness Maid*. At only 49 gross tons she was the smallest schooner that the Ashburners built at Barrow, and perhaps her size was limited by the available building space in the shipyard. She was destined for the short sea trade around the Irish Sea. Her launch marked a change in direction for the Ashburners, who in the next eight years would largely concentrate on building this type of small schooner. The first master of the *Furness Maid* was a Tarleton-born seaman, Capt. John Latham.[37]

Despite this beginning of a change of emphasis for the shipyard, the next vessel was a far cry from the small schooners of the short sea trades. The *James & Agnes*, of 131 tons (about 220 tons burthen) and 93 feet in length, was the largest two-master ever built by the Ashburners, and she was to spend her early life almost entirely on deepwater. Apart from her size, she had other features to distinguish her from her closest contemporaries. She was built to a high classification, 12 years A1 at Lloyd's, and was given an elliptical counter stern, an extravagance that North West shipbuilders only allowed themselves with their finest schooners. She

---

32. *Ulv.Adv.* 10th Sept. 1857. The regatta mentioned was organised by the Royal Mersey Y.C. and the Royal Western Y.C. of Ireland. It took place at Piel and was reported in *Ulv.Adv.* 18th June 1857.
33. Aled Eames, *Ships and Seamen of Anglesey* (2nd. printing 1981), Appendix 10.
34. *Surv.Rep.(Lord Muncaster)* LIV 15679 Box 14.
35. Launch is described in *Ulv. Mirror*, 25th Aug. 1860, p4. In the *Captains Register*, GLL 18567/1, Robert Ashburner is noted as having commanded the *Mary Jane* until 1866, firstly in the coasting trade and then in the Spanish, Baltic and Mediterranean trades. His career after this date is not mentioned.
36. See p61 for list of initial shareholders.
37. *Ulv.Mirror*, 11th July 1863. This launch report states that the first commander of the *Furness Maid* was to be Capt. Salthouse. This is contradicted by LRO Crew Lists and *LSR*.

was launched in October 1864 and her first master and managing owner was to be Capt. James Brockbank of Ulverston.

At the time of the launch of the *James & Agnes*, work on the construction of Barrow Docks was already underway. The Channel was being walled in, eventually to be sealed by lock gates to form a wet dock. The Ashburners would be obliged to relocate their shipyard and they agreed to its sale to the Furness Railway Company, who were responsible for the dock developments. They still had time to build one more small schooner. This last vessel from the Barrow Channel yard was the *Alice Latham*, the ninth schooner built there. She was a short sea trader of 140 tons burthen, built for the command of Capt. John Latham of Tarleton. She was launched by Eliza, daughter of Capt. Henry Bond jun., on the 7th September 1865.[38] After the ceremony a celebratory dinner was held at the Ship Inn, chaired by Thomas Roper. No doubt amongst the toasts was one to the future success of William Ashburner's new shipyard at Hindpool, for shortly after the launch the last of the yard's machinery was to be moved to its new location. Possibly there was also a toast to Richard Ashburner's new enterprise, for the launch of the *Alice Latham* marked the end of his involvement with shipbuilding. It seems that William had been the active partner in the shipyard, and Richard had only ever been credited as a co-builder of the *Jane Roper*. After his retirement he invested his capital in property and began to describe himself as a gentleman – the contemporary title of one who earned his income from investments rather than labour. He bought several cottages and also the Bowling Green Hotel in Barrow's Greengate, where many of the future launches of his brother's ships were to be celebrated. Upon his death in 1873 he left an estate of £5602, and since he was unmarried this was bequeathed to his brothers and nephews.[39]

---

38. *Ulv. Adv.* 14th Sept. 1865. This Capt. John Latham, b.1819, was ten years older than his namesake in command of the *Furness Maid*, to whom he was unrelated (Crew Lists of *Alice Latham* and *Furness Maid* at LRO). There seem to have been four unrelated Latham families from Tarleton providing captains for Barrow and Duddon schooners.
39. Papers relating to Richard Ashburner's estate, CRO Z712 & Z732.

3 THE RISE OF BARROW

Town and Port

In the ten years following William Ashburner's arrival in Barrow its growth had been relatively slow. Despite continuing discoveries of iron ore, there had been little industrial development beyond mining and shipping, and the town was inhabited by only about 800 people in 1857. In the following decade, however, Barrow was to experience an expansion of both industry and population that was almost without parallel elsewhere in Britain. By 1867, the year which saw the town's incorporation and the opening of the new docks, Barrow's population had increased twenty-fold.

William Ashburner witnessed this astonishing development. Upon his arrival from the Isle of Man he had built his first shipyard in what was essentially a rural environment. The yard had been bordered by only a handful of farms and houses, and had looked across Barrow Channel to the pastoral splendour of the Michaelson Estate on Barrow Island. By the time he moved to his second shipyard at Hindpool, the island, like most of the Barrow waterfront, had been acquired by the Furness Railway Company and was laid out for industrial use. Industries had already been established at Hindpool and the new shipyard was surrounded by works of various descriptions, with construction of the town's infrastructure, docks, railways and roads, proceeding apace. All this activity ultimately derived from the exploitation of iron ore, and it was powered by the ambitions of two men, the iron magnate H.W. Schneider and the railwayman, James Ramsden.

The Iron Industry

Ore mining and shipping were not large employers of labour, and it was only with the construction of the ironworks that Barrow began to increase in size and significance. The initiative came from H.W. Schneider, a London capitalist who had arrived in Furness in 1840 to prospect for iron ore. Having no initial success, he bought an existing mine at Whitriggs and began to export ore from Barrow, building a fourth jetty in Barrow Channel for the purpose in 1842. Prospecting did continue and eventually brought success, with the discovery of the massive Park deposit at Askam in 1851.[40] This mine was to prove to be the second largest ore deposit ever discovered in Britain, and was eventually to yield more than eight million tons of ore. Together with lesser ore discoveries made by rival companies, and the development of existing mines, Furness ore production began to increase rapidly. With the Furness Railway as yet isolated from the main railway network, the entire output was transported by sea. In 1857, when Furness ore exports reached their peak, 562,095 tons, 95% of production, was exported through the port of Barrow.

The ore mines were not to reach their peak of production for a further twenty five years. Ore exports declined because Schneider and his partner, Robert Hannay, built their own ironworks, after which an increasing amount of the ore was used locally. Construction of the works at Hindpool began in 1857, and was in part motivated by the forthcoming completion of the link between the Furness Railway and the main rail network at Lancaster. This would provide a ready means for importing the great quantities of Durham coal needed by the blast furnaces. The new furnaces produced their first pig iron late in 1859, and thereafter expanded rapidly. Other smaller ironworks were being built around Furness, and in 1864 the Furness Railway Company introduced the local manufacture of steel by the Bessemer process, forming the Barrow Steel Company for this purpose. In 1866 the two iron and steel companies amalgamated to form the Barrow Haematite Iron and Steel Company.[41] Eventually, in 1876, this

---

40. *F.& I.R.*, p203.
41. *ibid.*, p252.

company was to have sixteen furnaces in production, at the time the World's largest iron and steel plant.

These developments did not detract from the trade of the sailing ships. Not only did the steel and pig iron have to be exported, but such was the scale of the ironworks that eventually Barrow established a large import trade in ore.

Barrow Docks and Industrial Expansion

The formation of the Barrow Haematite Co. brought Schneider into the fold of the Furness Railway Company. Owned by the principal local landowners, it was this firm that was largely responsible for the development of Barrow. The driving force behind the company was James Ramsden, and his influence on the town can hardly be overstated. He had arrived at Barrow in the year before William Ashburner, as the first manager of the railway company, eventually becoming its general manager and then a director. His influence extended beyond the railway and he initiated the schemes for the steelworks, the docks, steel shipbuilding and jute manufacture, as well as involving himself in all the town's municipal affairs. His vision was of a port to rival Liverpool and a town of 100,000 people. Though this goal was too ambitious, defeated by the isolation of Furness and the ultimate exhaustion of the iron ore, his achievements were nevertheless extraordinary. The most enduring of these was the steel shipbuilding that still dominates Barrow's economy, but it was perhaps the dock developments that were his grandest scheme.

After the development of the ironworks, and the expansion of ore mining in the late 1850's, there became a need to improve Barrow's shipping facilities. Berthing space in the harbour was limited and, more critically, its tidal nature made it unsuitable for the larger ships employed in continental trade. Barrow's overseas exports were transported first to Liverpool or Bristol by coasting vessels, and then transferred to larger ships for passage across the Atlantic. The Furness Railway Co. sought to remedy this, and in 1863 an Act of Parliament gave them jurisdiction over the harbour and authority to build new docks. Although this would to some extent help the coasting vessels that competed with the railway for inland transport, the company had more to gain if it could establish Barrow as an industrial town and a major port for foreign trade.

The railway company's plan was to enclose Barrow Channel with lock gates and divide it to form two wet docks. The capital for the work, originally £137,000, was raised principally from the Duke of Devonshire and the Duke of Buccleuch, after whom the first two docks were to be named. The railway company bought up the land around the channel, including the whole of Barrow Island and, on the mainland side, the Ashburner shipyard. Work started in 1865, at first on what was to become the Devonshire Dock, at the Western end of the Channel. It was a massive project, taking more than two years to complete and at its height employing 2,000 men in its construction. The extent of Barrow's sea trade at this time, and the need for new harbour facilities, is illustrated by a report that on a single day in January 1866 more than 300 ships sailed from Piel Roads after lying windbound due to heavy weather.[42]

Alongside the docks were built wharves and warehouses, all amply supplied with railway sidings to allow the railway company ready access to the ships. The total development covered 450 acres, composed of about 100 acres of water area, 100 acres of wharves and the remainder intended as industrial sites, principally for shipbuilding. The dock entrance was sixty feet wide, more than adequate for the largest ships of the time, as was the minimum 22 feet of water maintained in the dock. Around the docks themselves were 1½ miles of stone quays, provided with more than ten miles of railway sidings and warehouses, four stories high, and with a total floor area of 1,700 sq. yards. These were provided with hydraulic cranes to allow unloading directly from the ships.

---

42. *Ulv.Mirror*, 13th Jan. 1866.
43. *Ulv.Mirror*, 31st Aug. 1867.
44. "Opening of Barrow Docks" in *Ulv.Mirror*, 21st Sept. 1867, pp6–7.

PLATE 3A: Barrow's Buccleuch Dock, crowded with sailing vessels in the 1880's. The brigantine on the right of the picture is drying her sails, and most of the other vessels appear to be schooners.

By the summer of 1867 the Devonshire Dock was largely completed and a grand opening was planned for September. However the pressure from shipping was such that James Ramsden decided to open for business before the official opening ceremony. On Saturday 24th August, 1867, the steam yacht *Dione*, with Ramsden, H.W. Schneider and their wives aboard, towed the first vessel through the dock entrance. She was the *W. & M.J.*, a new schooner being delivered from Gowan's shipyard at Berwick-upon-Tweed to Barrow's leading shipowner, James Fisher. For being the first ship to enter the new docks she was rewarded with an exemption from all future harbour dues.[43] The first vessel to unload a cargo there was the Ulverston schooner *Caroline*, four days later. She was soon followed by others and in the period until the opening ceremony there were always between fifty and sixty ships in the dock.

The formal opening took place on the 19th September and was a great event in Barrow. The many public celebrations were headed by a banquet for 1,200 people, held in the railway carriage shed. It was presided over by the Duke of Devonshire and William Gladstone, late Chancellor of the Exchequer and future Prime Minister, was the guest of honour.[44] There was more than just the new docks to celebrate, for the most optimistic of those present saw Barrow expanding to rival Liverpool as a deepwater port. There were plans to introduce new industries onto the land surrounding the docks, and sidings had already been laid to ensure that the railway company benefitted from these as well. In May 1870 William Gradwell's company started work on building a corn mill on the site of the old Ashburner shipyard. Soon after, a flax mill was built, also alongside the dock. Both provided more cargoes for the Barrow ships, with deepwater vessels importing maize, wheat and flax, and the jute and flour being carried outwards by the coasters.

Subsequent years saw some further major advances for Barrow's shipping. In 1868 a Customs House was opened, and it became possible for ships to be registered locally rather than at Lancaster. The first ship to do so was Fishers' schooner *Ellen Clifford*. Four years later, at the instigation of James Fisher, Barrow was separated completely from Lancaster's jurisdiction and became a port in its own right. The dock works proceeded, with the Buccleuch Dock being opened in 1873 [PLATE 3A] and the Ramsden Dock in 1879.

PLATE 3B: *The Hindpool waterfront in the 1890's. Although the Ironworks can clearly be seen, the only signs of the shipbuilding industry that once prospered here are the two grid-irons in front of the sea wall.*

Barrow's status as a town had been confirmed in June 1867, when it received its Charter of Incorporation. Local government passed into the hands of a local council, in the first instance nominated by the Duke of Devonshire. Not surprisingly, the council was drawn from local industrial interests, and its members were largely connected with the iron and railway companies. Ramsden was appointed as Mayor and Schneider became an alderman, and amongst the twelve councillors local shipping interests were represented by James Fisher, Joseph Rawlinson and William Ashburner.[45] Fisher was Schneider's shipping agent and Rawlinson, principally involved in mining, had his own fleet of ships and a shipyard at Hindpool. Only Ashburner could claim to be somewhat distanced from iron interests, and his appointment to the council illustrates the degree to which he had established himself in Barrow's business community in his twenty years in the town. He served on the council for six years, and later his son, Thomas, was to become an alderman.

Ashburner's Hindpool Shipyard

During its early quest to purchase land along Barrow's seafront, the Furness Railway Company had bought, in 1854, a large estate of 160 acres at Hindpool. The Ironworks had been built on the Northern edge of the estate and a road and railway ran South to the Barrow Channel wharves. The land between Ironworks Road and the Walney Channel foreshore had been laid out for industry, principally shipbuilding and timber yards. Amply provided with railway sidings and in close proximity to timber dealers and saw mills, it was therefore ideally suited to William Ashburner's purpose. He chose a four acre plot for the site of his new shipyard, midway between a planned graving dock and the already established yard of Joseph Rawlinson [PLATE 3B].

The new shipyard was opened in September 1865,[46] but it was only in May of the following year that the new patent slip was ready for use, when the Furness Railway Company's steamer *Helvellyn* was possibly the first ship to be repaired on it, prior to commencing her

---

45. F. Barnes, *Barrow and District* (1981) p108.
46. *Obit.(W.A.)*

summer passenger service between Piel and Fleetwood. Two months later the slip was being used to repair a large barque, and under construction beside her there were three new vessels.[47] The first of these to be launched was the *Nanny Latham*, a small schooner that was in service under the command of Capt. Thomas Latham before the end of the year. She was of almost identical size to the *Alice Latham*, as was the next schooner to be completed. She was the *Catherine Latham*, launched on the 7th May 1867.[48]

The Ashburners' shipyard was known as the Hindpool Shipbuilding Yard and Steam Saw Mill. About 70 men were employed there,[49] though by 1880 when the yard was probably at its busiest, there were more than a hundred employees.[50] Each day William Ashburner would arrive at the yard at 5.30 a.m., ringing a bell at 6 a.m. to start the day's work. He did this until his health prevented him, two weeks before his death. The working day was from 6 a.m. until 6 p.m., though on Saturdays the yard was closed at 4 p.m. For working such arduous hours, the Ashburners' carpenters were rewarded with the sum of four shillings and sixpence per day.[51]

Ships were built on two building slips at the sea wall [FIG. 3, PLATE 3C]. Each was served by a railway siding that allowed timbers to be carried from the saw mill. More sidings served the saw mill, bringing in the uncut wood from the adjacent timber yards. The patent slip was at the Southern edge of the shipyard. It provided a means of hauling ships out of the water and into the yard, and was therefore used for repair rather than building [PLATE 3D]. There was a breach in the sea wall about 15 metres wide and the walls came back into the yard for about 50 metres, after which the sides of the slip were built up with an earthen embankment. A double line of rails ran down the centre of this cutting, extending from the engine room at the head of the slip for 110 metres to the ordinary tide line at the sea wall, and then beyond to the low tide line. On these rails ran a wooden cradle onto which a ship could be floated, then hauled up into the yard. The windlass which pulled the cradle and its load out of the water was driven by a 25 h.p. steam engine and was capable of hauling up ships of 500 tons. The length of the slip in fact allowed it to accommodate two or even three ships and contemporary reports indicate that the Ashburners did do this. Probably they would have put a second cradle onto the rails behind the first ship, then run a cable beneath its keel to haul up the second ship.

The patent slip would have been used where work was required below the waterlines of the ships, such as yellow-metalling, or for extensive repairs or alterations. Ships less seriously damaged could be repaired on the foreshore, where there was a grid-iron laid at the foot of the sea-wall. The ships were floated onto this lattice of timber keel blocks and were then secured to the mooring posts above the wall. Many less sophisticated shipyards were provided only with such a grid iron, yet were still capable of undertaking repairs to damaged hulls and keels. Hugh Jones' yard at Millom was not equipped with a patent slip, and neither were any of the yards in the Ulverston Canal basin.

The steam engine that powered the slip's windlass was also used for driving woodworking machinery. This was housed in a saw mill adjacent to the engine room. In 1872 this machinery included morticing and moulding machines and lathes, used amongst other things for turning wooden treenails. Vertical and circular saws were added later, but at that time the sawing was done by hand. The saw pits were housed in the same building. On the South side of the yard was a row of buildings housing the pitch boiler, the blacksmith's shop and another sawpit. Above the sawpit was a carpenters' shop where items such as hatch covers, blocks and skylights were crafted. At the corner of the yard, adjacent to Ironworks Road, were paint

---

47. Reported in *Ulv.Mirror*, 19th May & 7th July 1866. The *Helvellyn* is described in *LSR* as an 87 ton schooner-rigged paddle steamer, built at Glasgow in 1847 and owned by James Ramsden, Secretary of the Furness Railway Co.
48. *Ulv.Mirror*, 18th May, 1867 – She was to be captained by Capt. John Latham of the *Elizabeth Barrow* and was named after his wife.
49. F. Leach, *Barrow-in-Furness, its Rise and Progress* (1872)
50. *F.P.& P.*, pp53–54.
51. *Obit.(R.A.)*

stores and the site office. A galvanising tank was also sited in the yard, introduced by Richard Ashburner.

The Ashburner sons

William Ashburner's three sons all served apprenticeships in their father's shipyard, and eventually each acquired a distinct role in its operations. Nevertheless, their father continued to supervise the running of the yard until shortly before his death, and it was he alone that was credited as the ships' builder in the Shipping Registers.

Richard, the second son, received formal training as a naval architect. It was probably in the late 1860's that he began to take a leading role as shipyard manager and designer. It was then that the yard changed its title to "William Ashburner & Son". Richard was also credited with the introduction of galvanising at the yard, which occured in 1868. Together with his family, he lived at a house on Ironworks Road, adjacent to the site. Richard Ashburner's principal distinction was that he was one of the few schooner builders who designed his ships on paper.[53] Naval ships had been designed in this way for many years, as were many large wooden merchant ships and all iron and steel ships. However, most small vessels were designed from carved wooden models. Three sets of Richard Ashburner's constructional drawings survived until the 1970's, the earliest being for the *William Ashburner*. Probably all the ships after this, and possibly some before, were also built from drawings.

Richard's elder brother, Thomas, had begun his own sailmaking and mastmaking business and in 1864 had constructed a building in Fisher Street especially for sailmaking.[54] His uncle, Robert Ashburner, was also associated with this business, and was also managing some of the early schooners. As the Ashburners bought back shares in vessels originally sold to other owners, and retained substantial holdings in the newly launched schooners, a fleet began to be built up. Thomas became their managing owner and by the early 1870's he was directing a small fleet of ten schooners, only one of which was not Ashburner-built. As he became more involved in ship management, the sailmaking business was put under the direction of William Hurford. It eventually became known as the Barrow Sailmaking Company and supplied sails for all the later Ashburner ships.

William, the youngest son, was first in charge of the ships' chandlery business, run from premises in Duke Street. He later became involved in cabinet-making and upholstery, and from 1872 worked from a 4,000 sq. ft. room at the shipyard. He seems to have been primarily involved in making and selling household furniture, rather than fitting out ships. Upon their father's death it was to be Thomas and Richard who would be largely responsible for carrying on the shipping business.

The first three-masters

Three-masted schooners were uncommon in British fleets before the 1870's, but thereafter it became the preferred rig for the larger schooners. The advantage over the two-masters was that their fore-and-aft sails were smaller and easier to work. This was especially beneficial when reefing in bad weather, and this meant that a smaller crew could be carried than on a two-master of similar hull size.

William Ashburner was the first of the Furness shipbuilders to launch a three-masted schooner, though in a national context he was relatively late to experiment with this type of rig. The *R.& M.J. Charnley* had taken over two years to build and was launched in a heavy storm on the 23rd May, 1868. She was bigger than the largest Ashburner two-master, the *James & Agnes*, and had a carrying capacity of 280 tons. She seems to have been something of an experimental ship for the Ashburners in areas other than her rig, for she was their first ship

---

52. BRL Port Map (1873)
53. *Mer.Sch.* p50.
54. In BRL *Mannex Directory 1866* Thomas Ashburner is listed as a shipsmith, sailmaker & mastmaker (T. Ashburner & Co.), but not as a shipping agent or owner.

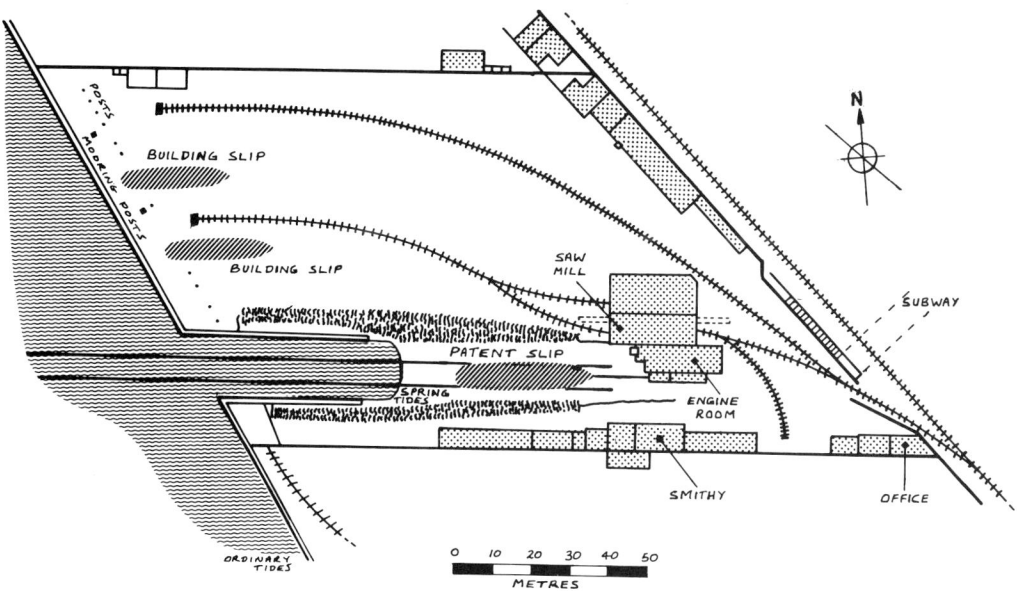

FIG. 3 William Ashburner's Hindpool shipyard,[52] as it would have been in November 1877, with the William Ashburner *on the patent slip and the* Mary Ashburner *and* Isabella *on the building slips.*

PLATE 3C: Barrow shipyards old and new. The two building slips of the Ashburner yard are in the foreground, and behind them an old trawler has been laid up in what remains of the patent slip. In the background is the VSEL Devonshire Dock Hall, said to be one of the most advanced shipbuilding facilities in the World (September 1990).

PLATE 3D: *The patent slip at the Solway port of Kippford. The schooner pulled up for repair is the Ashburners'* Margaret Ann.

in which iron bolts and fittings were galvanised. Otherwise they did not invest her with the high quality that they usually gave their larger ships, perhaps because they were again chanelling their money mainly into their shipyard. The *R.& M.J. Charnley* had the usual heavy frames and planking of an ore carrier, but most of her outside planking was pine and although her frames were of English oak, her deck beams were of inferior Baltic oak. She was classed only 8 years A1. She joined Thomas Ashburner's fleet and Capt. Robert Charnley left the *Lord Muncaster* to command her.[55] The schooner was destined to spend her first decade mainly in the Spanish ore trade.

The Ashburners continued to build small two-masters. The *Margaret Ann* was launched six months later, and she was followed by the *Henry & Mary*, launched in September 1869. She was christened by Mary Bond, sister of Capt. Henry Bond jun., the ship's first commander.[56] Another small schooner was on the building slip when the keel of the next three-master was laid, in February 1870. In contrast to the *R.& M.J. Charnley*, this ship was to be built to the highest standards, the Lloyd's surveyor having persuaded William Ashburner to build her under the rules of Lloyd's Special Survey. Her construction took more than three years, during which time the neighbouring building slip launched two more small schooners. The *Elizabeth Latham* was completed and launched in July 1870 and was followed by the *Margaret Banister*, launched on the 7th September 1871.

The new three-master was finally launched on the 26th April 1873, being christened *Mary Bell* by Ellen Latham, the daughter of her future captain. At 175 tons and over 105 feet in length, classed 12 years A1, salted and copper-fastened, the new ship was of a size and constructional standard that surpassed any of the Ashburners' previous schooners. Her command was given to Capt. John Latham, whose career with the Ashburners had started ten years previously with the *Furness Maid*. He had gained his master's ticket for foreign trade in 1869, and since then had been in command of the *James & Agnes*, sailing mainly to Spain and Portugal.[57] He was highly regarded by Richard Ashburner, who stated at the launch that he "did not think there was a captain sailing out of Barrow in whom any owner could have greater confidence in than Capt. John Latham".[58] The *Mary Bell* moved immediately into the deepwater trades for which she had been built. She carried iron ore to Cardiff, then sailed in thirteen days to Funchal, the main port of Madeira. She returned via Villa Real and Pomaron to Gloucester. She made two more voyages to these Portugese ports before the end of the year, returning firstly to Limerick and then to the Bristol Channel port of Pill.

By this time the first of the Ashburner schooners were being lost. In February 1872 the *Mary & May*, on a voyage from Barrow to Llanelly with pig iron, had struck between two rocks at St. Ann's Head, Milford Haven. All the crew survived and the iron cargo was salvaged.[59] *Lord Muncaster* went missing in the following year. These were ill omens for the *Mary Bell*, which early in 1874 successfully carried a coal cargo from Newport to Madeira. Her return cargo of copper pyrites was loaded at Pomaron for Gloucester. She put into Villa Real and left on the 2nd April, being last sighted by another ship four days later. Somewhere in the Bay of Biscay she disappeared, taking with her the crew of seven men, including Capt. Latham and his youngest son.[60] Being less than a year old, the *Mary Bell* had the shortest life of all the

---

55. Launch reported in *Ulv.Adv.*, 28th May 1868. Construction details from *Surv.Rep.(R.& M.J. Charnley)* WHN 2523 Box 3.
56. For launch reports see *Ulv.Adv.*, 12th Nov. 1868 (*Margaret Ann*) & 2nd Sept. 1869 (*Henry & Mary*).
57. GLL *Captains Register* 18567/9 – Certificate No. S 75,588.
58. Launch report in *B.Times*, 19th April 1873. Construction details in *Surv.Rep.(Mary Bell)* WHN 285 Box 3 – The surveyor wrote "A large quantity of high class material has been judiciously used in the construction of this vessel, with extra fastenings and superior workmanship."
59. *Lloyd's List*, 17th Feb.1872 – "Everything is gone except the bare hull, and that is much damaged and without decks".
60. Voyage details from GLL *Index to Lloyd's List*. Final cargo is given as sulphur ore in *Lloyd's List*, 9th July 1874 and copper ore in *Wreck.Ret.*

Ashburner schooners, and to lose their best and newest ship so early in her career must have been a severe blow to her builders.

The Ashburners' response to the loss of their flagship was to replace her with a new and even larger three-master. In contrast to her predecessor the *William Ashburner* would have a career of over seventy years, and was to become acknowledged as the finest of the wooden schooners built at Barrow. She was not only the largest, but also the last of the Ashburners' deepwater schooners, and perhaps if the *Mary Bell* had survived longer she may never have been built at all. Construction of the *William Ashburner* was started in March 1875 and progressed rapidly. Like the *Mary Bell*, and all the future schooners, she was built to Special Survey. Salted and copper-fastened, she was classed 11 years A1. The entire shipyard's effort was put into her building, there being no other new ships underway. She was completed in only nineteen months, and upon her launch in October 1876 her command was given to Capt. Robert Charnley.[61] Her first voyage was to Cardiff, almost a tradition amongst the Ashburner schooners, and then she went deepwater. By the end of the year she had visited her first foreign port, Palma on the island of Majorca. This was at the limit of the range of the *James & Agnes* and the Ashburners' other foreign-going schooners, but the *William Ashburner* would eventually travel to far more distant seas than the near Mediterranean.

---

61. Launch report in *B.Herald*, 21st Oct. 1876 p5. Plans of the ship are reproduced in Harold Underhill, *Deep-Water Sail* (1952).

4 SHIPBUILDING AT HINDPOOL

In the 1870's the number of shipyards operating in Barrow rose from two to four. The first yards, Ashburner's and Rawlinson's, built only wooden sailing ships and were started in response to the transport needs of local ore merchants. The next two shipyards reflected the change in Barrow's industry. They were motivated not by the need to transport goods away from Barrow, but by the opportunity to use the iron and steel manufactured there, and they both devoted themselves entirely to metal-hulled vessels. One of these yards was located at Hindpool [FIG. 4] and, at the start of its life at least, built sailing ships. The other, the Barrow Shipbuilding Company, was sited on Barrow Island and has concerned itself entirely with powered vessels.

The Barrow Shipbuilding Company achieved most of its fame under the name of Vickers and today is known as VSEL. It started life in 1871, a conception of the Furness Railway Company and backed by the considerable capital of that company's principal shareholders. It operated on a far grander scale than the Hindpool shipyards and, despite early mismanagement and labour troubles, soon out-distanced them in both tonnage and numbers of ships launched. The first of these was the steam yacht *Argus*, launched in May 1873, and she was followed by more than a hundred ships built in the next ten years, and these included large passenger liners and warships. Its subsequent success, primarily in building submarines, has given it a continuing role as the dominant force in Barrow's economy. Naturally its history has formed the major part of Barrow's history of shipbuilding, and this has been documented in several books.[63] The history of Barrow sailing ships, however, lies solely with the Hindpool shipyards.

Rawlinson & Reay

Joseph Rawlinson had been one of Barrow's principal iron ore merchants in its early days, and had built the second of Barrow's wooden jetties in 1833. In 1839 he had been joined in his business by an accountant from Sunderland, Robert Reay, who acted as his shipping clerk. By the following year the two men had become relatives when Reay had married Joseph's sister, Ann. Like his rival ore merchants, Harrison, Ainslie & Co., Joseph Rawlinson operated his own fleet of schooners, amongst which were the *Jane*, *Eleanor*, *Maid of Mostyn* and *Mineral*. These latter two ships were commanded by Reay's son from his first marriage, also called Robert. He had initially worked as a shipwright in Sunderland, both in shipyards there and as a seagoing carpenter. He had left this trade to command some of Sunderland's small coasting vessels and in 1849 he and his family had joined his father in Barrow. A few years later he retired from the sea and returned to his first profession, starting, with Joseph Rawlinson's backing, Barrow's second shipyard.[64]

The shipyard must have been one of the first industries established on the Furness Railway Company's Hindpool estate. A two-acre plot at the Northernmost end was leased to Robert Reay jun. in August 1856. Work must have quickly started on the construction of both the yard's patent slip and its first vessel. By September 1857 the patent slip was nearly completed and beside it stood a 140 ton (burthen) schooner, the *Gummershow*, ready for launching. She had been built from larch and her name derived from the Windermere plantation at which it had been cut. Her launch report makes it clear that she was designed and built by Reay, but the shipyard itself was described as Rawlinson's and the *Gummershow* was destined to enter his

---

62. From map in BRL Roberts' *Barrow and District Directory* (1886)
63. J.D. Scott, *Vickers: A History* (1963); T. Clark, *A Century of Shipbuilding* (1971); and Nigel Harris, *Portrait of a Shipbuilder* (1989).
64. *Reay.Hist.*

fleet.[65] All the subsequent schooners built by Reay went into the Rawlinson fleet, and it seems that the shipyard, unlike that of the Ashburners, was never an independant concern.

The next three schooners from the yard were named after the children of James Fisher who, with a fleet of about thirty vessels, was Barrow's leading shipowner at this time. The new schooners were named *Elizabeth Anne*, *Joseph* and *Francis*, and they were built in the years 1858 to 1861. They were slightly larger than the schooners that had so far been built by the

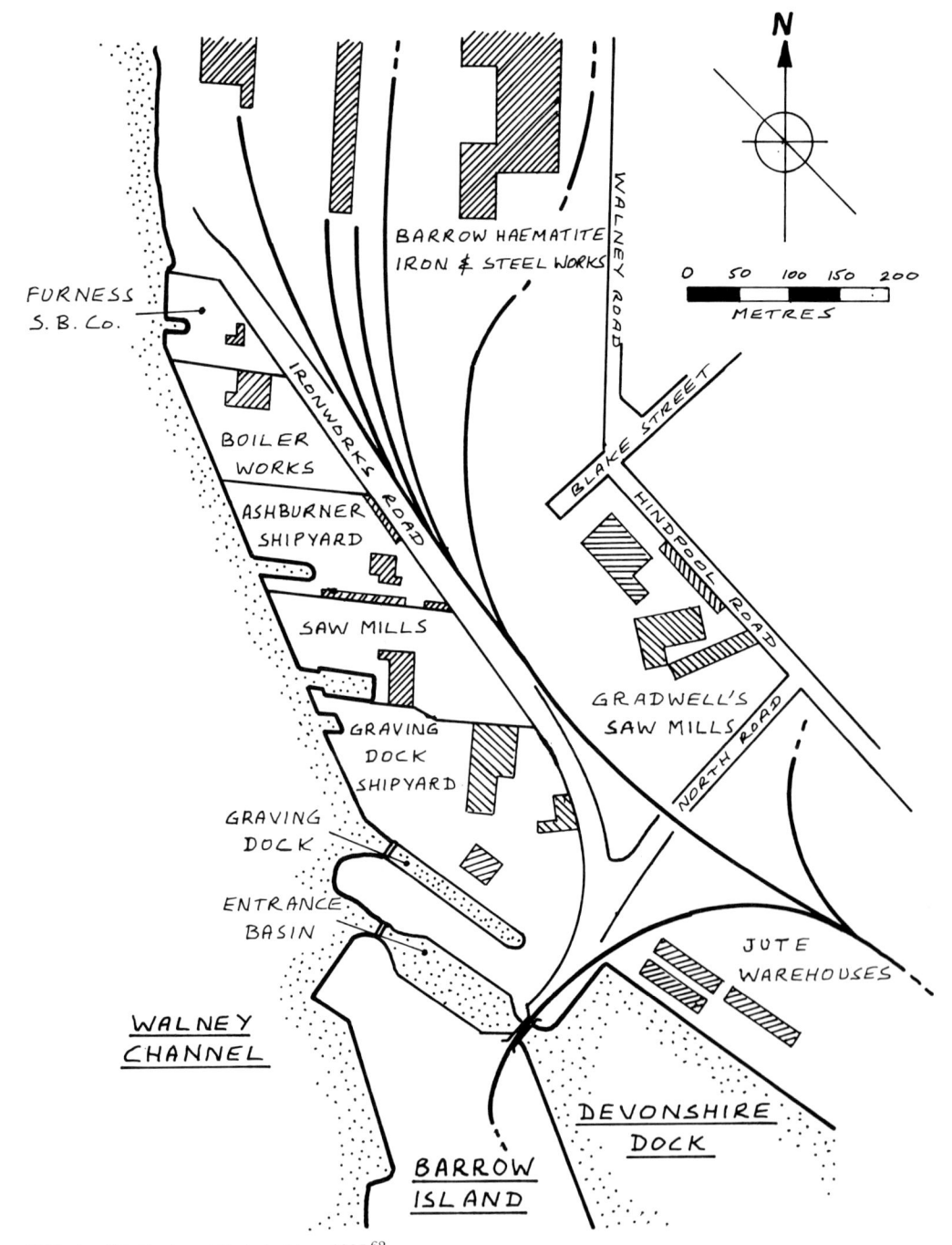

FIG. 4   Hindpool and its industries, 1885.[62]

Ashburners. The Rawlinson & Reay shipyard itself was smaller than the Ashburners' Barrow Channel yard and there only ever seems to have been one ship under construction at any one time. In April 1861 Robert Reay jun. lived at the site and was described as employing only eight men and three boys. Many yards could build a ship with this number of men, but perhaps the small number represented a temporary lull in its shipbuilding activity. It was only in July 1862 that Reay's fifth ship was launched, the schooner *Seven Sisters*. Two more schooners were built for the Rawlinson fleet in the next two years, and the *Betty Russell* and *Harry Russell* marked the end of Robert Reay's career in shipbuilding. The business had been a co-partnership between Reay, his father and Rawlinson, but Robert Reay sen. died in 1863 and his son retired from shipbuilding, transferring the shipyard lease to Rawlinson in the following year.

Joseph Rawlinson continued as sole proprietor of the yard, and began to build ships for other Barrow owners. Reay was replaced as foreman shipwright by John Peet and in 1865 the 350 ton (burthen) *R.F. Bell* was launched, for Samuel Jervis. She was the largest ship so far built in Barrow, and unusually she was rigged as a brig. The final ship from the yard, the even larger *Duke of Buccleuch*, was built in 1867. Also a brig, she and her predecessor were intended for the Mediterranean trade.[66] Brigs were only rarely being built on the West Coast of Britain at this time, where the schooner had become the almost universal choice of rig for the coasting and Mediterranean trades. The *Duke of Buccleuch* was fairly quickly sold to an owner at Cape Town, South Africa, and the *R.F. Bell* was eventually re-rigged as a schooner, in 1882. By this time, like the rest of the ships that had once sailed in Rawlinson's fleet, she had been sold to James Fisher.

James Fisher and the Furness Ship Building Company

After the launch of the *Duke of Buccleuch* Joseph Rawlinson retired from active involvement in shipbuilding. He sold his shipyard to James Fisher, who required facilities for the repair of his ever-increasing fleet. A new schooner, the *Beatrice*, was built but after two years in operation Fisher decided to form a separate company to take over his shipbuilding activities. He raised £10,000 capital by issuing 1,000 shares in the new venture, the Furness Ship Building Company. The first meeting of the new company was held in August, 1870. Among Fisher's fellow directors were his son, Joseph, William Chamley, Joseph Rawlinson, Capt. George Porter, who was a sailmaker, and John Hannay of the Ironworks.[67] Later they were joined by Capt. Robert Parkinson, one of the principal captains in Fisher's fleet. The new company continued to confine itself mainly to the repair of Fisher's own vessels and built only two more ships, both schooners for the same fleet. The first of these was the *Lily Baynes*, 100 tons, launched in 1872.

By this time the yard employed about fifty men. The shipyard itself was a two acre site at the end of the sandstone sea wall which ran from the entrance to the Devonshire Dock towards the Ironworks. The patent slip was operated by an 8 h.p. steam engine, which also drove a saw bench and other machinery. There was also a large blacksmith's shop, a joiners' shop and turning shop.

The last ship built by the Furness Ship Building Co. was the *Ellie Park*, launched in May, 1879. The company continued in business for many years, repairing the vessels of James Fisher. They eventually abandoned the smaller Northern yard and moved into the yard vacated by the Ashburners. They continued to repair ships but no new ship was built at either yard, and the business was eventually closed in 1900.

---

65. *Ulv.Adv.*, 10th Sept. 1857 – "The *Gummershow* was built and laid down from lines by Mr. Robert Reay jun., one of the firm we believe".
66. Launch of *R.F. Bell* in *Ulv.Adv.*, 1st June 1865. Launch of *Duke of Buccleuch* in *Ulv.Mirror*, 16th March 1867.
67. Share sale advertised in *B.Times*, 11th June 1870. First company meeting reported in the same newspaper, 16th July 1870.

The Graving Dock Shipyard[68]

The Furness Railway Co. had planned to build a graving dock (dry dock) even before the idea for the Devonshire Dock was conceived, and the first site proposed had been that of the Ashburners' first shipyard. However, it was only in 1870, after the Devonshire Dock had been completed, that work was started on excavating a graving dock. The site chosen was just North of the Devonshire Dock entrance, at the Southern end of the Hindpool sea wall. Once completed, probably by 1872, this dock was used for ship repairs, and a shipbuilding yard was eventually built alongside it. Unlike the other two Hindpool yards, this shipyard was interested in building only iron vessels, although wooden ships were sometimes repaired there.

The new shipyard was probably started in 1876 and traded at first under the name of David Noble & Co. Its proprietors were Noble himself, the shipwright, David Caird, a Whitehaven builder and Frazer Fowlie, a local shipbroker. Their yard was very productive in its first years, launching four sailing vessels in only fourteen months. The first to come off the slips was the schooner *Bridget Annie*, launched for James Ashcroft in September 1877. At 110 tons she was the yard's smallest vessel. Since those that followed her became progressively larger, it is possible that construction of all four started at about the same time. The schooner *Maggie Townson*, 149 tons, was launched for J. Walton & Co. in January 1878. She had only a short life, being run down in the Mersey later in the same year. Noble's third schooner had already been launched. She was the *Charles & Ellen*, of 158 tons. Her owner was Millom's William Postlethwaite and her first master was Capt. C.A. Reney, himself later to become prominent as a shipowner at Connah's Quay. The yard's final vessel was a 317 ton barque, the *Manx Queen*, which as her name suggests went to an owner in the Isle of Man. All four ships had been built from iron, to Lloyd's Special Survey, and were classed 100 years A1. Although built to a high standard, they were nevertheless purely sailing vessels.

The yard's name was changed to Caird & Purdie, James Purdie being a Liverpool shipbuilder. This also signalled a change in the type of vessels being built, for the yard's future now lay with steam. The *Espana* was the first steamship launched by the new company, in February 1881.[69] Other steamers followed in rapid succession and the yard had one final change of name, becoming the Graving Dock Shipbuilding Company. In 1882 it was advertised as being able to build vessels of up to 2,000 tons burthen. Thereafter it had only limited success, in part due to strikes and lockouts, and seems to have built no new ships after 1884. This was the end of shipbuilding at Hindpool, apart from a brief resurgence of activity during each of the two World Wars, for the Ashburner yard launched its final schooner in the same year.

---

68. Information from Carrie Garnett, Furness Maritime Trust.
69. *B.Times*, 5th Feb. 1881.

5 WILLIAM ASHBURNER & SON – SHIPBUILDERS

Construction Details

Barrow flats

In earlier years British sailing vessels had been classified by the shape of their hulls, but by the 19th Century this had changed to a classification based on their sails and rigging. A schooner was a fore-and-aft rigged vessel of two or more masts, differing from a ketch by having its largest boom-sail on the mainmast rather than the foremast. They became common in Britain from the 1830's and, unlike the American schooners from which they evolved, most British vessels carried some square sails on the foremast. Their hull design differed markedly in both shape and size, depending on the trade for which the ship was intended and upon the place in which it was built. The hulls of Furness-built schooners were especially distinctive, being adapted to the tidal harbours and heavy cargoes that characterised their major trades. To Devon seamen, whose own vessels were built on different lines, the Furness schooners became known as 'Barrow flats'. It was not a term that was used in Barrow or was even familiar to its seamen, but it serves to describe the type of schooner built there.

In its most basic form, the hull of a 'Barrow flat' was full-bodied and essentially double-ended, with full bows and, usually, a rounded stern. The design probably originated from the small 30 or 40 ton flats that had once traded in Morecambe Bay and along the Lancashire coast, and which themselves had much in common with river barges. They had a bottom that was largely flat, with a keel that was parallel to the waterline. This feature, together with their usually shallow draught, resulted from the type of harbours available in the North West, which often required ships to be grounded as the tide retreated. Under such circumstances, a ship sitting on an even keel would list only slightly [PLATE 5A]. The 'Barrow flats' would sit evenly on the mud, and this was a profound advantage in preventing damage. Ships built in ports with an ocean sailing tradition, such as those of Devon and Cornwall, had a keel which was deeper at the stern than at the bows. As the tide ebbed, such vessels would settle aft, but the bows would still be afloat and would tend to be pulled away from the quay. Such a process could cause twisting of the hull and could seriously damage its structure.[70]

The 'Barrow flats' were recognised as the most perfectly adapted schooners for the coasting trade. They could sail without ballast, an advantage in two ways, since it not only allowed the most productive use of hull capacity, but also did away with the often lengthy delays associated with the loading and unloading of the ballast. They were good sea boats, responsive when both light and loaded, and very manoeuvrable in strong tides and confined channels.

Round sterns and counters

The first three Ashburner schooners each had a square transom stern, and it was this type of stern that was seen on the great majority of British schooners. It was rarely seen on Furness-built vessels, for the 'Barrow flats', in their most primitive form, had a round stern with the sternpost and rudder mounted outside the hull. This was a strong and very practical design, for the lack of an overhanging counter meant that there was nothing to slam down as a vessel pitched in a rough sea. On more conventionally built schooners, such a motion could shake the hull severely. Most of the Ashburner schooners had round sterns, though at least in those later schooners that survived to be photographed, this has been modified somewhat by having the bulwarks flared outwards to enclose the rudderhead [PLATES 5A, 12C]. The most

---

70. *Mer.Sch.*, pp39–43 & p96. Also see Basil Greenhill, "Note on Barrow Flats", *Mariners Mirror*, 1961 pp149–151.

PLATE 5A: Isabella, *here seen beached at Par in the 1930's, had a round stern, typical of Furness coasting schooners.*

PLATE 5B: The elliptical counter stern of the William Ashburner. *The wrecked ship was photographed at Beachley in 1950.*

primitive types of round stern were deprecated because of their ugliness and possibly this minimal counter was added to improve their looks.

A great advantage of the round stern was that it was cheaper to build than the transom stern with all its complicated framing. In some cases, however, even North West shipbuilders were prepared to sacrifice practicality and economics in order to build a handsome ship. The best ships from their yards, the ones in which they invested most effort and took most pride, had an elliptical counter stern. The Ashburners gave such a stern to the *Mary Ashburner* and *William Ashburner* [PLATES 5B, 5C] and it was also given to their other deepwater schooners, the *Mary Bell* and *James & Agnes*. The *Mary & May* had what was described as an elliptical stern, though a painting of this early ship[71] shows that it is a development from the square stern of the other three schooners built for Harrison, Ainslie & Co. The *M.E. Johnson* is also described on her Certificate of Registry as having an elliptical stern, but reference to surviving photographs [eg. PLATE 12C] shows either that this was an error or she was substantially altered at some time.

Frames and planking

The 1737 Sailing Directions for Piel Harbour noted that "scarce any vessel but those built hereabouts would endure the hardships attending the ore traffic on this coast".[72] The tradition of building wooden ships of great strength was maintained in the Furness schooners of the following Century. As well as using the best materials for the frames, the frames themselves were massive, and were closely spaced. Such ships were able to resist much of the wear and tear associated with schooners designed on more classical lines, and were therefore more economical to maintain and tended to have a longer working life. In the last days of the schooners, in the 1950's, most of the wooden schooners still trading had been built in Lancashire, Cumberland or North Wales. They included three of the Ashburner schooners, four of the seven sailing vessels built at Millom, and others built at Connah's Quay and Runcorn.

The midship sections of the *Elizabeth Latham*[73] [FIG. 5] and *William Ashburner*[74] [FIG. 6] illustrate the nature of the frames and planking in these ships. Both had frames of English oak. In the *William Ashburner* these were spaced 2" apart at the floor, and were 11" × 13½" where they met the keel. In the smaller schooner the frames were less substantial, 8½" × 9" at the keel, and were spaced at 3¼" at midships and were adjacent to each other at each end of the vessel. Including the planking, the hull at the bows and stern was therefore solid wood, fifteen inches thick at the bilges.

The woods used in a ship's construction largely governed its Lloyd's classification. Each wood was classed for a number of years, according to its location in a vessel's structure. English oak, morra, greenheart and teak were classed 12 years wherever they were used. In contrast, pitchpine was classed 12 years only for outside planking to the bilges. In other locations it could be classed as low as 7 years – if used in the frames, for example. French oak was considered less worthy than English oak but better than other European oaks, and these were themselves classed higher than American oak. From such rules, a ship's overall classification could be calculated. It was based firstly on the lowest class of material used in the ship's construction. If this lowest class was unrepresentative of the overall materials, Lloyd's had a 'mixed material' rule, from 1870, allowing an extra year to be added. A further year could be added if the vessel was appropriately salted, and another if metal fastenings of a suitable standard were used. Most of the later Ashburner schooners were classed 9 years for

---

71. In *Barrow Evening Mail*, 17th Jan.1990 p29.
72. F. Barnes, *Barrow and District* (1981) p98.
73. Surv.Rep.(*Elizabeth Latham*) WHN 2226 Box 3.
74. Surv.Rep.(*William Ashburner*) WHN 3096 Box 3.
75. Table compiled from entries in *LSR*, *BSR* and *CSR*. The *Elizabeth Latham* had been recommended for class 10A1 by her surveyor but was marked down to 9A1 by the Lloyd's committee upon receipt of his report.

TABLE 5A: COMPARATIVE CONSTRUCTIONAL DETAILS OF THE ASHBURNER SCHOONERS[75]

NAME	YEAR BUILT	GROSS TONS	LENGTH (FEET)	BREADTH (FEET)	DEPTH (FEET)	MASTS	FIGUREHEAD	STERN	LLOYD'S CLASS'N
Jane Roper	1852	105	72.7	21.2	11.1	Two	Female	Square	11A1
Tom Roper	1857	120	80.0	21.3	11.0	Two	Male	Square	12A1
Lord Muncaster	1859	97	84.0	20.2	10.6	Two	Male	Square	9A1
Mary Jane	1860	99	83.2	20.5	10.4	Two	Female	Round	9A1
Mary & May	1862	97	82.0	20.3	10.4	Two	Female	Elliptic	9A1
Elizabeth Barrow	1863	96	80.0	20.5	10.3	Two	Female	Round	9A1
Furness Maid	1863	49	62.8	17.2	7.3	Two	None	Round	
James & Agnes	1864	131	92.5	21.9	11.4	Two	Carved knee	Elliptic	12A1
Alice Latham	1865	75	76.4	19.5	8.2	Two	Carved knee	Round	
Nanny Latham	1866	75	77.1	19.0	8.1	Two	Knee	Round	
Catherine Latham	1867	74	77.5	19.2	8.3	Two	Knee	Round	8A1
R. & M.J. Charnley	1868	155	97.8	22.5	12.0	Three			8A1
Margaret Ann	1868	77	78.2	19.5	8.2	Two	Knee	Round	8A1
Henry & Mary	1869	79	77.2	19.5	8.3	Two	Knee	Round	9A1
Elizabeth Latham	1870	77	76.6	20.1	8.2	Two	Knee	Round	9A1
Margaret Banister	1871	86	79.0	20.7	8.7	Two	Knee	Round	10A1
Mary Bell	1873	175	105.3	23.5	12.3	Three	Carved knee	Elliptic	12A1
William Ashburner	1876	205	115.1	25.1	12.8	Three	Scroll	Elliptic	11A1
Mary Ashburner	1877	106	88.2	21.8	10.0	Two	Scroll	Elliptic	11A1
Isabella	1878	97	88.5	21.3	9.0	Two	Scroll	Round	10A1
Useful	1879	99	89.3	21.3	9.1	Two	Scroll	Round	10A1
M.E. Johnson	1879	129	98.3	23.0	9.9	Three	Scroll	Elliptic	10A1
James Postlethwaite	1881	134	99.7	23.0	10.1	Three	Carved knee	Round	12A1
J. & M. Garratt	1884	104	92.4	21.5	9.2	Two	Scroll	Round	12A1

1. KEEL — AMERICAN ELM
2. KEELSON — GREENHEART
3. RIDER KEELSON — GREENHEART
4. FLOOR
5. 1ST. FOOTHOOK
6. 2ND. FOOTHOOK } FRAME — ENGLISH OAK
7. TOPSIDES
8. DECK BEAM — ENGLISH OAK
9. WATERWAY — PITCHPINE
10. SHELF & CLAMP — PITCHPINE

DEPTH OF HOLD 8 FT. 2 INS.

HALF EXTREME BREADTH 10 FT. ½ IN.

IRON KNEE

INSIDE PLANKING — GREENHEART, BULLETT TREE, PITCHPINE & RED PINE.

TREENAILS — LOCUST & E. OAK

BOLTS — GALVANISED IRON

GREENHEART, BALTIC & E. OAK

PITCHPINE

PITCHPINE

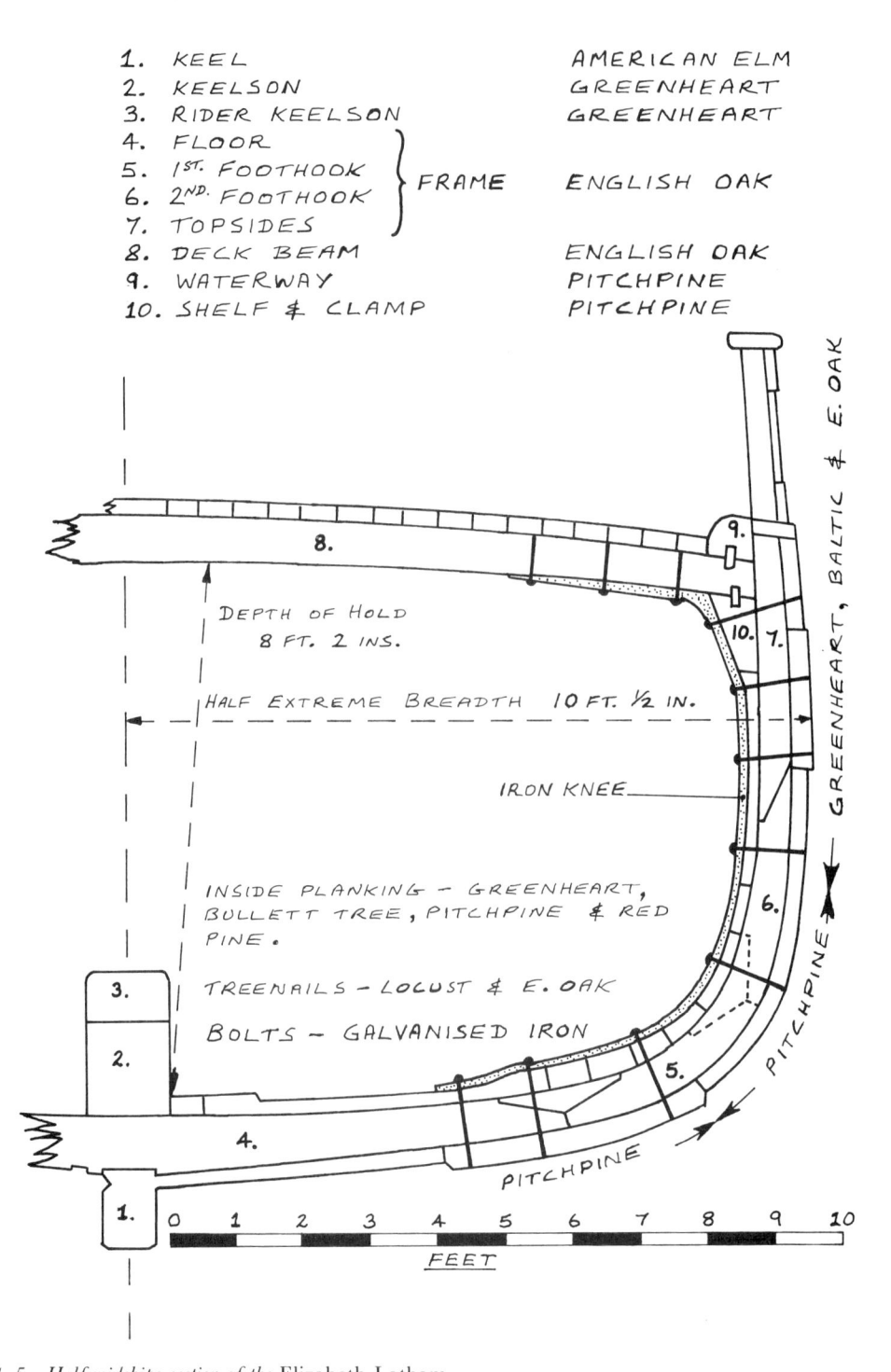

FEET

FIG. 5 Half-midships section of the Elizabeth Latham.

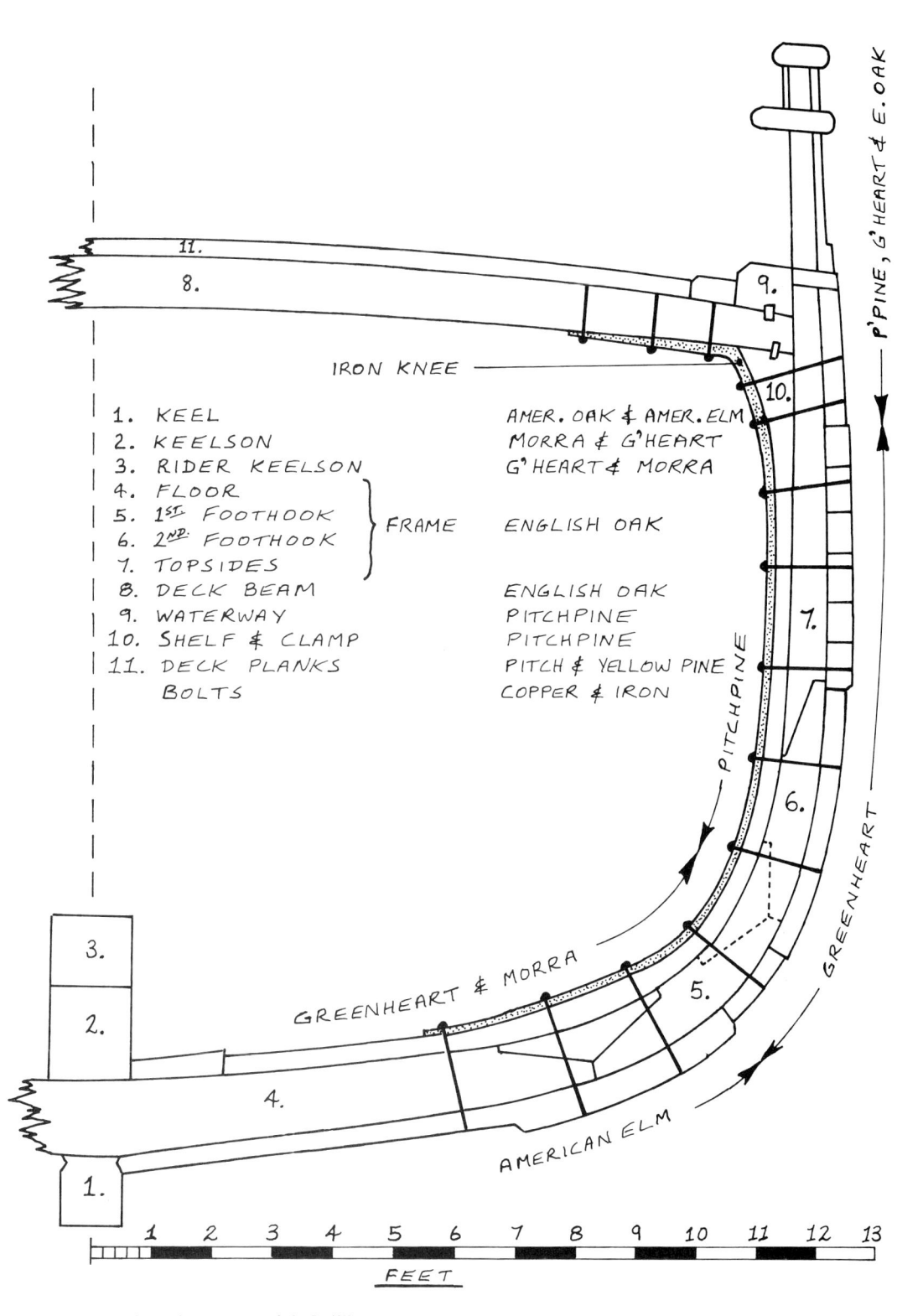

FIG. 6 Half-midships section of the William Ashburner.

materials, and then had extra years added under these rules, so that the best were classed 12 years A1 [TABLE 5A]. The *William Ashburner*, for example, was classed 9 years for materials (amongst other things, pitchpine was used for the waterways), an extra year for 'mixed materials' and a further year for salting – final class, 11 years A1. Although she was copper-bolted below the waterline, wooden treenails were extensively used for securing her planking, to such an extent that she did not qualify for the extra year for fastenings.

Salting was highly regarded by Lloyd's surveyors because it was a method of preserving timber from fungal decay. Rainwater seeping into the frames and collecting in the hull would promote this, and rotten structural timbers or planking could lead to a vessel's loss if not spotted in time. Salt water prevents fungal growth and is therefore a timber preservative. Salt was packed between the ship's frames and planking, for the full height of the hull at the ends and from the bilges to the level of the deck beams at midships. The deck beams themselves were sometimes cured in salt water prior to being fitted into the ship.

Yellow-metalling was another technique used for protecting the hull, in this case from the borings of the ship worms found in warm waters such as the far Mediterranean. Unprotected, a hull could be damaged irreparably in as little as twelve months. To counter this threat, British deepwater sailing ships had had their hulls below the waterline plated with copper from the 1700's. In the 1830's a cheaper brass substitute was invented, and this was known as yellow metal, or Muntz metal after its inventor. Prior to sheeting the hull, a felt layer was applied to the tarred hull, to prevent abrasion from bolts and plank edges. Only one of the Ashburner schooners is listed in Lloyd's Register as "felted and yellow-metalled". This was the *William Ashburner*, the only one of their schooners to trade extensively in the Mediterranean and the South Atlantic. The Ashburners did this work themselves a year after her launch, but the yard was certainly capable of carrying out this specialist work at an even earlier date. In 1870 the Norwegian barque *Meteor*, travelling on her maiden voyage from Porsgrund to New York, put into their yard to be so treated.[76] The *Mary Bell* was copper-fastened, indicating that she too would probably have been yellow-metalled if she had survived her first year.[77]

Speed

The underlying reasons for the design of the 'Barrow flats' have been given, and are largely based on the requirements of strength and longevity. The shape of the hull and their heavy construction mitigated against speed. William and Richard Ashburner both managed to overcome these limitations and designed ships that were considered to be fast, at least in comparison with their local rivals.

The Ulverston Mirror of the 3rd February, 1866 notes one smart passage by an Ashburner schooner, on one of the main coastal trading routes from Barrow:

> QUICK PASSAGE – The Schooner *Elizabeth Barrow*, Captain Latham, left Barrow on the 10th ult., bound for Newport, and there took in a cargo for Liverpool, and left that port for Barrow, at which place she arrived on the 2nd inst. She will be ready to leave Barrow this day (Saturday), with a cargo of iron ore.

However well the *Elizabeth Barrow* sailed on this voyage, it can be seen that her time would have depended on a great many things other than sailing speed. She left and entered three harbours, and in the channels to and from these ports her time would have been largely governed by the tides. Any delay in finding a berth or moving a cargo would have severely increased the journey time if it had caused the ship to miss a tide outwards. Once at sea, there were the vagaries of weather and winds to contend with. So much was left to chance that building sailing speed into a coasting schooner was not of prime importance. The fastest schooners were those which were designed to sail deepwater, and it is unlikely that the Ashburner schooners ever compared with these. The comparison of speed is best made against local rivals.

Claims regarding a ship's speed must always be treated with some suspicion, especially when made by masters or shipbuilders. Both Fishers' *Mary Sinclair*[78] and Ashburners' *Elizabeth Latham*[79] have been described as the fastest two-masted schooner sailing out of Barrow. That the claim for the *Elizabeth Latham* was made by an impartial observer gives it some credibility, though it is somewhat surprising that a small schooner designed for the short sea trades should be given this accolade. There are no surviving illustrations of her to reveal the secret of her speed, and the midships section [FIG. 5] and survey report show that she had all the usual features of a short sea trader. She was very heavily built and had markedly flat floors at midships. The date of her launch gives some substance to the claim, for she was built at the time when Richard Ashburner must have been starting to influence the design of his father's schooners.

There is some quantitative evidence for the speed of one of the earlier Ashburner two-masters. A notice published four years after her launch stated that the *Lord Muncaster* had sailed from Cardiff to Lisbon in five days and that this was a record, a good time for Ulverston vessels being nine days.[80] There is also a record of the form of this schooner [PLATE 2B] and it shows that she had clipper bows, with a great amount of sheer, and a rakish rig. Her length-to-breadth ratio, commonly related to speed, is one of the highest of the Ashburner two-masters. Perhaps not too much emphasis should be placed on this figure, as that of the *Elizabeth Latham* was one of the lowest.

The *William Ashburner* was also noted as a fast ship, credited with once sailing 240 miles in 24 hours with a full cargo of coal.[81] This is no bad performance for a deepwater schooner that still had many features of a 'Barrow flat'. It was also claimed that she had made a record passage to one of the South American ports.[82]

Building Costs

The lack of surviving records from the Ashburner shipyard means that the cost of building the schooners can only be estimated. It is known that Capt. Robert Latham purchased one of the first few shares in the *M.E. Johnson* at a price of £35 in January 1880, the ship having been launched at the start of October, 1879.[83] Assuming that the share was equal to one 64th of the building cost (including the Ashburners' profit) this equates to a total price of £2240 or £17 7s 3d per gross ton. The price of shares in the *Catherine Latham* sold three years after her launch indicates that she was valued at £1152, or about £15 10s per gross ton.[84] These prices compare relatively well with recorded prices for other locally-built ships.

The *Gauntlet* was a 110 ton two-masted schooner launched from Matthew Simpson's Glasson Dock shipyard in 1857. This ship, which eventually joined the fleet of James Fisher, was built at a cost of £1983 7s, according to surviving shipyard records.[85] The eventual sale price of the vessel would have been increased by about £150 to allow for the builder's profit. This would give a net cost of approximately £19 8s per gross ton. The purchase prices of three

---

76. *B.Times*, 2nd July 1870.
77. Copper bolts were used to prevent galvanic corrosion occuring between iron bolts and copper-based sheathing. This was believed to have caused the loss of some early coppered warships.
78. Alan Lockett, *Ports & People of Morecambe Bay*
79. *F.P.& P.*, p54. Joseph Richardson was editor of the Barrow Times. The claim is repeated in *Obit.(R.A.)* by Wm. Ashburner jun.
80. *Furn.Folk*, p37 – citing from a notice published 23rd May 1863.
81. *F.P.& P.*, p54.
82. *Obit.(R.A.)*. This possibly refers to a 40 day passage from Liverpool to Parahiba, Brazil reported in Shipping Intelligence, *B.Times*, 25th Jan. 1879 and noted 'quick passage'.
83. *Disb.Book*
84. Bill of Sale dated 1870, shown to me by Dorothy Latham. Her grandfather, Capt. Thomas Latham, paid £36 to Capt. John Latham for two shares.
85. D.R. McGregor, *Merchant Sailing Ships 1850–1875* (1984) pp94–100. Costs are also given for the *Margaret Porter*, a schooner launched for Barrow's James Fisher in 1856, and for other of the 14 schooners built by Simpson in the years 1849–79.

schooners built at Millom for the Duddon Shipping Association are also known and are equally comparable. The 113 ton *Nellie Bywater* was bought for £2400 in 1873, the 109 ton *Florence Petherick* for £2032 in 1890 and the 142 ton three-master *Happy Harry* for £2560 in 1894.[86] These equate to between £21 and £18 per gross ton.

The price of a ship depended a great deal on the quality of its materials and also on the classification for which her builder was aiming, so not too much should be made of the comparison of prices. Perhaps the relatively low price of the *M.E. Johnson* reflects the high degree of mechanisation in the Ashburner shipyard. Together with that of the *Happy Harry*, the other three master, it also seems to verify that three-masters were a better economic proposition than two-masters.

Launching

Some shipyards launched their ships as bare hulls, with the masts and rigging being added later in a fitting-out dock. The shipbuilders located by the Ulverston Canal basin, such as White, Charnley and Brocklebank, would have been obliged to do this in order to get their vessels under the Railway Bridge that crossed above the canal. There was a fitting-out berth on the seaward side of the bridge. From newspaper reports of launches it appears that the Ashburners launched all their schooners fully-rigged and ready to sail. Even where this is not specifically stated, it can be seen that usually within seven or ten days of launching most of their schooners had left Barrow on their maiden voyage, almost invariably with a first cargo of pig iron or iron ore. Newspaper reports usually confined themselves only to the bare details of a newly-launched ship. The following report is one of the most extensive, and appeared in the Barrow Times on Saturday, 16th July 1870.

LAUNCH AT MR. ASHBURNER'S SHIP-YARD, BARROW

Shortly after ten o'clock on Tuesday forenoon, a fine new schooner was successfully launched from Mr. William Ashburner's yard, in the presence of a considerable concourse of spectators. Her lines are very pretty for a wooden vessel and her appearance graceful. In length she measures 76 6-10ths feet; beam, 20 1-10th feet; and depth 8 3-10ths feet. She is 77 tons register and is classed A.1 at Lloyd's for ten years. Prior to the launch she was fully rigged, and her sails bent, ready for going to sea. A numerous company had assembled on board to participate in the exhilarating effects of her first dip into her native element. When the dog-shores had been knocked away a hydraulic lift capable of raising 150 tons was applied to her bows, when she glided smoothly and swiftly into the water. After her first plunge the anchor was quickly dropped, and she was pulled up amidst the most enthusiastic cheers from those on board and in the building yard. When she began to move upon the ways, the customary bottle of wine was broken on her bows, and she was christened the *Elizabeth Latham* by Miss Latham, a daughter of one of the owners. She is a sister ship to the *Catherine Latham*, which was built in the same yard three years ago and has been paying an excellent dividend to her proprietors ever since she was launched. The new schooner went into the dock in the course of the day, and will at once proceed to load a cargo of iron ore. Mr. W. K. Chamley is her managing director, and she is commanded by Captain James Latham . . . . . . In honour of the launch, on Tuesday a number of vessels in the docks and those lying off the Ironworks exhibited a profuse display of bunting.

After the launch, the Ashburners would host a celebratory meal either at their offices or a nearby hotel. Their guests would typically include men who had been involved in the ship's construction, prospective customers and shareholders, other local shipbuilders and the future captain. A substantial meal would be followed by a great deal of toasting and speech-making. Following the launch of the *Mary Bell*, for example, a meal at the Bowling Green Hotel was hosted by the three Ashburner sons. Their guests included representatives of the Furness Ship Building Co. and the Barrow Shipbuilding Co. Toasts were made to the Queen, the future

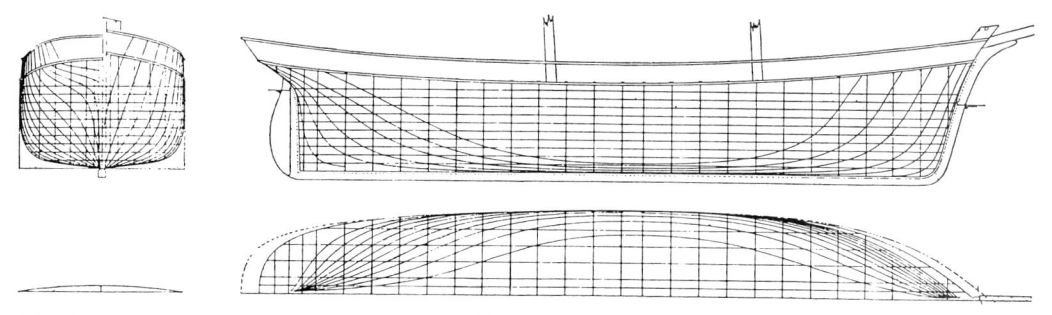

FIG. 7 Builder's draft of the Mary Ashburner.[88]

captain, the town and trade of Barrow, the sailmaker, and individually to William Ashburner sen. and both Thomas and Richard, as well as a number of guests. Replies to these toasts were by no means short, and covered such subjects as Samuel Plimsoll's newly-proposed marine safety legislation, the advantages of wooden ships over iron and the recent disastrous loss of the passenger ship *Atlantic* off the American coast. Guests spoke with pride of Barrow's recent development and expressed great hopes for its future. The final reply, by a local councillor presumably succumbing to the effect of such extravagant toasting, was an impassioned discourse on the problems of Barrow's sewers.[87]

Building the *Mary Ashburner*

The *William Ashburner* was launched on the 19th October 1876, and soon afterwards the Ashburners turned their attention to the building of their next schooner. She was to be a smaller vessel intended for the coasting trade, though she was to be built to the same high standard as her predecessor. This new ship was originally known simply as Yard No. 34, and only at her launch received the name of Thomas Ashburner's wife and ten year old daughter – *Mary Ashburner*. She was intended to be about 110 gross tons with a Lloyd's classification of 11 A1 and, like her two immediate predecessors, was to be built under the rules of Lloyd's Special Survey. Richard Ashburner designed her and produced a sheer plan, body plan and half-breadth plan from which his shipwrights could start their work [FIG. 7].

The *Mary Ashburner* was probably built on the same slip as her recently-launched sister ship. William Bath, the Lloyd's Whitehaven surveyor, made his first visit to inspect the newly-laid keel of the vessel at the Ashburner yard on the 6th November 1876. To fulfill the requirements of the Special Survey rules, the *Mary Ashburner* would have to have her materials and construction inspected at regular intervals. Over the course of the following year, the surveyor would visit the yard once or twice every week, so that the final survey, on the 29th November 1877, was the 72nd inspection of the vessel. Surveys for Lloyd's were necessary for insurance purposes and were in addition to mandatory Board of Trade surveys. Normally a survey would be carried out by examination of the vessel sometime soon after her launch. Special Survey was a more stringent test, the vessel and the materials used in her construction being liable to inspection at any time whilst she was in the shipyard. A vessel that had been built under such critical supervision was more attractive to shipping agents and other potential customers.

The 14½" x 11" keel of the new ship was 83 feet in length, made up of twelve 7 ft. sections of French oak and American elm, scarphed together and bolted with ¾" copper bolts. Onto the keel the timbers of the stem and stern of the ship were constructed. At the bows of the ship the

---

86. Trevor Morgan, "The Cumberland Connection: Hugh Jones, Shipbuilder, Millom", *Maritime Wales* (1983), pp69–95. Cost data is from Hodbarrow Mining Co. records at CRO.
87. Report of launch of *Mary Bell* in *B.Times*, 19th April 1873.
88. *Mer.Sch.*, p40. Reproduced with permission from Conway Maritime Press.

stem and knightheads were shaped from English oak. The sternpost was also of oak, and was supported by the deadwood of American elm. While this structure was being built on the slip, elsewhere in the yard the frames were being constructed. Loftsmen had translated Richard Ashburner's drawings firstly into full-size drawings on a floor, and then into full-size wooden patterns. These were taken to the sawyers who used them for guidance as they cut pieces of English and French oak into the component parts of the ship's frames. Each frame was made of seven pieces. The floor timber, which would straddle the keel, was scarphed on either side to the first foothooks. These in turn were scarphed to the second foothooks, and above these were the topside timbers. Each frame was assembled on the ground and once completed was hoisted into position on the keel, then bolted there with iron bolts. The frames were 11¾" deep at the keel and were 9¾" wide there. As the frames rose they became thinner, so that at the topsides they were only 6¾" × 5". The spacing between the floor timbers was 1½" at the ends of the ship and 2½" amidships.[89]

Once all the frames were in place a pitchpine keelson was laid into the hull. This was a massive piece of wood, 16¾" wide and 18" high, and running nearly the whole of its length. It lay above the frames and was bolted to the keel. Above the keelson, a smaller rider keelson was made from 6 ft. pieces of greenheart, 15½" × 12", scarphed and bolted together.

Richard Ashburner proposed that they dispensed with diagonal straps inside the frames and strengthened the hull instead with fourteen pairs of hanging knees, made of iron. He drew his idea as a midship section and, in February, sought the approval of the Lloyd's surveyor. After some discussion this drawing was approved and was ultimately appended to the Survey Report. It is drawn in pencil on canvas, to a scale of ½" per foot. Some of the sections are coloured with watercolour, and the scantlings and woods of the main timbers are noted in ink.

Out on the building slip the schooner's framework was being completed. A pitchpine shelf was constructed around the periphery of the ship, bolted to the frame heads. The shelf's function was to strengthen the top of the ship and to support the deck beams. There were seventeen full beams, together with three pairs of half-beams at the points where the two hatches would be located. The beams were each made from a single piece of oak, 9" deep at the centre and 8" wide, which spanned the 21 ft. breadth of the schooner. They were dowelled to the shelf. Beneath the shelf a pitchpine clamp piece was fitted. Later this whole construction was further strengthened by fitting the iron knees. These extended from the underside of the deck down to the floors. Above the beams, and dowelled to them, a pitchpine waterway was constructed. Like the shelf below the beams, this extended right around the periphery of the ship. It functioned to further strengthen the hull, but also to direct water from the cambered deck to the three wash ports and three mooring pipes on either side of the ship.

The two hatches of the *Mary Ashburner* were each formed by bolting fore-and-after timbers to two full beams, and then to the half beams in between. The main hatch between the masts was 12 ft. by 7 ft. and the smaller after hatch was 6 ft. by 6 ft. 6". Each hatchway was framed with galvanised iron coamings to prevent damage during the movement of cargo.

Richard Ashburner had not made any concessions to the weight of the frames of his new ship, and her planking too was as substantial as that of any schooner built in Furness, or indeed elsewhere. On the outside, this planking changed in materials and thickness. American elm, 3" thick, was used for the bottom planks. At the turn of the bilge these gave way to pitchpine planks, 4½" thick to resist wear due to grounding. Thinner pitchpine planking was used at the wales, and above this, around the topsides where the ship would contact harbour walls, 4" greenheart was used. Each plank was cut in the saw mill, then shaped by hand to the form of the schooner. It then went to the steam chest and, softened by the moist heat, was rushed to the side of the ship, bent to the shape of the frames, clamped and bolted into place. For the deck 3" planks of pitch and yellow pine were used. Inside the ship the planks lining the inside of the frame, known as the ceiling, were also being fitted into place. Rock salt was packed into the cavities formed between the planks and the frames, for the whole depth of the ship at either end and from the upper part of the bilges to the gunwale amidships.

---

89. *Surv.Rep.(Mary Ashburner)* WHN 3202 Box 1035.

PLATE 5C: Mary Ashburner, *painted in 1880 by William McIllvenney. She is shown entering Barrow Harbour, with Piel Island in the background. The flag on her foretopmast is the Ashburner houseflag.*

The hull form of the new schooner was now complete. Perched above the sea wall at the front of the shipyard, she could be admired by onlookers from the boats in Walney Channel, who could see that Richard Ashburner had added a fine elliptical counter stern to the traditional form of a "Barrow flat". Her bows could be viewed by passers-by in Ironworks Road, who could hear the ring of the caulking irons and see her hull darken and blacken as oakum was hammerred into her seams and sealed with boiling pitch.

The Ashburners always fitted-out their schooners before they were launched. Masts were cut, smoothed, bound and stepped into place. They were secured with their standing rigging and the bowsprit was fitted between the knightheads above the stem. The Ashburners had ceased giving figureheads to their schooners fourteen years earlier, and the stem of the *Mary Ashburner* was decorated with only a carved and painted scroll. Her rudder of French oak was mounted on iron pintles, and the steering gear and wheel were fitted. Unlike most of the other Ashburner schooners, the *Mary Ashburner* was given a wheelhouse, and into the after-part of this was a cavity for a permanent stern navigation light. Winch, windlass and pumps were put in place and her 15 ft. small boat was mounted on skids over the main hatch. Her two bower anchors had 60 and 75 fathoms of 1" chain, and kedge and stream anchors were also stowed.

Inside the ship the carpenters installed the bulkheads separating the crew's quarters from the cargo hold. In the stern the cabins for the master and mate were constructed, the master's cabin and companionway probably being lined with mahogany and lavishly decorated. In the bows of the ship the fo'c'stle accommodation for the rest of the crew would have been more basic. In between these spaces was the single hold, of sufficient size to stow 171.59 tons of cargo.

PLATE 5D: The Isabella, *seen here entering Newlyn Harbour in the 1930's, retained her original rig until her very last days. However, by the time this photograph was taken she had been fitted with an engine, revealed by the cooling water outlets at her waterline amidships.*

The Barrow Sailmaking Company provided a single suit of sails for the new ship. All the Ashburners' two-masters were double topsail schooners and had the same basic sail plan. The mainsail was the largest sail, and above this on the mainmast was a jib-headed main-topsail and, forward, a triatic-staysail. The foremast carried a boom-foresail and upper and lower fore-topsails on the yards. Some of the smaller schooners only carried three headsails, but the *Mary Ashburner* had, working forward, a fore-staysail, standing jib, boom jib and flying jib [PLATE 5C]. The Ashburners made their own blocks and it is likely that the standing and running rigging, of hemp and manilla, came from Henry Stuart's Rope Works.[90]

The *Mary Ashburner* was launched exactly one year after her keel had been laid, on the 6th November 1877. The *William Ashburner* had returned to the shipyard after her first year in service to be felted and yellow-metalled. She was relaunched soon after, being eased down the patent slip and then floated off the cradle to join her newest companion in Walney Channel.

The *Mary Ashburner* was towed into Devonshire Dock to load her first cargo of pig iron, and three weeks after her launch she sailed out of Barrow on her first voyage, bound for Cardiff under the command of Capt. Edmondson Charnley. Earlier that day William Bath had made his final inspection of the ship for Lloyd's. He accorded her the classification for which the Ashburners had initially aimed, 11 years A1 (9 years materials, plus additional years for mixed materials and salting). It is worth quoting from his final report: "This vessel is in scantlings and fastenings considerably in excess of the requirements of the Rules ... and the material and workmanship is of a superior quality."

The Final Schooners

Once the *Mary Ashburner* had been launched the Ashburners' two building slips were constantly occupied for most of the next few years. The two ships that followed her were also two-masted schooners designed for the coasting trade, and they were so similar that it can be construed that they were built from a single set of plans.[91] The *Isabella* [PLATE 5D], like her predecessor, took almost exactly a year to build and was launched on the 1st August 1878. The *Useful* was launched on the 22nd March 1879 by the wife of her first master, Capt. Robert Wright.

The *M.E. Johnson* and *James Postlethwaite* were probably also built from a single set of plans. They were both three-masters, though very shallow-draughted and designed for coasting rather than deepwater passages. The *M.E. Johnson* [PLATE 5E] was named after the wife of her first master, Capt. Robert Johnson, and it was this same lady who christened her when she was launched on the 1st October 1879. The *James Postlethwaite* [PLATE 5F] was built to a higher standard, 12 years A1 at Lloyd's, and was not launched until the 11th August 1881. Her first master was Capt. Robert Roskell.[92]

All these schooners joined the Ashburner fleet, and the *James Postlethwaite* was the last of their ships to do so. She was also the last in which William Ashburner participated. He died on the 5th November 1881, aged 72 years. He had caught a severe cold on a trip to Dublin three weeks earlier, and died as a result of a subsequent lung inflammation. He was buried besides his late wife in St. Mary's churchyard on Walney Island. During the day of the funeral, flags were flown at half-mast from most of the principal buildings of the Barrow dockyards, and from shipping in the port.[93] It was a fitting tribute to a man who had been associated with Barrow since its early days and had played a considerable part in its development. However, his industry was already outdated, and dwarfed by the newer

---

90. *Ulv.Mirror*, 27th April 1867 reports the opening of Henry Stuart's Steam Rope Works at Barrow. The first rope manufactured was 1½ inches × 70 fathoms, for James Fisher.
91. *Surv.Rep.(Isabella)* WHN 3254 Box 3 has a midship section annotated 'Yard Nos. 35 & 36'.
92. Launch reports in *B.Times*, 10th Nov. 1877 (*Mary Ashburner*); 3rd Aug. 1878 (*Isabella*); 29th March 1879 (*Useful*); 4th Oct. 1879 (*M.E. Johnson*); 13th Aug. 1881 (*James Postlethwaite*). Plans of the latter four ships are included in the unpublished manuscript of *Schooners' Sunset* by Douglas Bennet, held at the Merseyside Maritime Museum.
93. *Obit.(W.A.)*

PLATE 5E: M.E. Johnson, *possibly by Reuben Chappell, undated. Unlike the* William Ashburner *she was rigged without a topgallant and carried only three headsails. An unusual feature of her rig is that she carried a jackyard-topsail on the mizzen mast but a more easily handled jib-headed topsail on the main.*

PLATE 5F: James Postlethwaite *at Dover, 1922. She was fully re-masted after the First World War but this is probably her original form.*

industries that dominated the town. The value of William Ashburner's estate was calculated as £7051 – insignificant in comparison to the £100,000 capital raised to start the Barrow Shipbuilding Co. ten years earlier.

Only one more schooner was built at the Ashburner shipyard, and the launch of the *J.& M. Garratt* in April 1884 marked the end of wooden shipbuilding at Barrow. This last ship, a two-masted schooner, continued the usual high standard of the shipyard. She was classed 12 A1 and was built to Special Survey. She was sold to owners at Connah's Quay, the main port on the Dee River into Chester.

Wooden shipbuilding had begun to decline in Britain in the 1870's, and although some yards were to continue to launch ships for another thirty years, many others were being closed down. The last vessel to be built at Ulverston, the schooner *Ellen Harrison*, had been launched in 1878. The following year had seen the final launch by Barrow's Furness Ship Building Co., the schooner *Ellie Park*. The Ashburners seem to have closed down their shipyard in the year after the launch of the *J.& M. Garratt*. In January 1889 Peter Campbell, a shipwright and director of the Furness Ship Building Co., moved into the premises.[94] His company vacated the smaller Northern Hindpool yard and continued its repair operations from the Ashburner yard until the end of the Century. Matthew Simpson's yard at Glasson Dock was to continue building ships until 1907, in its later years under the name of Nicholson & Marsh. The Duddon Shipbuilding Co. at Millom was to continue longest of all, launching the last schooner built in England in 1913.

---

94. Notebook of Capt. Thomas Latham, shown to me by Dorothy Latham.

6 OWNERS AND SAILORS

The Schoonermen

The 1871 Census recorded 261 seamen at Barrow. Many of these would have been aboard ships in the harbour and were therefore unlikely to be resident locally. More representative of the size of the local maritime community was the fact that 301 Barrow seamen were absent from home aboard their own ships.[95] This was a great increase from the four local seamen listed in the 1851 Census, and like the rise in Barrow's population generally, which had grown to 17,992, was attributable to a large-scale immigration into the town. The schoonermen came from the Morecambe Bay ports, especially Ulverston, Lancaster and Fleetwood, but also from more distant places. Considering the great quantity of trade to South Wales, it is not surprising that Welsh surnames occur frequently in the crew lists of Barrow vessels. Within the Ashburner fleet in the 1870's however, the majority of seamen came from the small Lancashire port of Tarleton.

The Tarleton seamen

Tarleton lies on the River Douglas at its confluence with the estuary of the River Ribble, about nine miles South West of Preston. It was once a thriving port, mainly exporting Wigan coal that had been brought by barge, first along the Douglas Navigation, then from 1783 by a branch of the Leeds-Liverpool canal. The coal was shipped onto 30 or 40 ton flats for transport to the Morecambe Bay ports, Liverpool and Ireland. The magnitude of this trade was such that there was a Customs officer at Hesketh Bank nearby, and double lock gates were built at the head of the canal to form a 500 yard dock for the seagoing vessels. Customs returns show that in the years 1847 to 1852 about 300 vessels each year sailed to Tarleton. Incoming cargoes were Welsh slates, Furness iron ore and gunpowder from Ulverston, destined for use in the South Lancashire coal mines. The trade with Furness was substantial but Tarleton's trade slumped in the 1850's after the imposition of duties, to such an extent that the Customs officer was withdrawn in 1859.[96] Fortunately for its seamen, Tarleton's decline had coincided with the expansion of the Barrow fleets. First they began to man the Barrow ships, and eventually many of them moved with their families to live there, or at Ulverston or Millom. In common with William Ashburner, himself a Wesleyan, and also many of the North Wales seamen, the Tarleton men came largely from a non-Conformist background. Some of them were enthusiastic evangelists, and in the 1860's it was a common Sunday event to see Tarleton and Preston masters preaching from the bows of their ships as they lay moored in the Ulverston Canal basin.[97]

The extent of the exodus can be seen by examining the Tarleton Censuses of the period. In 1851 and 1861 there were many mariners listed there, with family names such as Iddon, Wignall, Banister, Edmondson, Latham, Fairclough and Geldart. By 1871 most of these had disappeared from the Tarleton Census, and were to be found instead in the newspaper lists of Barrow captains and the crew agreements of its ships. Such a movement of people was typical of Victorian Britain, and in Barrow it was mirrored by the immigration of Cornish miners and Staffordshire ironworkers.

As with many sailing communities, the Tarleton men preferred to crew their ships with men from their own locality, and often an entire crew could be drawn from a single family. In 1872 Capt. John Latham had his three sons, William, John and Thomas, sailing with him on the *Alice Latham*. The eldest of these was twenty years old and the two younger were aged fourteen

---

95. *The Barrow Pilot*, 20th May 1871.
96. From notes made by a Local History Society, at Ormskirk Reference Library.
97. *Furn.Folk*

and eleven. Men from nearby communities such as Preston and Lytham also appeared regularly in these crews, and in 1882 it was a Lytham man, Capt. Thomas Davies, that was in command of the *Alice Latham*.[98]

Tarleton had other maritime connections with Barrow. James Ashcroft was a shipowner, variously decribed as resident at Tarleton or Hesketh Bank until about 1865. He then moved to Barrow and amassed a significant schooner fleet. When the Customs House opened a few years later most of his ships were re-registered locally. Tarleton's small shipbuilding industry had even earlier connections with Furness. A 28 ton sloop, the *Newland*, had been built for Thomas Roper in 1859.[99] Ten years later Peter Lund built a 120 ton schooner. He was not able to fit her out himself, so the hull was towed to Barrow by a Preston tug. She was completed early in the following year and was named the *Sarah Jane* at her launch.[100]

Capt. Robert Charnley

The influx of Tarleton seamen into the Ashburner fleet began with Capt. John Latham's command of the *Furness Maid* in 1863. In the preceeding years the Ashburners had recruited their captains primarily from Ulverston, and it was one of these men who became the principal master in the fleet. Capt. Robert Charnley was a member of a seafaring family that was perhaps more closely involved with the maritime activities of Furness than any other. He was born at Ulverston in 1830 and was associated with the Ashburners from their earliest days at Barrow. During his career he had command of three of their finest schooners.

Robert Charnley's first contact with the Ashburners came in 1859 when he was given command of the newly-launched *Lord Muncaster*. He must have already been been successful in his profession for he bought shares in her and nearly all the succeeding Ashburner schooners. He was an uncertificated master, meaning that he was not formally qualified to take his ship outside the limits of the Home trade. The Mercantile Marine Act of 1850 had introduced the statutory system of masters' tickets for ships involved in Foreign trade, and these could be obtained in two ways. Men who had been in command of ships at the introduction of the system were granted Certificates of Service. Others were required to take an examination to gain a Certificate of Competency. Capt. Charnley eventually took this examination at 42 years of age, in Dublin in 1872, at which time he was in command of the *R.& M.J. Charnley*.[101]

Capt. Charnley had not however confined himself to the Home trade in the intervening years. The *Lord Muncaster* had made occasional foreign trips under his command, including her record-breaking passage from Cardiff to Lisbon. After he took command of the *R.& M.J. Charnley*, from her launch in 1868, this ship was almost constantly involved in foreign trade in the years up to 1872. Capt. Charnley had avoided the requirements of the Act by taking on a certificated master for these voyages. He himself was listed on the Crew Lists as either boatswain or purser, and for one voyage as 'supercargo'. The certificated master was only on board to comply with the requirements of the Act, and Capt. Charnley was still in effective command of his ship. This was a common practice amongst the uncertificated schooner captains, who despite their lack of qualifications had the confidence of the ships' owners, and more importantly, their insurers.

Capt. Charnley's ticket was for fore-and-aft rigged vessels only, meaning that he was effectively confined to schooners – no great disadvantage on the West Coast, and none at all within the Ashburner fleet. Since the crew's wages in a Furness schooner were paid from the master's share of its profits, it would no doubt have been of financial benefit to him to obtain his ticket and dispense with the need to carry a qualified master. Perhaps he was also clearing the way to take command of one of the large three-masters that the Ashburners were about to

---

98. LRO Crew Lists for *Alice Latham*
99. *LSR*
100. Launch reported in *B.Times*, 15th Jan.1870 – her sails were made by Capt. Porter, blocks by Mr. Sharp and rigging and cordage by Henry Stuart. Capt. John Taylor was her first master.
101. *Charn.Hist.* – Certificate of Competency No. 95924; also Application to be Examined, dated 3rd April 1872. Further information from *Captains Register*, GLL 18567/3 & 18567/17.

build. Four years after qualifying he was given command of the Ashburners' finest vessel, the *William Ashburner*, and at that time was described as the oldest master in the Ashburner fleet. He sailed her in foreign trade until 1891, when he seems to have retired.

Robert Charnley came from a large family and several of his brothers achieved distinction in maritime careers. Four of the brothers were schooner captains, and at various times had command of the Ashburners' *Mary Jane, Elizabeth Barrow* and *Lord Muncaster*. They were, however, each associated more closely with other Barrow shipowners. Edmondson commanded Jervis's *J.H. Barrow* for 14 years and Walton's *Mary Sinclair* for 21 years, and in between these two ships he took the *Mary Ashburner* on her first voyage. Richard Charnley fell from the rigging of James Fisher's *Elizabeth* on a voyage from Barrow to Rotterdam in 1865 and was drowned.[102] Thomas commanded schooners from the Rawlinson fleet, including his first Barrow-built vessel, *Gummershow*. Stephen Charnley had command of the *S.& E.A. Charnley*, a 101 ton schooner built for Richard Fisher at the Charnley shipyard at Ulverston in 1872, and wrecked on the South Stack, Anglesey, in July 1881.[103] The Ulverston shipyard was operated by William & Richard Charnley but it is not known if they were part of or related to the Barrow family. A fifth brother, James, was the first holder of a Trinity House pilot's licence for the port of Barrow, which he received in 1873. His pilot cutter *Argus* had been built by the Ashburners.

Lost at Sea

The seamen on the Ashburner schooners of course faced danger at sea, but it has to be said that their profession was less hazardous than working in Barrow's other main industries. The local newspapers of the mid-Victorian years only occasionally listed a shipping loss, but their pages are littered with reports of accidents, maiming and death at the ironworks and the mines. Even so, most of Barrow's maritime families suffered tragedy at some time, and often this was magnified because of the tradition of family members sailing together on the same ship.

Six of the Ashburner schooners were lost with all hands, a total of twenty nine men, and three of the five crew of the *R. & M.J. Charnley* were also drowned when she went down. And lives were lost in bad weather even when the ships themselves survived, men being washed overboard or falling from the rigging. One such accident was reported in 1867:

> LOSS OF AN ULVERSTON SAILOR – Intelligence has been received of the arrival of the schooner *James & Agnes*, Captain Brockbank, at Majorca, after a very rough passage. She encountered very heavy weather and we are sorry to have to record the loss of one of the seamen, named Henry Rawcliffe, who was washed overboard during one of the many gales she encountered after leaving Liverpool. Henry Rawcliffe was a native of Ulverston, and eldest son of Capt. W. Rawcliffe, late of the *Richard Roper*.[104]

In September 1887 the *Margaret Ann* gybed as she passed the Bar Lightship at Liverpool and her master was knocked overboard by the mainboom and drowned. She seems to have been something of a fated ship, for later one of her owners and his wife both died on board, although of natural causes. Not all of the dangers faced by the seamen were inflicted by the weather and the sea. The men who sailed the *William Ashburner* encountered hazards unknown to their colleagues on the other Ashburner schooners sailing in European waters. Townley Charnley, a crewman and brother of Capt. Robert Charnley, died of yellow fever in a South American port.[105]

---

102. *Ulv.Adv.*, 1st June 1865.
103. *B.Times*, 23rd July 1881, p5.
104. *Ulv.Mirror*, 2nd Feb. 1867.
105. *Charn.Hist.* – from family Bible loaned by Robert Charnley.
106. *LSR*

Ships' Shares and Shareholders

British-registered sailing ships were owned in sixty four shares, a requirement originating from the 1824 Merchant Shipping Act. Sometimes all the shares would be wholly owned by an individual or company, but this was exceptional amongst the small sailing ships. Most of these were owned by groups of shareholders, usually tied by family or business connections with the ship, or at least originating from the local community. A managing owner, or 'ship's husband' if he was not himself a shareholder, was responsible for handling the ship's accounts and distributing dividends to the shareholders. He received from the ships' masters their accounts, calculated the owners' dividend, arranged insurances and generally acted as the accountant for the ships' business, for which he received a fee. Often a ship's managing owner held a substantial number of her shares, though he would not always be the major shareholder.

The shares in the earliest Ashburner schooners were largely sold to men associated with the iron company Harrison, Ainslie & Co., the managing owner being Capt. Henry Bond of Ulverston. Thereafter the Ashburners retained shares in all their ships, some of which they managed themselves. Nevertheless, their combined holdings rarely exceeded 25 to 30 shares, the remainder being widely distributed, mainly amongst the local community.

The usual practice with the later schooners, from the *Nanny Latham* onwards, was for Thomas Ashburner to buy the shares in their entirety. Then over a period of months he would sell them, usually in ones and twos, and only rarely with more than five going to a single individual. Usually the first buyers came from the masters in the Ashburner fleet, other ships' captains (but never ordinary seamen) and men who had participated in the ship's construction, such as sailmakers and blacksmiths. Thereafter shares were sold to a variety of people otherwise unconnected with the sea. There was a spread of ownership through all social classes, though in general the shares remained with people living in Furness.

Table 6A shows the original shareholders in the *Mary Jane*. The Ashburner family had a total of 23 shares, of which most were in the hands of Robert, the ship's master and managing owner. Amongst the other shareholders are several who had shares in the earlier ships, and the Ashburners seem to have been able to rely on a large group of people who regularly invested in their new ships over many years.

TABLE 6A: Owners of the *Mary Jane* in 1860[106]

Robert Ashburner	Master Mariner	Barrow	12 shares
Richard Ashburner	Ship Builder	Barrow	5 shares
Joseph Roper	Shoe Maker	Liverpool	4 shares
Robert Harrison	Draper	Barrow	4 shares
Robert Bell	Examiner of Inland Insurance	London	4 shares
William Hawkrigg	Farmer	High Seathwaite	4 shares
Richard Kendall	Ironmonger	Barrow	4 shares
William Ashburner	Ship Builder	Barrow	2 shares
Richard Ashburner	Ship Carpenter	Barrow	2 shares
Thomas Ashburner	Ship Carpenter	Barrow	2 shares
Joseph Brockbank	Ship Carpenter	Barrow	2 shares
James Brockbank	Master Mariner	Barrow	2 shares
Robert Charnley	Master Mariner	Barrow	2 shares
Henry Bond	Master Mariner	Barrow	2 shares
Sarah Bond	Wife of Henry Bond	Barrow	2 shares
John Slater	Butcher	Barrow	2 shares
Robert Ainsworth	Grocer	Hawcoat	2 shares
John Jackson	Stationer & Printer	Ulverston	2 shares
Thomas Greenwood	Farmer	Walney Island	2 shares
Robert Greenwood	Gentleman	Walney Island	2 shares
John Bell	Joiner	Liverpool	1 share

Merchants of all types are very common in the lists of shareholders. Those such as the iron ore merchants, coal merchants and millers would have had a business interest in shipping. Others, such as the butchers, stationers and publicans, would have been successful businessmen who merely saw shipping as a profitable investment, the same motive that attracted men from the professions, including surgeons, solicitors, insurance agents, a minister and a newspaper editor. Some farmers also had sufficient income for investment, and there were other shareholders wealthy enough to disdain from nominating any profession and describing themselves merely as 'gentlemen'. The wealthiest in Barrow's community, the iron magnates and large landowners, invested their money in grander enterprises than the small sailing ships. At the other end of the social scale, a share in a new schooner would cost the equivalent of half a year's wages for a labourer. Nevertheless labourers, servants and other low-paid workers were able to afford shares in the smaller ships, and it says something for the confidence that these ships engendered that such undoubtedly hard-earned money was risked in this way.

Most of the shares sold outside the Furness district seem to have gone to family relations of the local shareholders, the Ropers of Liverpool being prominent. One outsider who had no family relations with the district was George Pullen, a commercial traveller from York who bought two shares in the *Elizabeth Barrow*. Perhaps this man had other connections with Furness shipping – the first Barrow lifeboat was named the *Commercial Traveller* and was a gift from their trade association.[107]

---

107. The lifeboat was built outside the district. Her delivery and launch is reported in *Ulv.Adv.*, 3rd Aug. 1865.

7 TRADES

Although it has been said that certain of the Ashburner schooners were designed with specific trades in mind, the ships once launched were by no means confined to these. They operated wherever there was a profit to be made, and in the hard times when this was not possible, they took cargoes wherever they could be found. For the purpose of describing their trading routes, it has been convenient to divide them into foreign, coasting and short sea trades. By legal definition, foreign voyages were those to ports outside Britain, Ireland and the European coast between the River Elbe (Hamburg) and Ushant (Brest). The coasting trade strictly embraces any passage within these limits, Home waters. However, many of the smaller Furness schooners confined themselves to operating in the Northern half of the Irish Sea, to such an extent that it is worth describing this separately as the short sea trade.

Foreign Trade

Only four of the Ashburner schooners operated primarily in foreign trade. They were the *James & Agnes*, built in 1864 and their largest two-master, and their earliest three-masters, the *R. & M.J. Charnley*, *Mary Bell* and *William Ashburner*. Several of the other larger two-masters sailed to the Mediterranean and the Iberian peninsula, but these were only summer excursions from their regular employment in the Home trade. Of the deepwater schooners, only the *William Ashburner* ever crossed the Atlantic or went South of the Equator, and she was the only Ashburner schooner to be felted and yellow-metalled. The other schooners largely existed in the ore trades to Spain and Portugal. Other Barrow shipowners were more adventurous than the Ashburners, and ships belonging to the fleets of Fisher, Kirkby and Jervis sailed regularly to the West Indies, Brazil and North America, and less often to South Africa and the Far East.

None of the Ashburner schooners operated in the foreign trade out of Barrow. The ore carriers sailed to and from the South Wales ports and the *William Ashburner* mainly sailed from Liverpool and London. Barrow's limited foreign export trade was largely confined to steel products and was dominated by the ships of James Fisher. In its early years there was a substantial import trade in timber, from the Baltic and North America. The Ashburner schooners were not involved in this. Though the *James & Agnes* spent the first sixteen years of her life entirely in foreign trade, she never crossed the Atlantic and only visited the Baltic once (in 1879), when her return passage was from Riga to South Wales. Her master for some of this time was Capt. Evans, who alternated tours of duty with Capt. Robert Charnley on the *William Ashburner*.

The Spanish ore trade

The main foreign trade for the Furness schooners was the ore trade from the Iberian peninsula. There were two great mineral-producing regions in Spain, both of which emerged into prominence in the 1850's and exported vast quantities of minerals for use in British industry. In the North, iron ore was mined in the Basque region and was exported through the ports of Bilbao and Santander. Equally important were the mines in Huelva Province in the South of the country, largely producing copper pyrites for export through Spanish and Portugese ports on the Guadiana River. The Furness schooners, specifically designed for the carriage of ore cargoes, were ideally suited to this trade, and their owners' business connections with the iron and steel companies that used the ore ensured that they were able to fully exploit this advantage.

For the Ashburner schooners, the copper ore trade was the more important, and their principal ports of call were Pomaron and Villa Real.[110] These were on the Portugese side of the Guadiana River, which flows into the Atlantic and formed the Southern border between Portugal and Spain. The Spanish ports of Ayamonte, La Laja and Huelva also shipped ore, and eventually Huelva was to become the principal port for the trade. The local mines produced cupreous sulphur ore (copper pyrites), and also smaller quantities of iron pyrites, manganese and lead ore. The pyrites was transported to Britain for extraction of iron, copper and/or sulphur, and the copper smelting works at Swansea was a major recipient.

Pomaron, thirty miles inland, was the river port closest to the mines. Like Barrow it owed its development to a railway link and port improvements financed by the mining company. The first ship was loaded at Pomaron on the 23rd March 1859, and in that first year 7,887 (metric) tonnes of ore was loaded aboard 41 ships.[111] In the following years it was often visited by the Ashburner schooners, but for the most part these voyages were undertaken only in calm weather during the summer. The *Jane Roper, Tom Roper, Lord Muncaster* and *Mary & May*, the four schooners operating for Harrison, Ainslie & Co., were involved, as were the *Mary Jane, James & Agnes* and *Elizabeth Barrow*. The pattern of trade was generally that these schooners would first load coal at Cardiff, Newport or Swansea. This was sometimes destined for Gibraltar (possibly for the stockpile of the British Mediterranean fleet), but coal was in constant demand for domestic use everywhere, and amongst the other ports of call were Malaga, Palma, Marseille and Barcelona. The ships would then sail light to one of the ore ports, usually Pomaron, and take aboard a return cargo.

The activities of the Ashburner schooners in 1865 can be used to illustrate their involvement in the copper ore trade. In that year Pomaron shipped 142,478 tonnes of ore aboard 544 ships, some of which were steamers. The *Mary & May* was the first Ashburner schooner to arrive in the Guadiana River, on the 29th May, from Newport via Lisbon (14 days to Lisbon, then 5 to Villa Real). She loaded a cargo at Pomaron, and was safely berthed at Liverpool by the time the next Ashburner schooners arrived. They were the *Lord Muncaster*, from Figueira, and the *James & Agnes*, from Seville. Many other Furness-owned schooners were sailing into the port. The *Lord Muncaster* came in with Jervis's *Carrie Bell*, and on the day they arrived the departing ships included Jervis's *Fanny Slater*, Fisher's *Lancashire Witch* and two Ulverston-owned schooners, the *William Stonard* and the *Gauntlet*. Both the *Lord Muncaster* and the *James & Agnes* loaded ore at Pomaron to return to Liverpool, the *Lord Muncaster* making a slow return passage, putting into Lisbon in a leaky condition and having to lighten her cargo. Only the *Mary & May* made a second Portugese voyage that year, taking 17 days from Newport to Lisbon and returning from Pomaron to Liverpool in 19 days. Lloyd's List does not record any foreign voyages in 1865 for the *Elizabeth Barrow* or the *Tom Roper*, though in the previous year, together with the *Mary Jane*, they had each made a single journey to Pomaron from Newport, returning to the Clyde. In the summer of 1865 however, Capt. Robert Ashburner was trading to Swedish ports, taking the *Mary Jane* from Newcastle to Landskrona and Halmstad, and the only voyage recorded for the *Jane Roper* in that year was from Newport to Brouwershaven, Holland.

Whereas most of the Ashburner schooners only sailed on foreign voyages during the summer, the *R. & M.J. Charnley* was involved in the Spanish ore trade for most of her early life, under the command of Capt. Robert Charnley until 1876. In 1880 she was the last Ashburner schooner to carry a foreign ore cargo, going from Liverpool to Gibraltar under the command of Capt. Griffiths, then to Huelva to load ore for Connah's Quay. This was her last foreign voyage and thereafter she operated in the coasting trade. Huelva had by this time become the principal Southern ore port. The *R. & M.J. Charnley* was one of 535 British ships that visited the port in 1880, and nearly half a million tons of pyrites was exported in that year alone.

The export of Spanish iron ore was even greater in magnitude than the copper ore trade. Until the late 1850's Malaga, on the Mediterranean coast, had been Spain's main ore

---

110. Voyage details in this chapter generally from *Lloyd's List* (or GLL Index) or the Shipping Intelligence columns of Barrow and Ulverston newspapers.
111. Pomaron and Huelva trade details from British consular reports, communicated by Robin Craig.

exporting port, though producing only about 50,000 tons per year. It continued with this trade, as did the other Mediterranean ports of Carthagena and Almeria, where at one time the Millom & Askam Iron Company owned a mine. However, the Basque ore, like the Furness ore, was non-phosphoric haematite, essential for producing the right kind of pig iron for the Bessemer process of steel-making. With the introduction of this process in the 1860's the increased demand for haematite in Britain benefitted the trade enormously, and Bilbao and Santander became Spain's main ore ports.

The Basque haematite was cheaply produced from open-cast mines and was in great demand in Britain, to such an extent that it contributed to a recession in the Furness ore industry in the mid-1870's. Even Barrow imported it, amounting to 13,874 tons in 1873.[112] The major recipients were the South Wales steelworks, but the Furness schooners also carried Spanish haematite to all the major iron and steel manufacturing regions, including the Clyde, Workington and, less frequently, Middlesborough. In 1873, for example, the *James & Agnes* brought two cargoes from Santander, one to Shields and the other to Saundersfoot. In the following year she carried coal from Cardiff to Lisbon, then sailed light to Bilbao to load an ore cargo for Maryport.

There were other mineral cargoes from Spain and Portugal, including calamine ore (zinc oxide) from Malaga and sulphur from Lisbon. Together with haematite and pyrites, their transport sustained the *James & Agnes* and the *R.& M.J. Charnley* throughout most of their early careers. By 1880 they had both ceased making foreign passages, and of the Ashburner schooners only the *William Ashburner* continued to sail outside Home waters.

The deepwater career of the William Ashburner

The *William Ashburner* voyaged further than any other of the Ashburner schooners, and was wholly occupied in foreign trade for the first eighteen years of her life. She was rarely, if ever, involved in the ore trades, and most frequently voyaged deep into the Mediterranean or to South and Central America.

After being yellow-metalled a year after her launch, the *William Ashburner* spent the following year sailing to the near Mediterranean and North Africa, her ports of call including Gibraltar, Menorca, Carthagena, and Larache on the Atlantic coast of Morocco. She returned from Larache to Liverpool and there loaded her first cargo for South America. Her forty day passage to Parahiba ended on Christmas Eve, 1878 and was claimed as a 'quick passage'. This Brazilian port was to be one of her principal destinations in future years.

For all this time the ship had been under the command of Capt. Robert Charnley, and he continued with her throughout the following year. Her voyages were particularly wide-ranging. Returning to London from Parahiba, the ship loaded an outward cargo for Port Natal, South Africa. This voyage down the West Coast of Africa and around the Cape of Good Hope took more than three months, and was to be the only time she ever ventured into the Indian Ocean. She did not return directly to Britain, but headed for Brazil, putting into St. Helena and arriving eventually at Pernambuco, a second Brazilian port at which she was to become a regular visitor. She ended the year where she had started it, berthed at Parahiba.

The *William Ashburner* returned to Liverpool, but her next South American cargo was loaded at Troon for Berbice, Guyana. She then sailed light to Kingston and then St. Ann's Bay, Jamaica, from where she returned to London. Capt. Charnley took a well-earned rest, and when the ship cleared from the West India Dock for Pernambuco in September 1880, it was Capt. Evans, from the *James & Agnes*, who was in command. For the next ten years these two men would alternate tours of duty.

Table 7A gives a record of the ship's movements in 1881. The return cargo from Parahiba to Greenock was sugar, and the transatlatic crossing to Queenstown (now Cobh) in Ireland took forty six days. Capt. Charnley resumed command at Greenock and Capt. Evans returned temporarily to the *James & Agnes*, which by now had ended her days on deepwater. The

---

112. *F.& I.R.* p382.

TABLE 7A: Movements of the *William Ashburner* in 1881, taken from the Shipping Intelligence columns of the Barrow Times.

Pub'n Date	Details of Movements
1/ 1/1881	Evans, at Pernambuco, Nov. 30.
8/ 1/1881	Evans, at Pernambuco for Parahyba to load, 5.
29/ 1/1881	Evans, at Parahyba to load for Greenock, 22nd Dec., expected to leave 1st instant.
12/ 2/1881	Evans, left Parahyba for UK 14th Jan.
5/ 3/1881	Evans, at Queenstown from Parahyba, waiting for orders, 2.
12/ 3/1881	Evans, at Greenock from Parahyba, 9.
26/ 3/1881	Charnley, at Greenock, 24.
23/ 4/1881	Charnley, left Greenock for Naples, 18.
14/ 5/1881	Charnley, at Naples from Greenock, 12.
28/ 5/1881	Charnley, at Naples for Gallipoli, 19.
25/ 6/1881	Charnley, at Gallipoli for Canea, island of Candia, to load, 12.
16/ 7/1881	Charnley, at Canea, ready to leave for Goole, 3.
27/ 8/1881	Charnley, at Goole 22nd from Canea.
10/ 9/1881	Charnley, at Goole loading for Messina, 7.
17/ 9/1881	Charnley, left Hull for Messina, 15.
22/10/1881	Evans, left Plymouth for Messina, 1.
12/11/1881	Evans, at Messina for Kata Kolo, Greece, to load for UK, 3rd.
17/12/1881	Evans, at Catacolo ready to leave for UK, 25th ult.
31/12/1881	Evans, at Plymouth from Catacolo, for orders, 29.

TABLE 7B: Movements of the *William Ashburner* in 1885-87, taken from Lloyd's Weekly Shipping Index.

Pub'n Date	From	For	Latest Report
1885			
Jan. 2	Teignmouth Nov.21	Genoa (Italy)	Ar. Dec.20
Mar. 6	Genoa Feb.9	Barranquilla (Colombia)	Cd. Gibraltar Feb.26
Aug. 21	Colon (Panama) Jul.6	New York	Ar. Aug.4
Sep.25	New York Aug.21	Madeira	Ar. Sept.17
Oct.30	Madeira Oct.2	Faro (Portugal)	Ar. Oct.16
Dec. 4	Tavira Oct.30 (Portugal)	Leith	Ar. Dec.1
1886			
Feb.12	Leith Jan.19	Buenos Ayres	Sd. Falmouth about Feb.10
May 28	Leith Jan.19	Buenos Ayres	Ar. Apr.25
Aug.20	Paysandu (Uruguay)	Bahia (Brazil)	Ar. Jul.20
1887			
Mar. 4	Bahia Dec.18	New York	Ar. Feb.17 * Mar.4
Jul.22	Pointe a Pitre (Guadeloupe)	Marseille	Ar. Jul.12
Sep.16	Marseille Aug.10	Lisbon	Ar. Aug.27
Sep.30	Lisbon Sept.12	Liverpool	Ar. Sept.25

*Mar.4, Page 3: NEW YORK Feb.16 – The *William Ashburner*, Charnley, which arrived here yesterday from Bahia, reports :- Jan.10, during a heavy Northerly gale shipped a sea, which stove in bulwarks etc., and washed everything moveable from the decks.

remainder of the year was spent in the Mediterranean trade. Messina is on Sicily, and Naples and Gallipoli are also Italian ports. Candia is now known as Crete and Canea was its main port. The outward cargo was olive oil.

For the next ten years the *William Ashburner* sailed in these and similar trades, crossing the Atlantic many times [TABLE 7B]. Shipping reports only rarely mentioned cargoes, so it is only possible to speculate about what she was carrying; sugar, rum, coffee, cotton, timber and hides from Brazil; sugar, rum and cotton, also spices, from the West Indies; and hides, tallow, bones and boneash from Uruguay and Argentina. The outward cargoes would mostly have been coal, and perhaps also steel rails and machinery.

Towards the end of her deepwater career the *William Ashburner* began to sail regularly to Uruguay. Capt. Charnley retired in 1891 but Capt. Evans continued with the ship, sailing her from Cardiff to Montevideo, and then to Fray Bentos, an inland port on the Uruguay River. The return passage with a cargo of tallow took fifty two days to Queenstown. The ship continued in the Uruguay trade, visiting Montevideo, Fray Bentos and Paysandu. Capt. Evans retired and the ship was briefly commanded by Capt. D. Thomas and Capt. J.G. Learty. Her last deepwater passage was in 1894 and it was Capt. Learty who was in command. Having arrived from Antwerp, the *William Ashburner* started yet another year at Parahiba. Her return passage took her first to Barbadoes, then Trinidad. On her way to London's West India Dock she took thirty six days from Trinidad to Gravesend.

The schooner was put into the trade between Gravesend and Guernsey, but after a seemingly trouble-free existence on foreign voyages she soon encountered one of the frequent hazards of the coasting trade. Returning from Guernsey in December she collided with a steamer off South Benfleet. The crew abandoned her for the safety of the steamer, the *Normand*, but a boatman was put aboard and managed to run the damaged vessel onto Blyth Sands. The following day she was pulled clear by a tug and towed to Gravesend's Cherry Garden Pier. She was badly damaged on her port side and was taking in water. A temporary patch stopped this and at the end of her last year of deepwater passages the *William Ashburner* was sailing 'round the land' for repair at the North Devon port of Appledore.

The Short Sea Trade

For the Furness schooners the boundaries of the short sea trade could be said to be Dublin, Holyhead and the River Dee to the South. To the North, the limits were the River Clyde and the Ulster port of Larne. Within this area were the great ports of Liverpool, Glasgow and Belfast, and scores of smaller ports and harbours on the British and Irish coasts, as well as several on the Isle of Man. The carriage of the raw materials for industry, building materials, coal and foodstuffs between them was so substantial that many small schooners only rarely had to leave the Northern half of the Irish Sea in their search for work.

The Ashburners built several small two-masted schooners for the short sea trade. The smallest schooner, the *Furness Maid*, was also the first. She was 49 tons and 63 feet in length. After her came six schooners of almost identical size, the *Alice Latham, Nanny Latham, Catherine Latham, Margaret Ann, Henry & Mary* and *Elizabeth Latham*. Of 75 gross tons, they were about 77 feet in length with a draught of about 8 feet, each vessel having a cargo capacity of about 140 tons. The last of the Ashburners' short sea traders, the *Margaret Banister*, was slightly larger. They were all built in the years from 1865 to 1871, and their building was only interrupted by the launch of two deepsea schooners. Their building coincided with the great upsurge in export of iron ore from the Duddon, and it can be assumed that this was what influenced the Ashburners to change from building larger schooners. Both the Duddon and the Dee estuaries, a principal destination for the ore, had narrow, shifting channels and crowded, tidal harbours, best served by small and shallow-draughted vessels.

Most of the Ashburners' short sea traders worked for long periods in the Duddon ore trade, and often several would arrive or leave Millom together. In the 1870's the *Alice Latham, Elizabeth Latham* and *Catherine Latham* frequently sailed together on the journey to Ellesmere Port, where the Hodbarrow Mining Company had a stockpile. The import trade into the

Duddon was small, and largely confined to timber for use in the mines. Therefore the return passages were often to Barrow, usually with coal. The schooners would then sail light to the Duddon for their next ore cargo. Return cargoes from Belfast and other Irish ports seem to have been difficult to find, and often schooners would arrive light in the Duddon from Northern Ireland. The Furness masters would have been well-acquainted with the Duddon shipping agents, and perhaps it was the knowledge that they could always fix a cargo there that kept them from straying too far from this port.

There were many cargoes carried other than ore and coal, and many other ports visited. The short sea traders were the most versatile of ships, and the opportunity to carry even small quantities of goods often attracted them to the isolated communities and small harbours which abounded around the Irish Sea. Taking examples from the Ulster coast alone, between Londonderry and Dundalk, there were the major ports of Belfast and Larne, then Carrickfergus, Holywood, Whiteabbey and Groomsport on Belfast Lough. On the Down coast, Kilkeel and Annalong exported granite, and also Newry and Warrenpoint on Carlingford Lough, exporting sand and foodstuffs. On Strangford Lough there was Killyleagh, and Red Bay in Antrim exported iron ore. None of these small ports was a regular visiting place, but each at some time received an Ashburner schooner, and together with similar ports in England, Scotland and the Isle of Man they played their part in keeping them in constant employment.

Despite these occasional excursions to small harbours, it was still the larger ports shipping the raw materials and products of industry that were most frequently visited by the short sea traders. They were Liverpool, Garston, Ellesmere and Birkenhead on the Mersey, Saltney and Connah's Quay on the Dee, Barrow itself and the coal and steel ports of Cumberland and Scotland, such as Workington, Whitehaven, Ardrossan and Ayr. Ore, iron and steel, coal and to a lesser extent, building materials, made up the great bulk of their cargoes.

If the short sea traders were confined to the Irish Sea because of their small size, then this was related to their cargo capacity rather than their ability to weather rough seas. On occasion they did venture outside their usual trading area, and when they did so it was more often through the North Channel to ports on the Scottish Islands or the West coast of Ireland. These small schooners were generally manned by a crew of three men, but on such longer voyages they would usually have an extra man in the crew. In July 1874 the *Henry & Mary* went from Ballina on the West coast of Ireland to Liverpool, and then from Runcorn to the Orkneys (presumably with salt for the fishing industry). But the bulk of her trade was within the Irish Sea and when she went missing at Christmas, 1879, it was on a voyage from Liverpool to Douglas with coal. Capt. James Tinsley and two others were lost with her.[113]

The *Alice Latham*, early in her life, had been under the managing ownership of Millom's William Postlethwaite. In 1878 another of the Ashburners' short sea traders, the *Nanny Latham*, also joined his fleet, for what were to be the last years of her life. In October 1881 a great gale swept the country for several days and caused havoc all around the coast, with many ships being wrecked or sunk. In the Dee River the tide rose to eight feet above its normal level and sank all the fishing boats. The *Nanny Latham*, anchored in Mostyn Roads, was torn from her moorings and found herself cast ashore at Llanerchymor. Fortunately she had only grounded on a sandbank and had suffered no substantial damage. Within a week she had been towed clear by a tug and was bound for Ballyraine in Ireland. She made the Northerly passage safely and picked up a return cargo of potatoes at Lough Swilly, Co. Donegal. Her destination was Cardiff, but the weather was still atrocious as she headed for the North Channel. She was caught in the grip of a force ten gale from the South West, and on the 22nd November she was swept onto rocks at Portantruan on the island of Islay.[114] Capt. Charles Griffiths and his two crewmen survived but the *Nanny Latham* was a total wreck.

The *Furness Maid* was sold in 1886 to John Lavery, a Carrickfergus merchant. He

---

113. *BSR* and *Wreck.Ret.*
114. *Wreck.Ret.* and *Lloyd's List*, 26th Nov. 1881.
115. LRO Crew Lists of *Furness Maid*.
116. *Lloyd's List*, 9th May 1891.

PLATE 7A: *This painting of the* Catherine Latham *is owned by the descendants of Capt. Thomas Latham. She was his last command upon his retirement from the sea in 1878, after a career of 27 years, to take charge of the Walney Island ferry.*

commanded the ship himself for a few years, and in this time she made some of her most hazardous journeys, braving the seas of the Pentland Firth to carry cargoes to Port Dundas and Pittenweem on the East coast of Scotland.[115] Eventually the owner's son, Bailey Lavery, took over her command, and it was under him that she was lost. On the night of 7th May 1891 she was off Brodick Head, Isle of Arran, carrying what was described as 86 tons of dross, bound for Carrickfergus. The steamship *Comorin*, heading out of the Clyde, ran into her stern. With her rudder and sternpost carried away the *Furness Maid* sank almost immediately, but the crew had time to launch their small boat and were safely picked up by the steamer.[116]

In the year after her launch the *Furness Maid* had been regularly employed carrying sand from Fleetwood to Ulverston. Several of the short sea traders found fairly constant employment in a single trade at various times during their career, and ultimately some were sold to merchants who operated in these trades. The *Catherine Latham* [PLATE 7A] was one such vessel, and largely earned her living in the brick trade out of Connah's Quay. Another was the *Margaret Ann*, for whom another building material provided a constant livelihood in the last twenty years of her life.

The Margaret Ann *and the Granite Trade*

Dalbeattie can be used as an example of the smaller ports served by the short sea traders. It was on the Scottish side of the Solway Firth, sited a few miles inland on the River Urr. There was a small harbour, capable of taking at most only sixteen small schooners, and close by were the two industries that gave the ships their cargoes. Alongside the quays was a small fertiliser factory that imported bonemeal and guano. This itself was at the foot of the granite quarry which, together with the quarry at Creetown, gave the port its principal export. The granite was carried, either crushed or as setts, to Liverpool, Preston and Manchester. The return cargo was often guano, brought to Liverpool by a deepwater vessel and then distributed around Britain and Ireland by the coasting schooners.

Dalbeattie and Palnackie, the other port on the Urr, had their own sailing ships, but it was an occasional visiting place for the Furness schooners. It would not have been one of the most popular. The River Urr was difficult to navigate and it took time and hard work to get the schooners across the bar and up the narrow and winding river. In March 1894 the *Alice Latham* grounded there and was severely damaged, taking a cargo of bonemeal up to Dalbeattie.[117]

One Ashburner schooner, however, became a regular visitor to the port. The *Margaret Ann*, the thirteenth Ashburner schooner, launched in 1868, was first commanded by Capt. James Sumner of Tarleton. She had been initially involved in the iron ore trade to the Dee River. Her registry had been transferred to Chester in 1897 when she was owned by John Coppack of Connah's Quay. Within three years she had been sold to an owner in Co. Down and by 1902 she was owned by Margaret Stitt of Dumfries, the wife of the ship's master.[118] The *Margaret Ann* was put into the granite trade and in the years until the First World War she made regular trips from the Solway. Mrs. Stitt sailed with her husband and died on board the ship in October, 1903. The schooner was sold to Alexander Wilson of Dumfries, but she stayed in the granite trade and her registry was transferred to the Scottish port.

Capt. J.A.J. Williams wrote an account in the magazine "Sea Breezes" of how, as a 15 year old boy, he absconded from his deepwater sailing ship and briefly joined the *Margaret Ann*, in Salthouse Dock, Liverpool in 1899.[119] He was the fourth crew member. The schooner loaded fertiliser at Canada Dock and sailed for Dalbeattie. Her crew included the master's wife and a brief call was made at the Isle of Man to row the small boat ashore and gather the vegetables for the evening meal from a field. This would officially have been classed as an act of piracy, but it was apparently a common practice amongst the Irish Sea schooners. When the *Margaret Ann* reached the mouth of the River Urr she had to be kedged across the bar. The river was too narrow to sail in so a Clydesdale horse towed her upstream. It took them three tides to reach their destination, which Capt. Williams thought resembled a farmyard. The schooner was grounded for unloading the fertiliser and loading a return cargo of granite setts for Preston. Once refloated the schooner was towed back down river by the horse.

The *Margaret Ann* spent twenty years in the granite trade. In 1917 she was sold to a Wexford coal merchant, Patrick Donovan, and she became the first of the Ashburners' wooden schooners to have an engine installed.[120] In December 1918 she was heading out from Britonferry to Wexford with a cargo of coke. Her new engine failed her as the she weathered a severe gale. She was soon dismasted and the crew were forced to abandon her, being taken off by the steamer *Montcoffer*. The *Margaret Ann* was swept into Freshwater Bay, Milford Haven, and struck bow first on the beach. Gripped by the sands, she was helpless as the Atlantic breakers pounded at her sides. Within a day the sea first carried off her deck fittings and bulwarks, and then tore loose her sternpost and rudder. A brief examination by the local Lloyd's surveyor was enough to confirm that she was a total loss.[121]

Trading history of the Margaret Banister

The *Margaret Banister* was the largest of the short sea traders built by the Ashburners. She was launched in September 1871 and her first master was Capt. Thomas Banister, after whose wife

---

117. GLL *Lloyd's Weekly Index*, 8th Nov.1890.
118. *CSR*
119. "Adventures in the *Margaret Ann*", in *Sea Breezes*, Feb. 1948 p120.
120. J. Copland, "The *Margaret Ann* and Other Solway Sailers", *Sea Breezes*, April 1949 p206. See also letter from James Reay in the same journal, March 1948 p178.
121. *Lloyd's List*, 18th to 24th Dec.1918. Her master was Thomas Morris.

the ship was named.[122] He kept her command for seven years, during which time the ship was under the managing ownership of John Bell of Ulverston. In August 1878 Capt. Banister was given the command of the Ashburners' newest schooner, the *Isabella*, named after his daughter. The launch of a new ship was often an occasion for the Ashburner captains to play musical chairs with their ships. Capt. John Hughes left the *Twin Brothers* at Ellesmere to take command of the *Mary Ashburner*, then at Chester. The master of that ship travelled up to Millom to take over the *Margaret Banister*, which had now joined the Ashburner fleet. Capt. Robert Latham came from a Tarleton family and had served in Ashburner schooners since the age of 12, when he had been cook in the *Furness Maid*, commanded by his father in 1863. In 1875, after his father and brother had drowned with the *Mary Bell*, he had graduated to his own first command, that of the *Elizabeth Latham*. He had stayed with her for two years, and then transferred to the *Mary Ashburner* for six months.[123] He was a close friend of Capt. Banister, who was also from a Tarleton family, and when he eventually left the *Margaret Banister* it was to replace his friend as master of the *Isabella*.

Robert Latham's account book for the *Margaret Banister*, which he commanded from September 1878 to April 1882, illustrates the nature of the work carried out by the short sea traders.[124] During the three years and six months of Capt. Latham's command the schooner only ventured outside the Irish Sea on four occasions, to St. Valery-sur-Somme, Swansea, Newport and Stornoway. Her main trade was between Barrow, Workington, Liverpool and the Dee River, and ore, iron and steel were her major cargoes.

The goods carried during Capt. Latham's first full year in command are detailed in Table 7C. The ship largely depended on four regular trades, though there was no constant pattern to these and many times the ship sailed light, illustrating that cargoes were often not immediately available. Ore from Duddon was a regular cargo, but it can be seen that by this time Barrow's ore trade had largely given way to the export of steel. The ship also profited from the flour mills that had been built alongside the Devonshire Dock, taking several cargoes to the Isle of Man. The cereals, wheat and maize, taken from Liverpool were probably being distributed after arrival there from overseas. Of all her cargoes in that year, it can be seen that the last, gunpowder from Ulverston, was the most lucrative of all. It brought in a total freight of £57 10s, exactly £20 more than if the *Margaret Banister* had carried a full cargo of 150 tons of pig iron from Barrow to Newport. Even with such high profits gunpowder was not a popular cargo. Crews were always aware of the hazards, and were placed under restrictions about the use of fires aboard the ship, and also upon docking and cargo handling procedures. Ulverston once nearly suffered a catastrophe when one of three gunpowder ships in the Canal basin caught alight whilst loading, and was only saved by two brave crewmen who boarded the ship to extinguish the fire.[125]

The trade of the *Margaret Banister* in the following year was similarly haphazard. She participated in another of the steady Furness ore trades, carrying iron ore from Red Bay to Barrow at 3/– per ton. In July, at the beginning of the Scottish herring fishing season, she took salt from Weston to Stornoway for 7/– per ton. Towards the end of 1880 her trade became more regular, and for all the following year she was involved in a fairly routine circular trade between Liverpool, Weston (on the Mersey) and Workington. She carried purple ore from Weston to Workington, then steel or pig iron back to Liverpool, then sailed light to Weston for more purple ore. She would make the run from Weston in about four days, but it once took her thirteen. The fastest return journey was two days. Only occasionally did she deviate from this trade over the next year, and then it was to take flour or foodstuffs to Barrow and return to Liverpool with steel. For the last two months of Capt. Latham's command she was on a

---

122. *BSR*.
123. Crew Lists for *Furness Maid* (LRO), *Elizabeth Latham* (CRO) and *Mary Ashburner* (CRO). His Marriage Certificate states that he was a seaman on the *Henry & Mary* in 1874.
124. *Disb.Book*. These are described by Dr. Dennis Chapman in "The Ashburners and the Coastal Schooners," *Trans.Liv.Naut.Res.Soc.*, vol.10 pp40-48.
125. *Furn.Folk*.

TABLE 7C – Cargoes carried by the *Margaret Banister* in 1879.

Loaded		Discharged		Cargo	Tons	At (per ton)
Jan.8	Duddon	Jan.17	Connah's Quay	Iron Ore	141	3/6
Jan.24	Duddon	Jan.27	Fleetwood	Iron Ore	150.55	2/6
Feb.5	Duddon	Feb.14	Saltney	Iron Ore	148	3/6
Feb.27	Barrow	Mar.6	Connah's Quay	Flour	107.75	3/–
Mar.11	Barrow	Mar.18	Liverpool	Steel Rails	126	4/6
			Douglas	Empty Sacks	3	5/–
Mar.21	Liverpool	Mar.24	Barrow	Wheat	143.5	3/–
Mar.26	Barrow	Mar.31	Douglas	Flour	108.5	5/–
Apr.9	Barrow	Apr.18	Ramsey	Flour	114.05	6/–
Apr.19	Ramsey	Apr.25	Liverpool	Gravel	142	3/–
Apr.30	Barrow	May.6	Douglas	Flour	110	5/–
May.8	Douglas	May.15	Barrow	Stone	134	2/6
			Empty	Sacks & Beans	3.25	5/–
May.22	Barrow	May.29	Douglas	Flour	108.6	4/6
May.31	Duddon	Jun.6	Connah's Quay	Iron Ore	145.5	2/6
Jun.9	Connah's Quay	Jun.16	Holyhead	Bricks	135	3/–
Jun.23	Barrow	Jun.27	Liverpool	Steel Rails	159.75	4/6
Jul.1	Liverpool	Jul.7	Barrow	General	109.15	4/–
Jul.8	Barrow	Jul.15	Liverpool	Steel Rails	139	4/6
Jul.18	Liverpool	Jul.21	Barrow	Wheat	141.5	3/–
Jul.25	Barrow	Aug.1	Ellesmere Port	Iron Ore	147.5	2/4
Aug.5	Liverpool	Aug.15	Ayr	Indian Corn	132.5	4/3
Aug.19	Ardrossan	Aug.26	Liverpool	Pig Iron	145	3/9
Aug.30	Garston	Sept.21	Swansea	Copper Ore	140	4/9
Sept.27	Swansea	Oct.1	Garston	Copper Ore	100	5/–
Oct.4	Liverpool	Oct.8	Barrow	General	100.5	4/7
Oct.10	Barrow	Oct.18	Liverpool	Steel Rails	82.5	4/6
			Ellesmere Port	Pig Iron	60	2/9
Oct.22	Liverpool	Oct.30	Dublin	Wheat	142.5	5/6
Nov.5	Duddon	Nov.14	Garston	Iron Ore	134.25	2/9
Nov.19	Garston	Nov.24	Douglas	Coal	131.3	3/6
Nov.27	Douglas	Dec.8	Barrow	Stone	122.75	2/3
Dec.10	Barrow	Jan.1	Newport	Pig Iron	30	5/–
(Dec.12	Ulverston)		Newport	Gunpowder	?	£50 total freight

regular route carrying gravel at 2/6 per ton from Barrow's Piel Island to Liverpool, returning light.

During these three and a half years the *Margaret Banister* traded largely in steel, ore and pig iron [TABLE 7D], and this was entirely characterisitic of Furness schooners of her type. However, to have carried coal only once in this time is certainly unrepresentative, so possibly Capt. Latham had some particular reason for avoiding this cargo. There were two disadvantages to carrying coal – it was dirty and it was inflammable. It was no worse than iron ore for covering a ship in dust, and his disbursement books show that Capt. Latham was quite prepared to carry coal in the *Mary Ashburner* and *James Postlethwaite*. More probably there was something about the ship which made her unsuitable for it, and a poorly ventilated hold could be the explanation. If ventilation ports were absent or blocked, the consequent accumulation of coal gas would have created a severe risk of explosion.

The Coasting Trade

The coasting trade was carried out all around the coasts of Britain and Ireland, and with the ports on the continental side of the English Channel, between the Elbe and Ushant.

TABLE 7D: Summary of cargoes carried by the *Margaret Banister* (September 1878 to April 1882).

Cargo	Times carried	Average (Tons/journey)	Tons carried	%
Steel	29	132	3831.45	24.1
Purple Ore (Fluorspar)	23	141	3239.25	20.4
Iron Ore	14	139	1946.3	12.2
Pig Iron	13	120	1560.0	9.8
Copper Ore	2	120	240.0	1.5
Gravel	11	142	1566.85	9.9
Stones & Boulders	3	131	393.75	2.5
Bricks & Tiles	2	130	260.0	1.6
Coal	1	131	131.3	0.8
Flour	7	111	780.25	4.9
Other Foodstuffs	7	118	824.45	5.2
Salt	1	142	142.0	0.9
General Cargoes	9	78	702.05	4.4
Unrecorded	2	143	285.65	1.8
Totals	124	128	15903.3	

Deepwater vessels that had outrun their Lloyd's classification, their 'insured life', ended their days in the coasting trade, but many more were built specifically for it. Shallow-draughted schooners such as the *James Postlethwaite* and *M.E. Johnson* were never intended to sail on deepwater, and even if the opportunity had arisen, their masters lacked the necessary qualifications for foreign voyages.

The coasting schooners were larger than the short sea traders, which carried about 140 tons. The *Mary Ashburner* could load about 180 tons but needed five men to sail her, one more than the smaller schooners, and the *James Postlethwaite* could take another sixty tons, but needed usually six crewmen. The balance of cargo capacity and crew numbers, together with the length of voyages undertaken, were vital factors in the economic performance of the ships. Without much more financial information than is available, it is impossible to determine which type of schooner was the most profitable. It can only be assumed that the builders, shareholders and captains were well versed in such details, and that therefore these hull sizes were those best-suited to the coasting trade. The *R.& M.J. Charnley* had been designed for foreign trade, and could carry 280 tons with a crew no larger than that of the *James Postlethwaite*. However, her deep draught would have hindered her access to harbours, and there may not always been enough cargo available to fill her hold. As a coaster she was probably no match for her smaller rivals.

The work of Thomas Ashburner's coasters in September 1881 can be used to illustrate the variety of their trades, and it can be seen that in their search for profits the schooners had spread far and wide. The *James Postlethwaite* had sailed on her maiden voyage from Barrow, carrying iron ore to Newport. She then sailed to Par, so her second and third cargoes were probably coal and China clay. The *M.E. Johnson* had also left Barrow early in the month, loaded with pig iron for Le Treport. She returned from the French port to Ellesmere. The third three-master in the fleet, the *R.& M.J. Charnley*, was trading between Newport and Plymouth. Of the two-masted coasters, only the *Twin Brothers* visited a continental port in this month. She travelled from Ayr to Britonferry, then Neath to Le Treport, returning to Runcorn. Meanwhile the *James & Agnes* and *Mary Ashburner* had both left Runcorn, bound for Newcastle. The *James & Agnes* went 'north about' and arrived at Newcastle after her smaller rival. Her own return passage was to Greenock, again 'north about', whilst the *Mary Ashburner* loaded a cargo at South Shields and headed South for Poole. The *Mary Jane* started the month in Ireland, travelling from Tralee to Gloucester, then to Sharpness. For the whole month the

Elizabeth Barrow was confined to her home port, probably undertaking repairs at the Ashburners' shipyard. The *Isabella* and the *Useful* busied themselves in the short sea trades, visiting the Dee River, Duddon, Isle of Man and Belfast.[126]

The main cargoes of the coasters were largely the same as the short sea traders – coal, industrial raw materials and products, and building materials. Where coal was carried it was mostly from South Wales, Lancashire or Cumberland. The East coast coal trade was not favoured by the West Coast schooners, and the Ashburner schooners only began to appear there regularly in the 1890's as cargoes became harder to find. It was a dangerous coast with few save havens, even the major ports being difficult to enter during bad weather. The prevailing winds suited square-rigged ships better, and for this reason the commonest rig on the East coast was not the schooner but the brig. Nevertheless the Ashburner schooners did go to the East coast when necessary, and the *R. & M.J. Charnley* was lost there, on a voyage carrying granite from Aberdeen. The *Mary Ashburner* also had several bad experiences in the North Sea. On New Year's Eve, 1894, she was badly damaged by a fire at South Shields, started after a coal-trimmer had left his lamp in the hold. In 1899 she collided with the Tay Bridge whilst under tow and lost both topmasts. A few years later she survived a collision with a steamer off Coquet Island, shortly after leaving Amble with a coal cargo.[127]

The coasters sometimes visited France, Germany and the Low Countries. The *M.E. Johnson* and the *Elizabeth Barrow* visited Antwerp and the *Jane Roper* was lost on a voyage to Hamburg. More commonly visited ports on the French Channel coast were St. Malo, St. Valery, Cherbourg and Dieppe.

It can be seen therefore that the Ashburners' coasting schooners showed no great preference for Furness ports and were entirely free-ranging in their search for cargoes. If anything, they were most commonly seen in South Wales ports and the Mersey. One of the great schooner trades in which they did not regularly participate was the carriage of slates from North Wales. Welsh slates were widely used for housebuilding, but ports such as Portmadoc, Bangor and Amlwch were well-provided with their own vessels and the Ashburner schooners seem to have only rarely carried this cargo. A much more common cargo was China clay, carried North from Cornwall by schooners from many different home ports.

The China Clay Trade

The process for glazing pottery using China clay was patented in Britain in 1768. The great potteries of Staffordshire began using it soon after. The only large source of China clay in Europe was South Cornwall, and for the whole period of their existence the carriage of clay cargoes was one of the principal schooner trades. The clay was transported by sea to North West ports, where it would be unloaded onto barges for the journey inland by canal. The Cornish schooners were the main beneficiaries of this trade, usually carrying clay North and returning South with coal. Cornwall had no indigenous coal, and this two-way trade eventually attracted Welsh and North West vessels, amongst them several of the Ashburner schooners.

Ports were developed specifically for the clay trade. In Cornwall, they were first Charles-town, from 1795, then Pentewan, from the 1820's, and Par, ten years later. Fowey was also involved and by the end of the schooner period, between the Wars, became the principal Cornish clay port.[128] In the North West the clay was received first at Liverpool, and later at Runcorn. After the opening of the Ship Canal on the 1st January 1894, Manchester also received many clay traders.[129]

---

126. Shipping Intelligence, *B.Times*, Sept. 1881.
127. T.J. Latham, "The History of the Topsail Schooner *Mary Ashburner*", *Maritime Wales* (1990) pp35-43.
128. George Bainbridge, *The Wooden Ships and The Iron Men of the Cornish China Clay Trade* (1980).
129. Shipping Intelligence, *Manchester Guardian*, 1898 *passim*.

Virtually all of the Ashburner schooners that left the Irish Sea must have carried clay at some time. The account book of the *James Postlethwaite* shows that in 1885 she carried clay on three journeys, amounting to over 600 tons. The *Mary Ashburner* was a clay trader for much of the later part of her career, and was lost on a voyage from Charlestown to Runcorn in 1913. The *Elizabeth Latham* was lost whilst travelling in the opposite direction, carrying coal from Manchester to Pentewan in 1898.

TABLE 7E: Cargoes carried by the *James Postlethwaite*, May 1884 to October 1885.

Loaded		Discharged		Cargo	Tons	At (per ton)
1884						
May 7	Fleetwood	May 26	Plymouth	Coal	208	4/–
Jun.4	Plymouth	Jun.13	London	Bricks	220	4/3
Jun.24	Medway	Jul.8	Eriskay	Cement	160	9/–
				Cement	40	7/6
Jul.22	Ayr	Jul.31	Newport	Pig Iron	220	3/6
Aug.2	Newport	Aug.12	Dundalk	Coal	214	4/6
Aug.13	Dundalk	Aug.19	Whitehaven	Timber	43.5	4/–
Aug.23	Whitehaven	Sept.8	London	Stones	210	7/6
Sept.12	London	Sept.26	Dublin	Patent Manure	204	5/–
Sept.30	Holyhead	Oct.4	Liverpool	Scrap Iron	150	5/–
Oct.8	Liverpool	Oct.24	Belfast	Maize Corn	204.5	4/–
Nov.12	Kirkcudbright	Nov.25	Cardiff	Pit Wood	132	7/6
Nov.28	Cardiff	Dec.5	Fowey	Coal	207	4/–
Dec.12	Fowey					
1885						
		Jan.6	Runcorn	China Clay	197.5	3/6
Jan.13	Birkenhead	Jan.23	Cardiff	Cement	205.75	4/6
Jan.24	Cardiff	Feb.24	Pentewan	Coal	204	4/6
Feb.28	Pentewan	Mar.10	Southampton	Clay	207.5	4/–
Mar.14	Southampton	Mar.25	Llanelly	R'way Chairs	160.5	3/–
Mar.31	Llanelly		Not stated	Coal	205	4/–
Apr.14	Duddon	Apr.23	Saltney	Iron Ore	217	2/6
Apr.28	Connah's Quay	May 6	Barrow	Coal	167.5	1/10½
May 9	Barrow	May 22	Le Treport	Pig Iron	210	8/–
Jun.5	Southampton	Jun.10	London	Gov't. Stores	241	4/–
Jun.17	London	Jul.9	Workington	Cement	205	5/–
			Douglas	Powder	2	£2
Jul.13	Harrington	Jul.25	Brest	Pig Iron	152	7/3
				Coal	51.5	7/–
Jul.31	Pembrey	Aug.13	Castletown	Coal	210	4/–
Aug.24	Garston	Sept.8	Brixham	Coal	208.5	5/–
Sept.23	Charlestown	Oct.7	St. Valery	Clay	200.25	6/–
Oct.12	St. Valery	Nov.5	Chester	Not stated	165	4/–

Summary	Cargo	% tonnage
	Coal	30.9
	Cement	11.3
	China Clay	11.2
	Pig Iron	10.7
	Scrap Iron	5.7
	Bricks	4.1
	Iron Ore	4.0
	Timber	3.2
	Others	18.9

The clay trade was one of the last havens for the sailing ships. Between the wars there was a fleet of auxiliary schooners sailing regularly from Fowey to London with clay, and carrying cement to Penzance on the return passage. One of these schooners was the *William Ashburner*, which had been fitted with a motor in 1925 and was able to make this passage in about five days. She continued in this trade, under the command of George Kearon, of Arklow, until the outbreak of the Second World War. During and after the War the few schooners surviving in Ireland also carried China clay.

Trading history of the James Postlethwaite

After leaving the *Margaret Banister* Capt. Robert Latham took command of first the *Isabella* and then the three-masted schooner *James Postlethwaite*. His disbursement book [TABLE 7E] shows that he was far more adventurous with this ship, travelling regularly to the South coast and France. It is even possible that his first four voyages constituted a complete circumnavigation of Britain, depending whether he went from the Medway to Eriskay, a port in the Hebrides, by the 'north about' route around Cape Wrath or 'south about' around Land's End. There were three voyages to French ports and only one each from Barrow and the Duddon. Certainly there was little opportunity for the men in the coasters to see their families.

The cargoes carried by the *James Postlethwaite* were more varied than those of the *Margaret Banister*, and the greater proportion of coal cargoes was certainly more typical of the schooner trades.

8   THOMAS ASHBURNER & CO. – SHIPOWNERS

Schooner Management

Although Thomas Ashburner & Co. was listed in some Barrow directories under the heading of 'shipbrokers', there is no other evidence that the Ashburners arranged cargoes for their ships. James Fisher largely monopolised Barrow's iron and steel exports, and the limited extent to which the Ashburner schooners sailed from Barrow seems to indicate that it was left to the ships' masters to fix cargoes. The Ashburners were managing owners, their function being to find buyers for the shares in newly-launched schooners, and then to receive accounts from the ships' masters and distribute profits to the shareholders.

It was the master's responsibility to keep accounts for each voyage and calculate the net profit. Capt. Robert Latham's disbursement book lists for each of his voyages in the *Margaret Banister* the freight rate and the total tonnage carried, and a detailed listing of the voyage expenses. One such voyage account is shown in Table 8A. As in this example, freight rates were usually given on a tonnage basis, though for small quantities of cargo a lump sum was sometimes paid. The 'amount' was the gross freight received by the master upon the Bill of Lading being signed off after the cargo's discharge.

A high proportion of the gross freight went to cover the ship's voyage expenses. The first expense was the broker's commission, most often 2½% of gross freight as in the example. Often masters would contact a broker at their port of destination in advance, to ensure that a return cargo was quickly available, so telegrams are a frequent entry in the disbursement book. Once the master had signed the broker's charter party, upon which rates of freight, demurrage and commission were detailed, he could proceed to load his cargo. Wherever possible this was done by the crew, since this was to the master's financial advantage. However, this was not always possible without outside help, so men for loading and trimming the cargo were often hired, and sometimes also the necessary gear, such as spars, baskets and weigh scales. Further expenses were incurred leaving the port and entering the port of destination, perhaps including the cost of tugs and pilots, and also the taxes levied for the use

TABLE 8A: A typical account for a single voyage of the *Margaret Banister*.

30th August 1879				21st September 1879			
Loaded Copper Ore at Garston Dock, Liverpool				Discharged at Swansea			
	£	s	d		£	s	d
Towing Out, Prince's Dock		10		140 tons			
Commission		16	6	@ 4/9 per ton			
Clearance & Stamp		3					
Dock Dues		12		Amount	33	5	
Trimming		12		Expenses	10	2	6
Allowance & Dock Gatemen		7					
Telegrams		2			23	2	6
Reporting & Lights		4	9				
Pilot from Sea		8		Ship's share	11	11	3
Towage in & up to Middle Bank		19					
River Pilot		5					
Cranage @ 5d per ton	2	18	9				
Slinging @ 3d per ton	1	15					
Bank Allowance		9	6				
	10	2	6				

of canals, harbours and wharves. It all added up to a high proportion of the gross freight, about 33% in the example but sometimes as high as 50%.

Throughout the duration of Capt. Latham's command the *Margaret Banister* was worked under a system that can be called "sailing by halves". The expenses were subtracted from the gross freight and the ship's net profit was divided in two. One half, the "ship's share", went via the managing owner, Thomas Ashburner, to the shareholders. The other half was retained by the ship's master. Each had to meet further expenses from his part of the profit.

The master paid the crew's wages and for their food. Since these costs were of no interest to the ship's owners, they are not detailed in Capt. Latham's disbursement book. However, wages are sometimes listed in Crew Agreements, and on the *Mary Ashburner* in 1908 the crew were paid by the month, £3 15s. for the mate and £3 10s. for the able seamen. These rates of pay were little changed from those of the 1870's and may well have been supplemented by extra payments for working cargoes. Supplies are sometimes also detailed on Crew Agreements, but more often are simply described as 'sufficient without waste'. The different interpretation of this phrase by the master and the crew was sometimes a cause for conflict, and some ships with miserly masters were avoided by seamen wherever possible. Even the most generous of masters would have provided a relatively sparse diet, of meat perhaps once a day, augmented by ships' biscuits, some vegetables and tea and sugar, probably at a cost of less than one shilling per man per day.

After paying for the crew's food and wages, the master retained the remainder of his half-share for himself. A capable and hard-driving master was therefore able to accrue considerable sums for himself, and very often these profits were reinvested in his or other ships. Capt. Robert Latham bought one or two shares in all the ships that he captained, as well as in a few others from the Ashburner fleet. His father, Capt. John Latham, bought ten shares in the *Mary Bell*[130], a capital sum equivalent to ten years' wages for an ordinary seaman. In contrast, Capt. Robert Charnley preferred to spread his investment, buying a few shares in virtually all of the Ashburner schooners.

The Ashburner captains were required to present their disbursement books to Thomas Ashburner for settlement twice a year, a fortnight before the last Saturday in April and October. The 'ship's share' was summed for each half year, and from this the managing owner would make any payments that were the owners' responsibility, prior to dividing the profit into dividends for the shareholders. The owners were responsible for all repairs to their ships. Minor repairs were made by the crew, but any materials that had to be purchased were charged to the owners. Capt. Latham kept a separate list of such materials in his disbursement book, an example of which is given in Table 8B. These costs were reimbursed to him at the settlement of his account. The list includes not only repair materials, but also consummables needed for running the ship: Coal for heating and cooking; sulphur for fumigation; candles for lighting the hold when moving or trimming cargo; Colza oil for burning in navigation lamps. In other years such lists included quantities of rope, canvas and twine for repairing sails and rigging, various spars and timber, and a host of minor implements such as brushes, spades, hooks and shackles. Major repairs were paid for directly by the managing owner, on behalf of the other shareholders.

Insurance was also the responsibility of the owners, as indicated by an entry in Capt. Latham's disbursement book in Oct. 1879. A dividend of £2 was paid on behalf of a 1/64th share in the *Mary Ashburner*, but from this was deducted 12s. for insurance. Amounting to about 2% of the ship's value, this may well have represented the cost of entering her into a mutual insurance fund. 'Mutuals' were the commonest form of insurance for small sailing ships and were usually organised within the ship's home port. A fee of 2 to 3% of the ship's value was charged upon her entry into the fund. If the ship was lost, or damaged, then the costs would be divided between all the members of the fund in proportion to the total amount each had insured with it.[131] At least one such 'mutual' was operating in Furness, the Barrow-

---

130. *BSR*
131. See *Mer.Sch.*, p126 for description of 'mutuals'.

TABLE 8B: Cost of supplies charged to the owners of the *Margaret Banister* in 1879.

		£	s	d
Belfast	Blacksmith		10	
Connah's Quay	3 lb. of nails			10½
	Blacksmith		2	4
	1 gallon Colza oil		4	
	Coal		2	
Swansea	Coal		2	6
	Black paint		1	9
	Coals		2	6
Barrow	Candles		1	6
	Glass in globe lamp		4	3
Liverpool	Blacksmith		10	
	1 lb. of plate nails			4½
	Coals		2	
	Sky light glass		1	7
	Cork fender		3	6
Ellesmere	Coals		4	
Ayr	Deck brush		1	3
	1 gallon Colza oil		3	9
	Coppell varnish		1	4
	4 lb. black paint		1	
	1½ gallons boiled oil		4	1½
	6 lb. sulphur @ 4d per lb.		2	
Garston	Deck scrubber		1	8
	TOTAL	4	1	3½

in-Furness Mutual Ship Insurance Company.[132] In later years, when many of the Ashburner schooners were sailing out of Connah's Quay, some were insured with the Dee Ship Owners' Mutual Insurance Association Ltd. The *James & Agnes* was one such vessel, and upon her loss in 1909 her owners were paid a claim of £550.[133]

After making payments for repairs, consummables and insurance, and subtracting his own fee for managing the ships, Thomas Ashburner was left with a sum available for distribution to the shareholders. A dividend could vary wildly from year to year, as indicated in Table 8C. It depended firstly upon the ship's trading performance, but could be reduced substantially if there were significant repair costs, or perhaps if there had been an unusually high number of losses amongst the ships of the mutual fund. Sometimes such costs would be greater than the income generated from the ship's trading account, and in these cases a 'call' would be made to the shareholders, asking them to contribute further monies. However, this would have been an unusual event, primarily occurring when the ships were repaired in preparation for their major surveys. For the most part ships did earn profits for their shareholders. Capt. Latham's 1/64th share in the *M.E. Johnson*, bought for £35 in 1880, earned him £2 9s. 8d. for the half-year ending January 1881 and £1 8s. 7d. for the half-year ending May 1885. These are equivalent to an annual return of 14% and 8%, markedly better than the 5% interest that would have been paid by a bank at this time.

Capt. Latham 'sailed by halves' in the *Margaret Banister* and the *Mary Ashburner*, and for his first five months in command of the *James Postlethwaite*. In October 1885, however, his disbursement book begins to show a different system. The 'ship's share' became one third of

---

132. From its establishment in the 1850's membership was confined to Barrow-owned vessels until 1881. Then it was turned into a limited liability company (*B.Times*, 5th March 1881, p5) and was opened to all vessels owned in ports on the West coast of England and Scotland or the East coast of Ireland.
133. *Report of Inquiries into Wrecks 1909/10 (James & Agnes)*, at D.o.T. Marine Division Library, Holborn.

Table 8C: Dividends paid to Capt. Robert Latham, 1885.[134]

	8th May, 1885 £ s d	31st October, 1885 £ s d
1/64th *Isabella*	2 7½	19 1
4/64th *James Postlethwaite*	4 8 4	6 18 6
1/64th *M.E. Johnson*	1 8 7	—
1/64th *William Ashburner*	1 15 1½	4 18 2½

gross freight receipts and he stopped recording the port expenses, indicating that he was paying these himself from his own two-thirds share of the freights. This was known as 'sailing by the thirds' and was the commonest form of running coastal shipping around Britain.[135] It was more favourable to the master when he was engaged on longer voyages, where expenses were less than 33% of gross freights. In the short sea trade, where expenses usually exceeded this proportion, the system of 'sailing by halves' was more beneficial to the master.

The Ashburner Fleet

Of the first ten schooners built by the Ashburners at Barrow, only the *Mary Jane* was retained under their own management from the date of her launch. The others were either managed by their masters or by people associated with Harrison, Ainslie & Co. The *Mary Jane* was managed by Capt. Robert Ashburner, continuing after his retirement from the sea in 1866 until his death in 1878. He was then described as a sailmaker, so it is likely that he was associated with Thomas Ashburner's sailmaking business in the last years of his life. Probably it was his experience that persuaded his nephew to move into ship management. The *Nanny Latham*, launched in 1866, was the first schooner in which all the shares were initially assigned to Thomas for resale, a system adopted for all the subsequent schooners. The two succeeding schooners, the *Catherine Latham* and *R.& M.J. Charnley*, seem to have been the first to be retained under the management of Thomas himself. Thereafter, by assuming the management of his father's earliest schooners, and by retaining control of most of the new schooners, Thomas enlarged his fleet to a significant size.

Capt. Brockbank's *James & Agnes* started 1869 at Pomaron. He returned to Newport and made a further voyage to Portugal, this time returning to Runcorn. The schooner's next voyage to Portugal was started at Troon in August, but this time it was Capt. John Latham who was in command, for Capt. Brockbank had relinquished both her command and management.[136] Soon after Capt. James Pernie's *Elizabeth Barrow* also joined the Ashburner fleet, as did the *Alice Latham* and *Henry & Mary*, both of which left the management of Capt. Henry Bond in the following year. Another schooner to join the fleet at about this time was the *Twin Brothers*, a two-master built by John Dawson at Liverpool. She had been owned since her launch in 1865 by Samuel Jervis, a Barrow shipowner. Apart from the later steel schooner *Result*, and briefly James Ashcroft's *Christiana Davis*, she was the only ship bought by the firm that had been built outside the Ashburner shipyard. Having been built to Special Survey, it is likely that she was of sufficient quality to satisfy the high standards that the Ashburners demanded of their ships. She was eventually sold to William Hurford and was wrecked at Ballinacourty Lighthouse near Dungarvan, Ireland, in April 1909[137] [PLATE 8A].

Despite these acquisitions, Barrow's 1871 commercial directory still listed Thomas Ashbur-

---

134. *Disb.Book*
135. See *Mer.Sch.*, p127 for description of 'sailing by the thirds'.
136. Voyage details from *Lloyd's List*. Capt. Brockbank, b. 1819, continued his career in other Furness schooners in the foreign ore trade, commanding Postlethwaite's *Millom Castle* and Fishers' *Mary Watkinson, Morris's, Joseph* and *Francis* (GLL *Captains Register*, 18567/16).
137. *Lloyd's List*, 3rd & 5th April 1909. The *Twin Brothers* had been carrying coal from Newport to Dungarvan. Capt. Whelan and his crew saved themselves by rowing ashore in the ship's boat.

PLATE 8A: The Twin Brothers *was wrecked at Ballinacourty Lighthouse, Dungarvan, Ireland in April 1909. She was one of only three schooners in Thomas Ashburner's fleet that had been built away from the Ashburner shipyard.*

ner simply as a sailmaker, and it was only in the next directory, published in 1876, that he appeared as a shipowner. By this time the *Elizabeth Latham* had returned to the fleet. She had spent her first two years under the management of William Chamley, one of the directors of Fisher's Furness Ship Building Co. The *Margaret Ann* had briefly joined the fleet, but had quickly been resold, and the *Mary Bell* had been launched and lost. In that year too, with the launch of the *William Ashburner*, the fleet had acquired its flagship.

By the time William Ashburner died in 1881, his son's fleet had grown to its largest size. Six schooners had been launched in the previous seven years and the fleet numbered fifteen vessels. The *Margaret Banister* had been bought back from John Bell, an Ulverston shipowner, in 1878, and the *Henry & Mary* had become Thomas Ashburner's second shipping casualty. Other losses were to follow.

Late in July 1884 the *Elizabeth Barrow* was chartered by Harrison, Ainslie & Co. to deliver a cargo of iron ore from Barrow to Saltney. Capt. John Foulkes had her command, and when he left Barrow he took with him a crew of two seamen and a boy, and also his wife and two children. Entering the Dee estuary without a pilot, the schooner fell victim to the shifting sands, grounding heavily on the East Hoyle Bank. With his ship taking in water, Capt. Foulkes decided to put his family into the small boat and lowered it into the sea. The crew remained on the grounded schooner whilst the steam tug *Derby* came to their assistance. A tow-line was given and the tug succeeded in pulling the schooner clear of the sandbank. However, the *Elizabeth Barrow* was too badly damaged below the waterline to survive, and within a few minutes she had filled with water and sunk. The crew had taken to the rigging and went down with the ship, but all managed to pull themselves out of the water and climbed further up the rigging to be rescued, with great difficulty, by the tug. Capt. Foulkes' family was retrieved from the small boat, and all seven people were safely landed at Connah's Quay. The *Elizabeth Barrow* was twenty one years old when she was wrecked and was valued at £600, but she was uninsured and the full cost of her loss was born by Thomas Ashburner and his fellow shareholders.[138]

Three years after the wreck of the *Elizabeth Barrow* the Ashburner fleet lost one of its largest schooners. The *R.& M.J. Charnley* had sailed from Aberdeen, bound for Hull with a granite cargo. On the night of the 14th December 1887, at 4.30 a.m., she was off Flamborough Head when she crossed the bows of a Liverpool steamer, the *Barden Tower*, heading for Middlesborough. Too late the schooner changed her course and the steamer struck her with terrific force amidships. She was literally cut in two, sinking immediately upon impact and casting at least some of her five crewmen into the water. The steamship captain put about to search for survivors, and was able to retrieve two from the water, an able seaman from Glasgow, James Thompson, and the ship's cook, Henry Kennedy. The other three men, the master, mate and another able seaman, were drowned.[139] The increasing occurence of steamships in coastal waters posed a great hazard to wooden sailing ships, and in future years several more of the Ashburner schooners were to be lost by collision.

The steel schooner Result

Despite the loss of some of its largest schooners the Ashburner fleet was still highly successful, though by 1890 most of its vessels had acquired Dee River masters and were operating primarily from Connah's Quay. One of the most successful of these was the *Useful*, under the command of Capt. Robert Wright. He had originated from Tarleton and had sailed for the Ashburners as man and boy, having been given command of first the *Margaret Ann* and then the *Useful*, from her launch in 1879. He had moved to live at Connah's Quay rather than Barrow, and earned his living largely in the short sea trades between the Dee River ports, the Isle of Man, Ireland and Furness. As his ship reached the end of her insured life, his success encouraged the Ashburners to supply him with a new and larger schooner.

Their own shipyard was by now closed down, and the Ashburners had to look elsewhere for a builder. By this time too, iron and steel schooners were commonly appearing in the fleets of their rivals. Such vessels had greater carrying capacity than their wooden counterparts of similar dimensions, and were also more durable and cheaper to maintain. They had appeared at Barrow first in James Ashcroft's fleet and had begun appearing in the fleet of James Fisher in 1885. By 1890 four metal-hulled schooners had been delivered to Fishers from the Carrickfergus shipyard of Paul Rodgers, with two more on order. Undoubtedly the Ashburners had inspected these vessels at Barrow and must have been impressed by the quality of them. Paul Rodgers was commissioned by the Ashburners to build what was to be both his and their last schooner. The design of this vessel was a collaborative effort between Rodgers, Richard Ashburner and her future captain, Robert Wright. The steel schooner was to work in the same trade as the *Useful*, carrying heavy cargoes into narrow estuaries, and therefore had to have all the requirements of a typical "Barrow flat". However, her designers were concerned with more than just functional details. Since the closure of his shipyard, Richard Ashburner had been largely involved in designing yachts, and Rodgers too was a distinguished yacht-builder. Using the skills gained in this work, they aimed to invest their new schooner with both speed and a graceful appearance. The design evolved at a series of meetings between the three men, and eventually a set of plans was drawn by Richard Ashburner to describe the result of their discussions. And the *Result* was the name decided for the new ship.

Rodgers probably started construction of the *Result* early in 1892. However, as work proceeded he was overtaken by financial difficulties and was forced to sell his shipyard to a shipbuilder from Ayr. When the *Result* was finally completed her builder's name was listed as Robert Kent & Co. They themselves suffered financial misfortune, possibly as a result of the considerable investment they had made in improving the shipyard, and less than two years after the takeover they too were bankrupted. The *Result* was long gone by this time, having

---

138. *B.Herald*, 29th July 1884, p4. Also *Lloyd's List*, 25th & 26th July 1884. *Wreck.Ret.* incorrectly gives the master's name as J. Pernie.
139. *North-Eastern Daily Gazette* (Middlesborough), 15th Dec.1887. *Wreck.Ret.* gives master's names as W. White.

PLATE 8B: Result, *probably at Connah's Quay. She has her original rig, with yards to set double topsails, so the photograph must date from before 1909.*

been launched early in January 1893.

The *Result* [PLATE 8B] had been built to Special Survey and was classed 100 years A1. Her frames and plates were of steel and she measured 122 gross tons. Her dimensions characterised her as a coasting schooner, for she was very shallow-drafted, having a depth of hold of only 9.1 ft. At 102.0 ft. in length and 21.7 ft. in depth, she was longer and narrower than the Ashburners' previous three-masted coasters, the *M.E. Johnson* and *James Postlethwaite*. The grace of her hull was augmented by a counter stern, and she had clipper bows with a handsome sheer. Her initial rig had more in common with a deepwater vessel than a coaster, for she carried double topsails and a flying topgallant on her foremast. In this her designers had been over-ambitious, and soon after her launch the lower masts were reduced in height by several feet and the topgallant-yard was removed. Surprisingly she had an open wheel, but there was an aft shelter used as paint locker and lavatory. She was initially owned by Thomas Ashburner & Co. and was registered at Barrow.[140]

As the final product of two of the most skillful of all the schooner-builders, it is not surprising that the *Result* has been described as the finest small sailing vessel ever built in Britain. In part this was due to her looks, but was also a tribute to her speed. In a straw poll conducted amongst schoonermen in the 1940's by Basil Greenhill, the *Result* was acclaimed as one of the fastest of the later schooners, especially when sailing to windward.[141] Furthermore, these qualities were not achieved by compromising her cargo-carrying ability, for she was to have a long, varied and successful career which outlasted that of all her contemporaries.

Some short sea traders lost

With the arrival of the *Result* the Ashburner fleet was increased in size to thirteen ships. In the five years following her arrival the four smallest schooners were either sold or wrecked.

The *Margaret Banister*, bound from Ballina to the Bristol Channel with a cargo of 70 tons of oats, was wrecked at Lenadoon Point, Co. Sligo on Monday, 1st October 1894. Her crew of five survived and over the following five days strenuous efforts were made to save her cargo as well. These were described in a dramatic series of telegrams (ten, over five days) sent to the underwriters at Lloyd's. The ship was firmly grounded and her keel was smashed. She was also shipping water, and by the time a tug from Ballina put men aboard the wreck on the Wednesday morning the water was two feet deep in the hold. Despite these considerable difficulties they were able to remove fifty tons of oats on that first day. Work continued throughout the night, the water in the hold rising to six feet, only two and a half feet from the underside of the deck. Even so, more of the cargo was saved, and when the tug returned to Ballina on Thursday night she carried with her fifty five tons of sound oats and ten tons damaged. This left only five tons still aboard the fast disintegrating vessel but still the tug returned to the wreck. By the following morning even this had been salvaged. On Saturday afternoon the last plaintive telegrams were sent to Lloyd's by Capt. William Iddon – "Bottom seriously damaged, keel gone, bad prospects saving vessel, if weather breaks will go to pieces".[142] The weather did break and the *Margaret Banister* was lost on one of the few journeys she had ever made outside the Irish Sea in her twenty three years.

Four years later the *Catherine Latham* was sold by the Ashburners and very soon afterwards her sister ship was lost. The *Elizabeth Latham* sailed from Manchester on Wednesday, 13th July 1898, bound for Pentewan in Cornwall with a coal cargo. She had a crew of four men, the master being Capt. James Bennet of Connah's Quay. Accompanying him were his wife and

---

140. Michael McCaughan, "Result goes Home", *Ships Monthly*, March 1980, pp20–23.
141. *Mer.Sch.*, p44.
142. *Lloyd's List*, 2nd to 8th Oct. 1894.
143. Wreck reported in *Liverpool Journal of Commerce*, 18th July 1898. Further details in letters included with Crew Lists, CRO Z3231.
144. Richard Ashburner's Cash Book, CRO 755.
145. *LSR*

two children. By Saturday afternoon the schooner had negotiated the Manchester Ship Canal and was heading through the Crosby Channel for the sea. This was not the luckiest of places for this ship, for twenty five years earlier she had collided with, of all things, the Crosby Lightship. However, Capt. Bennet probably did not know this, and even if he had it would not have caused him any worry. In the sheltered waters of the channel, beating into a moderate head wind and with the tide behind her, this fast little schooner was in her element. Accompanying her was another ship, the 4637 ton steamer *Chancellor* of the Charente Steam Ship Co. She was also heading out to sea, bound for Calcutta, and in the charge of the company's own pilot. Near the Lightship she slowed her engines as the *Elizabeth Latham* was sighted on her port side. The schooner was crossing the bows of the steamer and the pilot expected to pass behind her stern. If she had stayed on course she would have been safe, but Capt. Bennet unexpectedly tacked across the wind. Perhaps he was too confident in the speed of his ship, or perhaps the wind dropped, but he was not able to cross the steamer's bows for a second time. The *Chancellor*, unable to manoeuvre herself in the confined channel, struck the *Elizabeth Latham* square amidships, and almost immediately the schooner began to sink. Her crew and Capt. Bennet's family took to the rigging to save themselves as she started to go down. The steamer's boat took them off and it was said that Mrs. Bennet was the calmest of all the survivors.[143] All seven people were saved, though William Beeks, the 25 year old mate, got entangled with the gear as the mainmast came down, breaking his left leg. Even the ship's dog was taken aboard the *Chancellor* before the *Elizabeth Latham* finally disappeared beneath the water. The steamer anchored in the channel and a tug boat took the rescued people to Liverpool landing stage. William Beeks was taken to the Northern Hospital and the *Chancellor* proceeded on her voyage in the evening with only a few scratches on her paintwork to mark the incident. There was no official inquiry into the cause of the collision. Since the weather was fine and there was good visibilty, it seems that the *Elizabeth Latham* was the only Ashburner schooner whose loss was directly attributable to poor seamanship by her crew.

Early in 1900 the *Alice Latham* was repaired at Robert Cock's Appledore shipyard and then sold, for £430,[144] to John Monaghan. She sailed for him for eleven more years before being sold in 1911 to shipbreakers at Kilmore, Co. Wexford.[145] With her sale the Ashburner fleet had been reduced to its final form. At the turn of the Century there were nine vessels remaining, and these ships were all to survive until the Ashburners finally sold the fleet in 1909.

9   SHIPOWNERS AND SHIPBUILDERS OF FURNESS

The Barrow Fleets

As already described, small sailing ships were mostly owned by groups of shareholders. Outside Furness the ships were often managed by their masters or their brokers, but even the most successful of these had usually only a handful of ships in their fleets. In Furness the pattern of management was different. The area relied heavily on seaborne transport for its imports and exports, and its economy was dominated by a few massive enterprises. Both Barrow and Millom owed their existence to iron ore and relied on the companies that ran the ironworks and the mines for their trade. Shipowners and brokers connected with these companies built up the largest fleets of sailing ships in the country.[146] Most notable amongst them were the Barrow fleet of James Fisher and the Millom fleet of William Postlethwaite. The Ashburner fleet, never more than fifteen schooners, was far smaller, as were all other Barrow fleets, such as those of Geldart, Ashcroft and Jervis. One of the earliest fleets was that of Joseph Rawlinson, already mentioned in Chapter 4. Isaac Kirkby had several ships sailing in foreign trade in the 1860's and 1870's, and in the latter decade Walton & Co., agents for the Furness Iron & Steel Co., operated a small number of ships. All these companies were involved with transporting cargo. James Little & Co. was the only Barrow shipping line to be substantially involved in carrying passengers.

The fleet of Samuel Jervis

Samuel Jervis began his fleet with four schooners bought new in 1862. They were the *Francis*, built at Runcorn, *Twin Sisters*, *Fanny Slater* and *Carrie Bell*. This last ship was built at Glasson Dock, and in the following year she was joined by another schooner from the same yard, the *J.H. Barrow*. Jervis was a shipowner, owning most or all of the shares in these vessels himself. They operated in the coasting and Spanish ore trades, but Jervis soon set his sights on more distant shores. In 1865 he bought his largest ship from her South Shields builders, the 235 ton barque *Isaac & M. Kirkby*. She was intended for the West Indies trade but was lost within a year of her launch, being wrecked on the Castille Reef, a few hours out of the Cuban port of Cienfuegos, bound for New York.[147] In the same year Jervis also bought Joseph Rawlinson's *R.F Bell* and the schooner *Twin Brothers*. This latter ship was built by John Dawson at Liverpool, and when the Jervis fleet was finally disbanded in 1870 she came under the management of Thomas Ashburner.

James Ashcroft's Fleet

James Ashcroft was a Tarleton shipowner who moved to Barrow in the mid-1860's. He owned a fleet of similar size to that of the Ashburners, amounting to twelve vessels in 1877 and operating primarily in the coasting trades. The best of them was the *Eugenie*, a yellow-metalled brigantine built by Hugh Williamson at Whitehaven in 1863. She sailed deepwater to the Mediterranean and in the Scandinavian timber trade. She was sold to William Bell of Ulverston in 1886 and was run down off the S. E. coast of Ireland two years later. There were two other ships from Williamson's shipyard in the Ashcroft fleet, the schooners *Lady Lilford* and *Christiana Davis*. Amongst the other small coasters were three 87 ton schooners, all built at

---

146. BRL *Barrow Commercial Directory 1871* lists as shipowners: James Ashcroft, Miss Bond, W.K. Chamley, James Fisher, Joseph Fisher, R. Fisher, James Little & Co., G. Porter and A. Sumner. Ship brokers are listed as J. Carter, W.K. Chamley, I. Clark, Curwen Bros., James Fisher, R. Fisher, W. Gawith, J. Geldart, J. Mawson and J. Walton & Co.
147. *Lloyd's List*, 16th Aug.1866.

Liverpool in 1856. The *Gilbrow, Lindal Moor* and *Whitriggs* were bought by Ashcroft from Thomas Roper in 1874, and were all named after mines worked by Harrison, Ainslie and Co.

James Ashcroft was the first Barrow shipowner to realise the potential of metal-hulled sailing ships. He bought the iron-hulled schooner *British Queen* from her Preston builders in 1864. She operated in the Mediterranean and Baltic trades and eventually joined the fleet of James Fisher. When Fishers finally sold her in 1924 she was the last of Barrow's sailing ships. Ashcroft's second iron schooner was the *Bridget Annie*, the first launch from the Barrow shipyard of D. Noble & Co.

Ashcroft's fortunes as a shipowner began to decline in the early 1880's and several of his ships were acquired by other Barrow owners. *Maria McMillan*, an Ardrossan-built schooner originally owned by Fisher, went to Walton & Co. The *Christiana Davis*, a small schooner built in 1864, was mortgaged to Thomas Ashburner in 1883 and she briefly joined the Ashburner fleet. Within a year the ship had been sold to him outright and he in turn had quickly sold her to William Hurford, the Ashburners' sailmaker who was beginning to acquire and manage a small fleet of his own.

James Geldart's Fleet

Capt. Geldart had started his career as a seaman and had been master of the *Tom Roper* for several years early in her career, sailing her to Spain and Gibraltar. After retiring from the sea he established a ship chandlery, one of several located in Hindpool Road close to the Devonshire Dock. In about 1870 he also began to act as broker for the ships of Harrison, Ainslie & Co. William Ashburner's first three schooners, the *Jane Roper, Tom Roper* and *Lord Muncaster*, all sailed in James Geldart's fleet, and only the *Tom Roper* survived the experience.

The *Lord Muncaster* was the first to be lost. The third of the Barrow-built schooners, she had been sailing for fourteen years when, in February 1873, she left Newport on what was to be her final voyage. Under the command of Capt. J. Blundell and with four crewmen she was bound for Waterford with a cargo of coal. No more was heard of her and she was listed as 'Missing' in Lloyd's List on the 15th May. Two months later the same journal reported that a red and blue-painted pine boat, marked with her name and that of Capt. Thomas Charnley, had been picked up near Ile de Sein on the Atlantic coast of Brittany.[148]

Some of the vessels in the fleet were wholly owned by Geldart himself. One of these was the *Ada*, a 133 ton two-masted schooner, the last vessel built at the Charnleys' shipyard at Ulverston and completed by John Peet in July 1876. She was unique amongst the Furness schooners in that she was decorated with painted ports. She was also to become one of the longest survivors, ending her days as a floating museum at Newquay, and being finally broken up in 1954. Two other Ulverston-built schooners, the *Mary Atkinson* and the *Warsash*, were owned by the iron company, and had come from the shipyard of William White. They were part of the Geldart fleet that numbered eight schooners in 1877.[149]

Late in 1886, at 34 years of age, the *Jane Roper* seems to have been in a dire state of repair. In November, bound for Hamburg from Bangor with slates, she slipped her moorings off Ramsgate and narrowly avoided grounding before being assisted into the harbour. She was in a leaky condition and had lost her anchor, chains and some yards and sails. Perhaps foolishly her master continued almost immediately with the voyage. A month later the *Jane Roper* was in the North Frisian Islands off the German Coast. She foundered in a force 11 gale off the island of Amrum on the night of the 18th December. Capt. J. Price and his three crewmen were lost with her.[150]

The Geldart fleet operated until the mid-1890's, when James Geldart died and its management passed briefly into the hands of his son. The remaining ships were soon sold, the *Tom Roper* going to J.C. Hornby of Liverpool.

---

148. *Lloyd's List*, 15th May & 19th July 1873.
149. Geldart's other ships were the *Thomas Pearson, Lorn* and *Hope*.
150. *Lloyd's List*, 9th & 10th Nov. and 18th & 22nd Dec. 1886.

James Fisher and Son

The fleet of James Fisher dominated the port of Barrow, having more sailing ships than all the other owners together. At its height in the 1870's it was the largest fleet in Britain and numbered more than eighty ships. The bulk of their work was in the coasting trade, but Fishers traded to all five continents and many of their ships went deepwater. The great majority of them were schooners, but there were several of the other popular types of small merchant vessels.

James Fisher was a local man, born in 1822 at the Old Farm House, very close to where later William Ashburner was to have his first home in Barrow. In the 1851 Census he was described as a farmer of 58 acres. In his early days, like all the local farmers, he would have had some business hiring carts to the iron companies, for transport of the ore from the mines to the loading quays. With the arrival and expansion of the railway this business was entirely lost. However, Fisher had started to acquire shares in ships during the 1840's and by the middle of the next decade he had a small fleet under his management. He bought his first new ships in 1856 and thereafter his fleet grew in parallel with Barrow's increasing trade, aided by his association with the major Furness iron company. H.W. Schneider had sought James Fisher's advice on the location for the first blast furnaces to be built at Barrow. Construction of these furnaces was completed in 1859 and Fisher was rewarded by being appointed shipping agent to Schneider. Ultimately when Schneider, Hannay & Co. merged with James Ramsden's steel company in 1866, to form the Barrow Haematite Iron & Steel Co., Fisher was retained as the shipping agent.[151] The iron and steelworks was destined in the next ten years to become the largest in the World. James Fisher's fleet exported ore, pig iron, steel rails and other products to all parts of Britain. This trade was mainly carried out by schooners, but in the mid-1860's the demand for Barrow's iron and steel in North America and the opening of Barrow docks brought about the inclusion of a large number of barques into the fleet.

From 1867 James Fisher himself ceased active involvement with shipping. This was managed by his son, John, whilst he himself concentrated on the exploitation of an iron ore deposit at Glenravil in Co. Antrim. The ore was shipped from Red Bay primarily to Barrow, Morecambe and several Welsh ports. When Fisher died in 1873 the mines there were producing exports of 25,000 tons per year.

Table 9A[152] gives an illustration of the activities of the Fisher fleet at one point in time, in November 1877. Most of the vessels listed are in the coasting trades, but this probably understates Fishers' involvement in deepwater trades. The fleet then numbered about seventy vessels, and amongst those that were unreported are many that were likely to have been on foreign voyages. These included, for example, the barque *Kate Rousfield*, the barquentine *Bella Tumulty*, and two yellow-metalled schooners that commemorated the family of Fisher's business associate, the *Rose Schneider* and *Nelly Schneider*.

Of the forty six vessels that are listed, thirty four were schooners, and the remainder is made up of four barques, three brigs, four brigantines and only a single barquentine, the 197 ton *J.E. Fisher*. The largest vessels were the barques, and the largest of these was the 795 ton *Reliance*, followed by the *Margaret* (505 tons), *Sea King* (441 tons) and *Clara* (276 tons). The three brigs, *Annie Ripley*, *Buccleuch* and *Eleventh Lancashire*, were all close to 210 tons. The brigantines *Bidsie & Bell*, *Frank M. Fisher*, *Scottish Maid* and *Lancashire Witch* were slightly smaller, ranging from 100 to 200 tons. The largest schooner was the 183 ton *James W. Fisher* and the smallest was the 47 ton *Maid of Irvine*.[153]

Of the larger ships, the *Reliance* and the *Margaret* were built in Canada and were bought second-hand. It was the smaller *Sea King* that was really the flagship of the Fisher fleet. She was bought new in 1866, together with a sister ship, the *Lizzy*, from their builder, Wray of Burton Stather in Lincolnshire. She was too large to be accommodated in Barrow Harbour

---

151. *F.P.& P.*
152. *B.Times*, Shipping Intelligence, 10th Nov. 1877.
153. Rig and tonnage from *Lloyd's Register of Shipping*, 1877/8.

TABLE 9A: VESSELS OF MESSRS. FISHER & SON

Name of Ship	Captain	At	For/From
Alice Fisher	Conway	Barrow	for Larne
Annie Ripley	Casey	Barrow	
Beatrice	Forshaw	Holyhead	for Swansea
Betty Russell	Lewis	Barrow	
Bidsie & Bell	Comley	Cadiz (SPAIN)	from Swansea
Brandon	Davies	Workington	for Belfast
Bridget Smith	Halsall	Barrow	for Dublin
Buccleuch	Ball	Barrow	
Charlotte Helen	Dickinson	Londonderry	
Clara	Brooks	Barrow	for Algoa (BRAZIL)
Dreadnaught	Bogan	Barrow	
Eleventh Lancashire	Richards	Palma (SPAIN)	from Newport
Elizabeth Alice	Parkinson	Runcorn	for Newcastle
Emma	Hunter	Barrow	
Francis	Summers	Barrow	for Swansea
Frank M. Fisher	Williams	Runcorn	for Cette (FRANCE)
Gauntlet	Selby	Fleetwood	
George & Mary	Davies	Barrow	for Dublin
Harry Russell	Hughes	Swansea	for Belfast
Hematite	Croasdell	Barrow	for Saltney
Holly How	Mayor	Lancaster	for Londonderry
Isabella Hall	Jones	Barrow	
James W. Fisher	Richards	Hamburg (GERMANY)	for Ardrossan
J.E. Fisher	Ridge	Cette (FRANCE)	for Tarragona (SPAIN)
Joseph	Wilding	Barrow	
Joseph Fisher	Iddon	Barrow	
J.T.S.	Iddon	Runcorn	for Saltney
Julia	Pernie	Antwerp (BELGIUM)	for Newcastle
Lancashire Witch	Edmondson	Barrow	for Dublin
Lily Baynes	Bond	Barrow	for Cork
Maid of Irvine	George	Barrow	
Margaret	Bennett	Miramichi (CANADA)	for Bristol
Mary Ann	Edmondson	Glasgow	from Isle of Man
Mary Watkinson	Watkinson	Cork	for Barrow
Morecambe Belle	Owens	Youghal	for Barrow
Morris's	Gracie	Whitby Roads	
Petrel	James	Barrow	
Princess Louise	Forshaw	Holyhead	
Reliance		Barrow	
Rusko Castle	Iddon	Barrow	
Sarah Anne	Llewellyn	Milford Haven	
Scottish Maid	Griffiths	Barrow	for Swansea
Sea King	Griffiths	Elsinore (DENMARK)	for Barrow
Seven Sisters	Evans	Barrow	
Telegram	Iddon	Barrow	
William & Sarah	Evans	Barrow	for Porthcawl

prior to the opening of the Devonshire Dock. There were other complications – her builder had been bankrupted before she was completed and there were legal difficulties associated with the purchase. The *Sea King* traded to Australia and the Far East, and she was returning from Macau when, nearly four years after her launch, these were finally resolved. A month later, in June 1870, she paid her first ever visit to her home port, to load a cargo of steel rails for New York.[154] She was eventually sold by Fishers and went missing in August 1883, on a voyage from the West Indies to London.

Several of the other ships were eventually lost in far off places. The *J.E. Fisher* grounded on a reef off the Brazilian coast in February 1878, on a voyage from Santos to Pernambuco,[155] and the *Frank M. Fisher* was abandoned by her crew on a voyage to Trinidad seven years later. Both ships were yellow-metalled and had been built at the Berwick shipyard of Messrs. A.B. Gowan & Son. This yard built more ships for the company than any other. In May 1870, when the *R.E.A. Parkinson* was launched by them, she was the 22nd vessel that they had built for Fishers,[156] and at least seven more followed her. The longest survivor was the schooner *Mary Watkinson*, built in 1872 and lost by collision off the Lizard in December 1927, carrying coal from Runcorn to Looe.

After the first few years Fishers bought most of their smaller vessels new, or occasionally bought them from less successful Barrow owners. The firm did not favour local shipyards. One of the few Ulverston vessels to ever enter their fleet was the brig *Annie Ripley*. She came from the shipyard of John Wilson in 1864, and in her best days traded across the Atlantic. The schooners *Gauntlet* and *Julia* came from Matthew Simpson's yard at Glasson Dock and were bought from Ulverston owners. All the ships built at Barrow's Rawlinson & Reay yard also appeared eventually in the Fisher fleet, excepting only the *Duke of Buccleuch*, and there were of course the three schooners subsequently built by Fisher at the same location.

Other ships came from a wide variety of shipyards from all around the British coast, a large number coming from Scottish shipyards. The best of these was the 118 ton *Mary Sinclair*. Named after the wife of a Barrow surgeon, she was built by Hugh Barclay at Ardrossan in 1876 and was owned in her early years by Walton & Co. For most of her early career she was commanded by Capt. Edmondson Charnley, from the time he left the *Mary Ashburner* in 1878 until his death on board in 1897. Sold to Grounds of Runcorn in 1921, she spent her last years in the China clay trade. This ended in February 1936 when she collided with a mooring buoy in the Mersey and was badly holed. Condemned as a wreck, her final indignity was to be used as a towing barge.

Amongst the last sailing vessels bought by Fishers were twelve three-masted schooners from the Carrickfergus shipyard of Paul Rodgers. They were magnificent vessels, all built to Special Survey, the first six from wood and the remainder from steel. The *Fanny Crossfield* and *Mary Miller* were the first, and they were to have the longest lives, the latter ship surviving as a pure sailing ship until her conversion to a houseboat in 1945. The other four wooden schooners, the *Mary Armstead*, *Louie Bell*, *Annie Crossfield* and *Edith Crossfield*, were all short-lived, as were most of the later steel schooners. The first of these was the *George B. Balfour*, Rodger's first metal-hulled schooner, launched in 1885. She survived for only eight years before being lost by collision in the English Channel. Rodgers was bankrupted in 1892,[157] and his last schooner, the *Ford Fisher*, was also the last new sailing vessel bought by Fishers.

Fishers owned or managed more than 160 sailing vessels in the years up to 1924,[158] and several of these survived into the 1940's, if only as houseboats or barges. Amongst these was the *Francis*, from the Rawlinson & Reay yard. She was still listed in Lloyd's Register in 1951 and was probably being used as a barge or hulk in the Bristol Channel. It was another Barrow-built schooner that was Fishers' last surviving trading ship. The *Ellie Park*, the final ship built by the Furness Ship Building Co., remained in their fleet until 1921. She was owned

---

154. *B.Times*, 30th April 1870.
155. *Lloyd's List*, 22nd March 1882.
156. *B.Times*, 7th May 1870.
157. Michael McCaughan, "Paul Rodgers, an Ulster Shipbuilder, and his Welsh Connections", *Maritime Wales* (1983) pp46-63.
158. From records compiled by Derek Blackhurst. A lower figure was given by J.W. Dodderidge in "A Famous North Country Fleet", *Ships and Ship Models*, July to Oct. 1939. These four articles describe the Fisher fleet, but they include many errors. No other records of some of the named ships can be located, and builders, launch dates and year and place of wreck are often given incorrectly.

in Annalong, Co. Down, in her later years, one of several schooners mainly employed carrying granite from that dangerous coast. Her career ended in November 1947 when, carrying a cargo of scrap iron from the Isle of Man to Connah's Quay, she foundered with the loss of two of her four crew. The only remaining vessel from the Annalong fleet was the *Nellie Bywater*, the first schooner built at Millom and one of several survivors from that port's large fleet.

The Duddon Fleets

Haematite ore deposits were not confined to the immediate district around Barrow. On the far side of the Duddon estuary a small mine at Holborn Hill had yielded an occasional cargo for ships arriving at Borwick Rails. Mining had been in progress since the 1850's and in 1855 Nathaniel Caine and John Barratt, prospecting at Hodbarrow Point, founded the Hodbarrow Mining Company. It was only in 1860 that they discovered any substantial ore deposits, but from that point the export trade developed rapidly and in 1866 about 140,000 tons was put aboard ships at Borwick Rails.[159] Iron ore was almost the only cargo outwards, and was most commonly sent to Bristol Channel ports, and to the Dee and Mersey where the mining company established stockpiles. Local use of the ore was promoted from 1865 by the building of blast furnaces at Millom and nearby Askam. The seaborne trade was thus extended to the import of coal and the export of pig iron. A wooden pier was constructed to allow ships to load and unload their cargoes. The Hodbarrow ore deposit proved to be greater even than the Park deposit at Barrow, and together they were the largest in Britain. Like Barrow, Millom grew from almost nothing to become a significant port and with an industry based entirely upon iron ore.

William Postlethwaite's Fleet

The Duddon had no substantial trade before the discovery of iron ore, and so in its early development it depended mainly on vessels from Barrow and Ulverston. In 1866 the Ashburner schooner *Alice Latham* came under the management of William Postlethwaite, secretary of the Hodbarrow Mining Company. Born in 1835, he was from a prominent local family and had been appointed as the mining company's first secretary in 1862. In 1866 he married Elizabeth Stonard Worthington, herself associated with an Ulverston shipping family, and they were to have one son, George, born two years later. The *Alice Latham* appears to have been the first ship managed by Postlethwaite, who was eventually to command the largest fleet operating out of Millom.

Postlethwaite managed the *Alice Latham* only for a year or so, but she was followed by a number of Ulverston-built schooners so that in 1871 he had four vessels under his management. At this time the mining company established the Duddon Shipping Association, whose ships were to be managed jointly by Postlethwaite, as company secretary, and the Duddon Harbourmaster, Capt. William Morgan.[160] Thereafter Postlethwaite began to expand his own fleet considerably. By the end of 1873 it numbered twelve ships, six more being added in the following year and another four in 1878, one of which was the Ashburners' *Nanny Latham*.[161] Upon his retirement from the mining company, Postlethwaite's fleet numbered twenty six sailing ships, second in size only to that of James Fisher. He had other business interests associated with Duddon shipping – a one third share in the local shipyard and a partnership in the Lady Kate Steamship Co.

Postlethwaite's schooners traded both in Home waters and to Europe and beyond, one vessel travelling to Australia and India. His coasting schooners were strongly built for the ore

---

159. *F.& I.R.*, p270. For a general history of the Hodbarrow mines see also Alan Harris, *Cumberland Mines*.
160. Trevor Morgan, "The Cumberland Connection: Capt. William Morgan and the Hodbarrow Schooners", *Maritime Wales* (1987) pp90.98.
161. Information on Duddon fleets from records of Trevor Morgan.

trade, the great majority of them coming from Ulverston shipyards. He also bought ships from the Amlwch shipyard of Capt. William Thomas, starting with the *Cumberland Lassie* in 1874 and followed four years later by the *Baron Hill*. Both ships were built from wood, but Thomas later adapted his yard to iron shipbuilding. Postlethwaite's first metal-hulled schooner had been the *Charles & Ellen*, launched from the Barrow shipyard of D. Noble & Co. in August 1878. Seven years later he bought William Thomas's first iron schooner, the 183 ton three-master *Elizabeth Peers*. Another of Thomas's iron schooners, the *Maggie Williams*, became the last sailing ship bought by Postlethwaite, upon her launch in 1892.

The Millom trade attracted steamships and eventually a few such ships began to appear in the Postlethwaite fleet. Nevertheless, the fleet declined in numbers, and when William Postlethwaite died at his home at Whicham on Christmas Eve, 1910, there were only five schooners remaining. They were briefly managed by his son, but within three years they had all been sold.

The Hodbarrow Schooners

The Hodbarrow Mining Company did not own any ships itself, but instead established the Duddon Shipping Association to manage a small fleet that would carry its ore exports. The mining company's secretary was always listed as their managing owner, but the ships' shares were widely distributed amongst the local community.

The Association's first ship was the *Burns & Bessie*, bought from the Charnley shipyard at Ulverston in 1870. From the same yard she was joined in the following year by the *Hodbarrow Miner*. In four years a fleet to thirteen schooners had been built up. Most of them had been ordered new, either from shipyards in Ulverston or North Wales.

Only five more ships entered the fleet after 1874. The first was the *Florence Petherick*, built locally in 1890. She was followed by two other locally-built schooners and also the *Donald & Doris*, built at the Amlwch shipyard of W.C. Paynter in 1897. The *Hannah Croasdell* was bought from Postlethwaite in the following year and remained with the fleet until 1908.

The Ulverston shipbuilders

Despite the efforts of the Ashburners and others at Barrow, Ulverston remained the major centre in Furness for wooden shipbuilding, right up until its last schooner was launched in 1878. Through the 1860's and 1870's there were four important shipyards located beside the Ulverston Canal, and the great majority of the ships launched there, mostly schooners, were destined to eventually join the Duddon fleets.

William Postlethwaite's first Ulverston-built vessels were the *Elizabeth Worthington* and *Mary Atkinson*, bought in 1867 and 1868. They had been built at the shipyard of William and John White, the principal Ulverston shipbuilders of their time. Like William Ashburner, they had received their training at the Petty & Postlethwaite shipyard. They built twelve schooners between 1861 and 1878, eleven of which went to Duddon owners.

In the 1870's six of the Whites' other two-masted schooners entered the Postlethwaite fleet, all bought new. The *Millom Castle* was the first of these, launched in 1870. She was sold by George Postlethwaite in 1912 and continued to trade until she was laid-up during the Second World War. She was joined by the *George 4th* in 1873, and then the *Kate*, *Edith* and *Mabel*. The last schooner built at the Whites' yard, also the last to be built at Ulverston, was the *Ellen Harrison*. She too joined the Postlethwaite fleet, immediately after her launch in 1878.

One of the Whites' earliest ships, the *Mary Goldsworthy* built in 1865, was acquired second-hand by the Duddon Shipping Association eight years later. They already had the *T.& E.F.* and in the following year bought the *Coniston* new. The 'Teeny Eff', only 63 tons, was reputed to be one of the fastest of the Duddon two-masters. She foundered with the loss of all hands in December 1914, whilst heading for the shelter of Ramsey Bay, Isle of Man. The *Coniston* too was lost with all hands, foundering as she crossed the Duddon Bar in September 1917, carrying pit props from Arklow.[162]

Another Ulverston shipyard, that of Richard and William Charnley, built eight vessels. Two went to the Duddon Shipping Association and three, the *Robert & Elizabeth*, *Maggie Brocklebank* and *Ann Crewdson*, to Postlethwaite. There were two other yards launching into the Ulverston Canal basin. Apart from Whites' and Charnleys', there were also the yards of John Rhodes and the Brocklebanks. Rhodes built only one vessel, the *Annie McLester*, launched in 1866. The Brocklebanks took over the Petty & Postlethwaite shipyard and built the *Ella Mary* in 1871 and the *William Brocklebank* in the following year. All three schooners were eventually bought second-hand by Postlethwaite.

There was another shipyard at the foot of the Canal. This was worked originally by the Schollick family, who built a large number of ships, primarily for their own fleet or that of the Stonard family. The foreman-shipwright, John Wilson, eventually took over the yard from the Schollicks. He was the only Ulverston shipbuilder of his period to build large vessels other than schooners. From his yard came the brig *Annie Ripley*, a transatlantic trader for Fishers, and the brigantine *Bessie Whinneray*. She was a Baltic trader in her early life and was reputed to have made a record passage from the Clyde to St. Petersburg in 1867.[163] Another of Wilson's brigantines involved in this same trade was the *Hannah Croasdell*. Together with a schooner from the same yard, the *William Rawcliffe*, she was bought by Postlethwaite in the 1870's. John Wilson died in 1867, but his widow, Margaret, continued to manage the yard. Her first vessel was the schooner *Mary Ann Mandall*, launched in 1868, and she built at least one other ship, the brigantine *Annie Brocklebank*, launched the following year. They both eventually joined the Postlethwaite fleet and, together with some of the other larger schooners, participated in the Spanish ore trade in their early years. The *Mary Ann Mandall* was later bought by Charles Reney of Connah's Quay and had a long life in the coasting trades, sailing from the Dee River until she was wrecked in the Mersey in 1930.

The Duddon Shipbuilding Company[164]

The Amlwch shipowner and builder William Thomas had been involved with the Duddon shipping trade since its earliest days. Eventually he was persuaded to open a shipyard there, in partnership with William Postlethwaite. This subsidiary of the Amlwch yard was also known as William Thomas & Co., and was started at Borwick Rails in 1870. At the head of the twelve man workforce was Hugh Jones, a foreman-shipwright from Amlwch. Work started on their first vessel, a 113 ton schooner ordered by the Duddon Shipping Association, almost as soon as the yard was ready in the following year. This first vessel was the *Nellie Bywater*, built to Special Survey and launched in December 1873. Like all other schooners built at this yard, she was strongly built for the iron ore trade, and this strength was to enable her to work a long career. Her full story has been told by her final owner, Capt. Richard England. One of the very last schooner captains, he was in command when she foundered off Plymouth in December 1951 with the loss of two lives.[165]

The Millom shipyard must have been primarily involved in repair work. Its second schooner, the *Countess of Lonsdale*, was built as a speculation and took over four years to build. Launched in 1878, she was managed for her first few years by William Postlethwaite before eventually William Thomas became her owner. For the next few years the shipyard concentrated on building steamers. Three were built, all for the Lady Kate Steamship Co., principally owned by Thomas Massicks, proprietor of the Millom Ironworks. The subsequent launch of the three-masted schooner *Greyhound* in 1886 marked the end of William Thomas & Co. at Duddon. The ownership of the yard passed to Hugh Jones and his brother, Micaiah, and it became known as the Duddon Shipbuilding Company.

---

162. Alan Lockett, *Northwestern Ships and Seamen* (1982) pp27-29.
163. Alan Lockett, *Northwestern Sail* (1978) p41.
164. Trevor Morgan, "The Cumberland Connection: Hugh Jones, Shipbuilder, Millom", *Maritime Wales* (1983) pp69-95.
165. Capt. Richard England, *Schoonerman* (1981) p210.

The first two ships from the yard under its new ownership were both schooners built for the Duddon Shipping Association. They were the *Florence Petherick*, launched in 1893, and the *Happy Harry*, launched the following year. The latter ship was a three-master named after Mr. Harry Arnold, a generally cheerful director of the Hodbarrow Mining Company. She was to have a long life, the last years of which were spent at Arklow in company with the Ashburner three-masters.
    By this time wooden shipbuilding had already ceased at Barrow and Ulverston, and was in decline elsewhere. To keep his workforce in employment, Hugh Jones built the *Becca and Mary* as a speculation. She was the yard's finest vessel, a 162 ton barquentine, built largely of teak and to Special Survey, with a Lloyd's classification of 14 years A1. After her launch in 1904 she was managed by Jones himself for nine years, before eventually being sold to Portugese owners. She survived until 1953 when she foundered off the coast of Newfoundland.
    The last vessel built by the Duddon Shipbuilding Company, and the last schooner built in England, was the *Emily Barratt*. Ordered by the Hodbarrow Mining Co. in 1910, she was launched on Easter Monday, 1913. She traded for the iron company until 1922, was then sold and continued to trade until 1960, interrupted in the War by a spell as an anchorage for a barrage ballon. She was subsequently used as a yacht, and has survived until today. She currently lies at Barrow and is owned by the Furness Maritime Trust.

10 YACHTS AND SMALL BOATS

William Ashburner jun., speaking for his brother Richard's obituary, estimated that one hundred boats had been built by the Ashburner family. The accuracy of this estimate is uncertain, nor is it known whether it included ships built at Greenodd or the Isle of Man. Apart from their twenty four schooners, the details of only a few other vessels that they built at Barrow are known.

An 1872 history of Barrow states that two pontoon hoppers were under construction in the Ashburner yard, each capable of carrying 150 tons.[166] This would make them about the same size as the smaller short sea schooners such as the *Elizabeth Latham*. They were probably destined for use in the construction of the Buccleuch and Ramsden Docks. Perhaps these hoppers were large enough to be given a Yard Number. There are no surviving Yard Books from the Ashburner shipyard but the Yard Numbers of a few of the schooners can be found in their Lloyd's Survey Reports. The *Mary Bell* was their 17th schooner built at Barrow and when she was started in February 1870 she was given Yard No. 29. The next schooner was *William Ashburner*, started in March 1875 and given Yard No. 33. The intervening numbers were probably given to the two pontoon hoppers and a pilot boat launched in 1871. Yard Nos. 34 to 36 were all schooners, the *Mary Ashburner*, *Isabella* and *Useful*.

Richard Ashburner built fishing boats at Greenodd and others were later built at Barrow – three of them were named *Gratitude*, *Champion* and *Ebenezer*.[167] They were described as trawlers and they were probably a type of boat much used around the Irish Sea and in Morecambe Bay, especially for trawling shrimps. Locally they were known as 'nobbies' and they were

PLATE 10A: Roa Island, at the entrance to Barrow harbour, was the location for many yachting regattas. Marine Terrace, behind Barrow's first lifeboat station, provided homes for several pilots and schooner captains. This photograph was taken in 1905 by J. Wells, from the mast of one of the pilot boats.

---

166. Francis Leach, *Barrow, its Rise & Progress* (1872)
167. *F.P.& P.*, p54.

shallow-drafted keelboats of 30 to 40 feet in length and with a low, square counter stern. They had to be strongly built to take the ground, and they had to be fast to bring the perishable catch quickly ashore. They were cutter-rigged with a running bowsprit and they usually carried a great area of sail.

Two other types of small boat had a requirement for speed that attracted the attention of Richard Ashburner. For the Barrow pilots the speed of their boats was an economic necessitity in their competition for work. The Ashburner brothers' involvement in yacht racing gave Richard the opportunity to pursue sailing speed in its purest form.

Pilot Boats

The Barrow pilots only had rights to pilot ships to and from their own port. On the South side of Morecambe Bay, Fleetwood also operated a pilot service, and their rights extended not only to their own port but to ships using Barrow as well. From the opening of the Heysham docks in 1904 the pilots of both ports were allowed to pilot ships to and from there. The boats from the two rival services would race each other to be first to land a pilot aboard any vessel bound inwards, sometimes travelling as far South as Anglesey. An illustration of the importance attached to the speed of their boats is that in the 1880's the Barrow pilots used a racing yacht for their work. The *Mosquito*, built in 1848 for Lord Londesborough and rigged as a cutter, had once sailed against the famous yacht *America*, losing to her in the Queen's Cup of 1851. She was re-rigged as a schooner for the seventeen years that she spent with the Barrow pilots.[168]

The first Ashburner pilot boat was built for James Ramsden. They began cutting out the timbers for her in July 1870 and she was launched the following year. She was cutter-rigged and was named *Argus*. Ramsden had ordered her because he was hoping to obtain control of the pilot service for the Furness Railway Company, but in this one area at least he was unable to extend his pervasive control over Barrow's institutions. The pilot service was put in the hands of Trinity House and Ramsden had no need for the new boat. The *Argus* was sold to James Charnley, himself the first pilot to be awarded a Trinity House licence for Barrow. The *Argus* served the pilot service for 35 years before being sold to owners in the Mediterranean. She was a sizeable boat, with a keel of 50 feet, a 15 feet beam and a draught of 7 feet. Pilot Charnley described her as being "as strong as a castle". A newspaper report at the time of her building states that the midships section of her keel was made from a 2½ ton iron casting produced by the Barrow Ironworks, and that it functioned in place of ballast. The *Argus* was originally copper-bottomed, and when the copper sheathing was eventually stripped from her, at a refit at the Furness Ship Building Co., it has been said that its sale paid not only for the yellow-metal that replaced it, but also for all the other repair work as well.[169]

Richard Ashburner had ceased even building yachts by the time that *Argus* was sold. However, the Charnley family and the other Barrow pilots must have been impressed by Richard Ashburner's original boat, and probably also by the success of his yachts. He was still designing boats and one of the last of these was the successor to the *Argus*. This new vessel was originally named after her trade, the *Barrow Pilot*, but became known as the "new *Argus*" after

PLATE 10B: Richard Ashburner's half-model of the cutter Rose. *The original is 930 mm. from stern to tip of bowsprit.*

PLATE 10C: Lu-lu, *ex- Rose, was owned at Tranmere Sailing Club in 1905. This boatyard photograph allows her hull-form, slightly lengthened since her launch, to be compared with that of her builder's model.*

her predecessor, the "little *Argus*". The new vessel was built by Nicholson & Marsh, who had taken over Simpson's Lancaster shipyard. Launched in 1907, this 74 ft. schooner was the last sailing vessel built at this yard after a history of 69 years. She was also the last sailing vessel built for the Barrow pilots, and when she was sold in 1919 she was succeeded by a steamboat.

Yachts

Racing regattas had been held as early as the 1850's at Barrow, usually at the South end of Walney Channel around Piel and Roa Islands. These were at first organised by yacht clubs from outside the area, and it was only in June 1871 that the Barrow Yacht Club was formed and held its first races. At that time there were 42 yachts owned by its members. Amongst them were Thomas and Richard Ashburner, who both were enthusiastic yachtsmen. Barrow's founding fathers were as well represented at the club as in all of Barrow's new ventures – the Duke of Buccleuch was Commodore and Sir James Ramsden was Vice-Commodore. Men such as these saw yachting as only a further means by which to demonstrate their wealth and achievement, and Ramsden, H.W. Schneider, James Fisher and others confined themselves to

---

168. Alan Lockett, *North Western Sail* (1978) pp16–20.
169. From an undated cutting from the *North-Western Daily Mail*, mid-1920's, reporting the retirement of pilot Henry Charnley, James Charnley's son.

PLATE 10D: Rose *under sail. Her gaff topsail has not been set.*

cruising in their own luxuriously-appointed steam yachts. In 1878 the club received the Royal approval and became the Royal Barrow Yacht Club, Thomas Ashburner later becoming its Honorary Secretary. He and his brother were yachtsmen in the true sense, and their interest in racing produced remarkable success, principally in boats they had designed and built themselves.

At least nine of the Ashburners' yachts are recorded in Lloyd's Register of Yachts, which only started in 1872. All of them were less than 40 ft. in overall length. The first was *Daisy*, a two-ton cutter designed by Richard Ashburner and launched in 1878. She was followed by two larger cutters, *Salmo* and *Rose*, launched in May, 1880. *Rose* was lengthened by two feet in the following year to bring her to 27 feet 8 inches overall, with a beam of 8 feet and a draft of 6 feet 6 inches. She was later bought by a Liverpool owner and by 1889 had been renamed *Lu-lu*.

PLATE 10E: Rose *at Rock Ferry, c. 1909. She is probably dressed for a regatta*

It can be assumed that the hull form evolved from that of the 'nobby', boats adapted for speed in the face of the short, steep seas characteristic of Morecambe Bay. This is particularly evident in the long run aft to a low counter stern [PLATES 10B, 10C]. At the bows the entrance is much deeper and sharper, a considerable development from that of the straight-stemmed, bluff-bowed trawl boats. The sail plan [PLATE 10D] is also very similar to that of a 'nobby', though for racing the cutter rig was augmented by a spinnaker.

Further yachts followed *Rose* at regular intervals. A three-ton cutter, *Lily* was built in 1882/3. By 1889 she was owned in Hamburg. *Rosebud* was built in 1884. The largest of the Ashburners' yachts was the eight-ton *Red Rose*. She was designed by the Glasgow designer G.L. Watson and was built in 1890. Their final two yachts were *Primrose* and *White Rose*. Unlike all her predecessors, *Primrose*, launched in 1895, was rigged as a sloop.[170]

The Ashburner yachts were highly successful. *Rose*, *Rosebud* and *Red Rose* all won trophies from the RBYC in their first year of competition.[171] *Red Rose* was owned jointly by Thomas and Richard and she was sold in 1897 for £200. The two brothers invested the money in what was to become their most successful and famous yacht, *White Rose*.

---

170. From *Lloyd's Register of Yachts*, 1878 to 1919.
171. Trophies still owned by the Ashburner family include silver chalices won by *Rose* in 1880 and *Rosebud* in 1884, and a silver drinking mug won by *Red Rose* in 1890. All presented to the Ashburners by Sir James Ramsden on behalf of the R.B.Y.C.

The Ashburners' racing success was largely local, against similar yachts built at Morecambe Bay and Duddon boatyards. The enduring success of *White Rose*, built in 1899, gives a better perspective on Richard Ashburner's qualities as a yacht designer. *White Rose* was originally a 30 ft. cutter of 6 tons, carrying just under 700 square feet of sail. She was soon lengthened three times, doubling her tonnage and bringing her to 39 ft. 6 ins. overall. With this increase in hull size came more sail, so that in her final form the Ashburners raced her with two jibs, a gaff topsail and a mainsail totalling 900 square feet. The Ashburners, both in their sixties by then, raced her themselves and were reportedly almost invincible in local races.[172]

The Ashburners ceased to appear in Lloyd's Register as builders in 1903, and as owners ten years later. According to the Register they still owned *White Rose* but she was sold during the First World War, soon after Thomas Ashburner had died. Her new owner removed her keel to profit from the then inflated price of lead. By the end of the War she was in new ownership and was not sailed again until 1925. With the yacht in a decrepit state, her owner decided to raffle her and she was won by a local yachtsman, Dr. Coffey. He refitted her, though giving her only an iron keel. She re-entered the local racing scene, again winning most of her races, and in 1928 she took the record for the passage from Douglas to Barrow's Piel Island. The Second War interrupted her career and she was again laid-up. In 1949 Fred Rollinson bought her and restored her to her former grandure, though with a more modern sail plan of only a 450 sq. ft. mainsail and 150 sq. ft. jib. She was again a winner, and in 1973 won the North West Veterans and Old Gaffers Race.

Thanks to the efforts of these North West yachtsmen *White Rose* survived even longer than the Ashburner schooners. Fred Rollinson donated her to the Furness Maritime Trust for the nominal sum of £1, and today, though in fine condition, she awaits further restoration at Barrow. She is a beautiful, elegant boat and Richard Ashburner could have wished for no finer memorial.

---

172. Alan Lockett, *Morecambe Bay*, pp4–8 gives a full history of the *White Rose*.

11 THE ASHBURNER SCHOONERS IN WALES

The Dee River Ports

The Dee River was one of the principal destinations for the Furness schooners, which supplied ore to the Mostyn ironworks and ore and pig iron to the steelworks at Shotton. Other industries along the Dee estuary were equally important to the profitability of the trade, for they provided the return cargoes. Brickworks and coal mines at Buckley and Point of Ayr, lead mines at Halkin, and a chemical works at Flint expanded during the mid-19th Century, to the point that the harbours at Connah's Quay and Saltney became far more important to the schooners than Chester, the principal Dee River port since Roman times [FIG. 8]. The few shifting channels into the river were marred by sandbanks and the harbours were small and tidal, making the shallow-drafted schooners and ketches the most suitable ships for the trade. Together with the general unsuitability of bricks and tiles as cargoes for steamships, the difficult navigation of the estuary ensured that the Dee River became one of the last homes for British sailing ships. Many of the Furness schooners were to end their careers there.

Connah's Quay

The Dee's main port from the mid-1800's was Connah's Quay, a connecting point to a good railway link to the Midlands. A thriving schooner fleet had been established there, based mainly on the import of iron ore and the export of bricks. A considerable part of this trade was with Furness, and in particular with the Duddon. Two of the seamen who had served in this trade were Capt. John Coppack and Capt. Charles Reney, and at about the same time in the 1880's they both retired from the sea to start shipbrokering businesses at Connah's Quay. By 1890 Reney was the principal local shipowner and Coppack had been joined in partnership by H.C. Carter.[173]

Not all of the Connah's Quay vessels were owned locally. The deepwater docks at Barrow had attracted steamers to the port, reducing the number of cargoes available to the sailing ships, and many of the Ashburner schooners increasingly began to sail from Connah's Quay. Though their shares remained largely in the hands of Furness owners, the schooners acquired local masters and effectively became Dee River traders. This process started in the 1880's, at first with the smaller schooners. The *Catherine Latham* was commanded by a Coppack from 1881 and the *Alice Latham* had her first Connah's Quay master in 1884, Capt. Benjamin Bennet. Later the *Margaret Ann* was bought outright by Capt. John Coppack.[174] Eventually even the larger schooners were given Dee River masters – Capt. Robert Foulkes in the *James Postlethwaite*, Capt. Tom Hughes in the *M.E. Johnson* and Capt. Tom Peers in the *James & Agnes*.

The final schooner built by the Ashburners operated from Connah's Quay for all her life. After her launch in April 1884 the *J. & M. Garratt* was sold in her entirety to Coppack, Carter & Co. Though John Coppack and Charles Carter retained joint ownership of 24 shares, they sold the rest to their fellow schoonermen, including members of the Garratt, Bennett, Vickers and Wright families. Coppack & Carter retained managing ownership for ten years, after which Capt. John Vickers took over responsibility. He had started a third shipbrokering business, which after his death was taken over by Capt. Ben Vickers, his brother. During all this time it seems that Capt. Joseph Garratt was master of the *J. & M. Garratt*.

The *Isabella* had been captained by Connah's Quay masters since 1891, when Capt. William Hughes took command. All the subsequent masters in the following twenty six years

---

173. Tom Coppack, *A Lifetime with Ships* (1973)
174. *CSR*

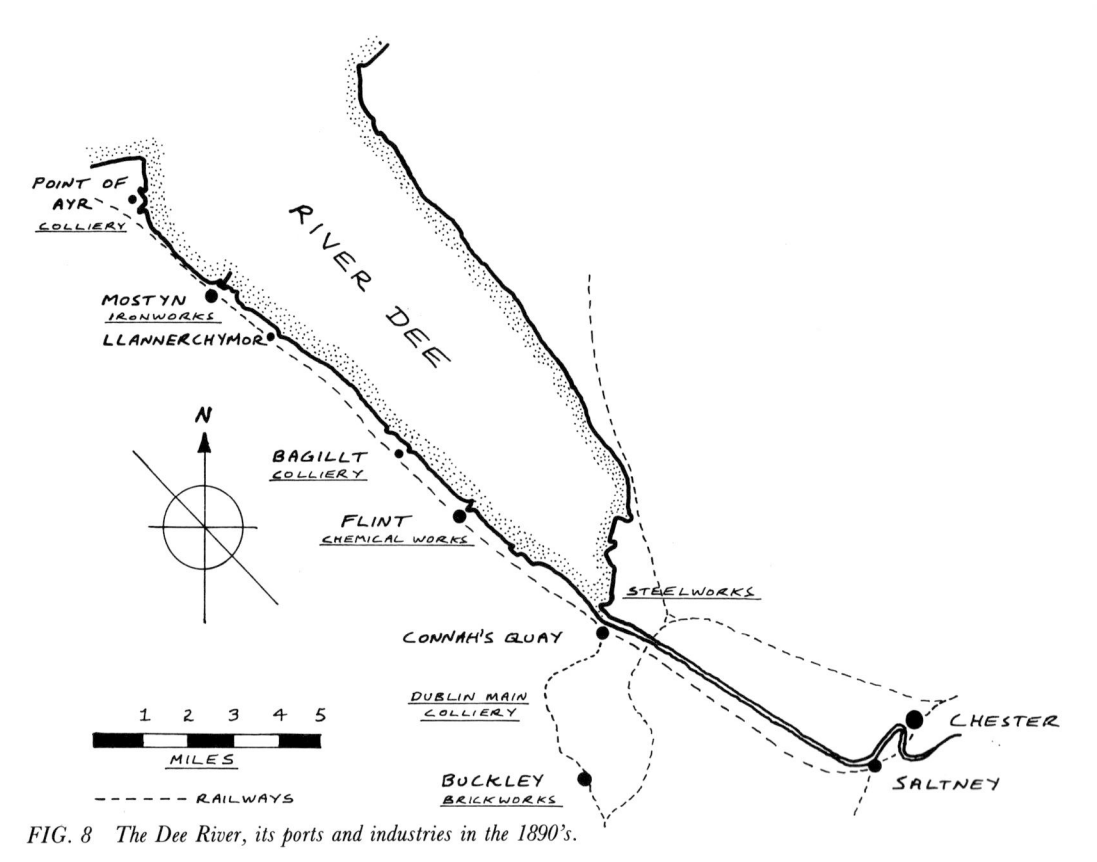

FIG. 8 *The Dee River, its ports and industries in the 1890's.*

joined her at Connah's Quay – they were Capt. Thomas Hughes, Capt. William James Coppack and then Capt. Humphrey Shaw.[175] His son, Capt. Hugh Shaw, sailed briefly on the *Isabella* and, in his autobiography, described her as a "fine fast sailer and a good one in which to get a living".[176] The *Result* too was a Connah's Quay schooner in her early life. Her first master was Capt. Robert Wright, who originated from Tarleton. Unlike so many of the other seamen from his birthplace, he moved not to Barrow but to Connah's Quay, illustrating the decline of Barrow as a schooner port.

Bricks and Tiles

Connah's Quay owed its development to the export of bricks and similar products. There were several brickworks nearby at Buckley, but the trade also included quarry tiles from Ruabon, glazed earthenware pipes from Lancashire and bricks and ceramic sanitary products from the Staffordshire potteries. Bricks were a most suitable cargo for sailing ships. Their fragility required that they be loaded slowly and carefully by hand, and they had to be protected with packing once stowed in the hold. To load a 150 ton cargo might take three days. At sea, a ship carrying bricks would damage its cargo if it attempted to proceed in weather conditions that were too rough. For these reasons, the brick trade was one of the last refuges of the sailing ships, for steamers required quick turnaround times in port and fast passages in all weather conditions in order to earn their keep.

The Ashburner schooner that was most closely associated with the brick trade from Connah's Quay was the *Catherine Latham*. William Hancock & Co., brick merchants at Buckley, had bought all 64 of her shares, for £450, in 1898. She traded for this company for seventeen years until her loss on the 13th February, 1915. Carrying bricks and tiles from Connah's Quay to Dublin, she sought refuge in the outer harbour at Douglas, Isle of Man. In a strong easterly gale she dragged her anchors and stranded below Fort Anne. Capt. T. Jones and his crew were saved by the Douglas lifeboat, but by the following morning their ship had filled and become a total wreck.[177]

The Schooner Auctions

After the closure of their own shipyard the Ashburners had ceased to repair their schooners themselves. The work was largely done at two highly respected shipyards, Robert Cock's yard at Appledore and the Butlers' yard at Connah's Quay. Periodically Thomas or Richard Ashburner would travel from Barrow to inspect work that had been done. On their visits to Connah's Quay they would stay at the home of Tom Coppack, a local shipowner and broker. It was to him that they went for advice and assistance when, in 1908, they decided to sell off the remaining nine schooners of the Ashburner fleet. To make profits in the British schooner trade by this time required a commitment that the Ashburners no longer felt able to make. The two brothers were both in their seventies and their sons had already established their careers elsewhere. Thomas's only son was a solicitor and of Richard's two sons, one was a clergyman and the other, a steamship master, was about to emigrate to Australia.

Thomas and Richard travelled together to Connah's Quay to consult Tom Coppack. One Saturday morning they met at his office in Church Street and devised their strategy for the sale. Their first concern was to attract the widest range of potential buyers, and to this end they draughted a letter to be sent to all the major schooner owners. They recognised that Irish owners were likely to offer the highest prices, for the trade to and from that coast was still bouyant. Arklow was the main centre for the Irish sailing ships and the principal families of that port, the Tyrrells, Kearons, Gregorys, Hagans and Halls, all received the letter. It also went to the Fleming family of Youghal, Capt. Curran of Dungarvan and many others in Ireland. In Britain the letter was sent to owners in places as distant as Cornwall and Ipswich. Welsh owners were told of the forthcoming sale verbally, but Coppack felt that many of these men were getting tired of the sea and would be unlikely to pay high prices.

The sale of the Ashburner schooners took place at Connah's Quay in three separate auctions spread over a period of six months.[178] The first auction took place in November 1908, and included the three oldest two-masters, the *Mary Jane*, *James & Agnes* and *Mary Ashburner*. They were pulled up onto the two beaches at Connah's Quay, to allow the prospective buyers to wander around them and thoroughly inspect their hulls and fittings. A local auctioneer who was inexperienced at selling ships was given charge of the sales. He caused some hilarity amongst the seafarers by referring to the bows and sterns of the ships as their sharp and blunt ends. This did not detract from the prices he achieved, which were said to be much above expectations.

The *Mary Jane* was sold for £555 to the family of her captain. Her new managing owner was to be a woman, the master's wife, Mrs. Mary Hughes of Shotton. This arrangement was by no means unusual in Wales, where family ownership of a vessel was much more common than in the North West. The *Mary Ashburner* also went to Welsh owners, but of a very different kind. William and John Thomas, of Amlwch, were successful shipbuilders, and like the Ashburners they managed a small fleet composed largely of schooners they had built themselves. These included wood and metal-hulled ships, all of which were highly regarded for the quality of their design. It is something of a compliment to the Ashburners that such respected shipbuilders chose to buy the *Mary Ashburner*, though no doubt they were influenced by Capt. John Hughes, an Amlwch seaman who had been her master for nearly all her life. The ship

---

175. *Documents relating to Isabella* (CRO BT/SR 4) include her Certificate of British Registry, listing all masters until 1927, and Wm. Ashburner's original builder's certificate.
176. From Capt. Hugh Shaw's edited autobiography – Norah Ayland, *Schooner Captain* (1972) p42.
177. *Lloyd's List*, 15th Feb. 1915.
178. *Chester Chronicle*, 27th Feb. 1909, reported the second auction and referred to the others. In *A Lifetime with Ships*, p55 Tom Coppack misrepresents these events as occuring on a single day. Sale prices are given in Richard Ashburner's Cash Book, CRO 755.

must have been in some state of disrepair because she was sold for £550, less than the smaller and older *Mary Jane*. Subsequently the Thomas's reconditioned her at a further cost of £638. Capt. Hughes was retained as master by the new owners.

The *James & Agnes*, the largest vessel, attracted the best price of the first auction. She was sold for £720 to James Horan, who was to be her future master and managing owner, together with George & Richard Kearon. They were all from Arklow in Co. Wicklow, Ireland. This port still had a large schooner fleet, and three other of the Ashburner schooners were soon to join their sister ship.

The second auction, held on the 25th February 1909, included a further three ships, the two remaining two-masters and the *William Ashburner*, the oldest three-master. Again there were potential buyers from all around England, as well as from Ireland, Scotland and the Isle of Man. However, two of the schooners were destined to stay at Connah's Quay. The *William Ashburner* and the *Isabella* were both commanded by local men whose families were anxious to preserve their livelihoods. The *William Ashburner* was sold for £1040 to Capt. Tom Bennett, a retired seaman himself and the father of Capt. Benjamin Bennett, the ship's current master. The *Isabella* was captained by Robert John Wright, son of Capt. Robert Wright of the *Result*. He and Tom Coppack each purchased a quarter share in the ship, which was sold for £590. The Ashburners retained a half share in her, and the younger Capt. Wright kept her command. Only the *Useful* was sold out of Connah's Quay. She was bought for £610 by Capt. John Gregory of Arklow, in partnership with the Kearon family. She was by far the smallest ship to go to the Irishmen, and perhaps she was too small for them, for she was destined to be sold back to Connah's Quay within a few years.

Six weeks later the third and final auction took place. The last three schooners were the newest three-masters, the *James Postlethwaite*, *M.E. Johnson* and *Result*. Again the Irishmen turned up in force, and there were men from Braunton and Appledore. They had already decided on the ships they wished to buy and the bidding was intense. The *James Postlethwaite* went to the Irishmen for £955. She was bought by Capt. Ned Hall, her future master, again with the financial backing of the Kearons. The steel schooner *Result* went to a Devon owner when Capt. Henry Clarke of Braunton made the winning bid of £1100. The highest price of all was achieved by the *M.E. Johnson*. Philip Kelly Harris, an Appledore shipbuilder, wanted her but could not match the bidding of the Irishmen. For £1110 the ship went to Capt. Frank Tyrrell and Capt. Thomas Price, and to their inevitable partners, the Kearons.

The price achieved by the *M.E. Johnson* was surprisingly high, since she was smaller and older than the *James Postlethwaite* and not very much larger than the *Result*. Presumably her price was driven up by competitive bidding between Harris and the Irishmen. Harris was certainly disappointed at his failure to secure her, for he asked Richard Ashburner to design a similar ship, which he would build himself. This vessel, the *P.T. Harris* was built at the New Quay shipyard at Appledore, which Harris had owned since the previous year. She was three years in construction, and was eventually launched in 1912. She was the last schooner built at Appledore and the last in which a member of the Ashburner family had participated. It is interesting that the Appledore men chose a 'Barrow flat' to be their last ship. The design of the Appledore schooners had previously reflected the deepwater sailing tradition of the port, which had at one time been much involved in the Newfoundland salt fish trade. This trade was still active but was slowly being taken over by steamers. For the Appledore men to depart from their own traditions to build a 'Barrow flat' was a sign not only that the future of the sailing ships lay primarily in the coasting trades, but also confirmation that the 'Barrow flats' were the schooners best suited to this trade. Unfortunately for Harris, they were not immune to all the vagaries of luck and bad weather and he did not get much happiness out of his new

---

179. *Mer.Sch.* p102.
180. Thomas Ashburner's obituary, *Barrow News*, 3rd May 1910, p10.
181. Loss described in *Mer.Sch.*, p195 & *Lloyd's List*, 13th Nov. 1911.
182. GLL *Board of Trade Official Inquiries 1914 to 1917*, Inquiry No. 7638. Letters from Wm. Thomas relating to the Inquiry are in Crew Lists, CRO Z3226.

ship. She survived only for five years before foundering in a gale off the Welsh coast.[179]

Thomas Ashburner survived his fleet by only four years, dying aged 78 on the 27th April 1913.[180] His wife and only surviving son died in the same year. Richard Ashburner lived to an even greater age, dying aged 85 on the 24th February, 1922. Their younger brother, William, survived them both, being 83 years old at the time of Richard's death.

Two Welsh Schooners Lost

A peculiar fact about the three schooners sold at the first Connah's Quay auction was that they were all to be lost in the five years prior to the First World War. In contrast, all six schooners sold at the succeeeding auctions would all survive at least thirty six years, beyond the outbreak of the Second World War.

The *Mary Jane* traded for Capt. Reney's agency for three years after her sale at Connah's Quay. She was lost on the morning of 13th November, 1911. She was travelling from Britonferry bound for Gosport with a cargo of coal, under the command of Capt. Hughes. On the afternoon of the previous day the ship had encountered heavy weather, suffering much damage and losing most of her sails. The following morning she was sighted near the shore at Watergate Bay, near Newquay in Cornwall. The lifeboat and rocket apparatus were called out, but the ship foundered and went to pieces before they arrived. Fortunately, the crew had already been taken from the badly leaking ship by the Cardiff steamer *Ruabon*, in extremely heavy seas ten miles north of Godrevy. They were landed safely at Penzance the same morning and seven of the crew of the *Ruabon* were subsequently awarded decorations for their part in the rescue.[181]

After her sale in 1908 to William Thomas the *Mary Ashburner* traded mainly on the China clay route between Runcorn and Cornwall. She regularly sailed South to the ports of Dartmouth, Teignmouth and Polperro, then picked up her return cargo of clay at Par, Charlestown or Pentewan. She remained in the charge of Capt. John Hughes, who had taken command of her within a year of her launch. He was 65 years old when the *Mary Ashburner* sailed from Charlestown at 5.30 p.m. on the 25th November, 1913. His ship was still rigged as a topsail schooner and was reportedly in good seaworthy condition. She was bound for Runcorn with 164 tons of China clay and carried a crew of five men, four of whom were from Anglesey. She never reached her destination. Two weeks later her small boat was found floating four miles East of Lundy Island by a Milford fishing boat, the *Queen Alexandra*. The overdue schooner was listed as 'Missing', it being assumed that she had sunk with all hands. A Board of Trade Inquiry into her loss, held at Liverpool in March 1914, established the story of her final voyage.

Two days after the *Mary Ashburner* had left Charlestown, the 1922 ton steamship *Castilian*, of Liverpool's Ellerman Line, had been travelling south on a voyage from her home port to Tangiers. At 7 p.m. on the 27th November, she was about sixty miles West of Lundy, steaming at her full speed of ten knots through thick fog. The ship's chief officer and a lookout were on the bridge. Too late they saw the white stern light of a ship right ahead. Despite stopping their engines and steering hard-a-port, the *Castilian* struck the unidentified ship with her starboard bow. As his ship sped past the stricken vessel, the lookout could only see that she was a two-masted sailing ship and that she had some square sails on her foremast. He thought that she had gone down almost instantly. Certainly the collision had been violent, because a schooner's main gaff and rigging was found lodged across the bows of his ship. The *Castilian* herself was only slightly damaged and she was put about and searched the area for two hours, without finding any further signs of wreckage or survivors. She eventually proceeded on her voyage, and the collision was reported to the ship's owners upon her arrival in Tangiers. Ultimately the Board of Trade were informed and they recognised the coincidence of the collision and the disappearance of the *Mary Ashburner*. At the Court of Inquiry William Thomas verified that the description of the gaff and rigging matched that of his vessel. The Court concluded that the *Mary Ashburner* had been run down by the *Castilian* and that she had sunk with the loss of all hands.[182]

PLATE 11A: J.& M. Garratt, *nearly fully loaded, lying at Bridgwater in April 1935.*

Connah's Quay and the Auxiliary Schooners

Auxiliary diesel engines began to be fitted into the schooners in the years before the First World War, a necessary adaptation brought about by increasing competition from alternative forms of transport. All the Ashburner schooners that survived the War were eventually converted to auxiliaries, starting with the *Result* in 1914 and the *Margaret Ann* four years later. The economic advantage that the auxiliary engine gave the schooners was a consequence of their liberation from the vagaries of wind and tide, a reduction in crew and the capability for making faster voyages. The auxiliaries were able to sail in light winds and against tides that would have previously kept them waiting in port. There was less need to hire tugs. Once underway, the auxiliaries could sail a course closer to the wind, shortening journies made to windward. On arrival, the auxiliaries could be unloaded and reloaded in turn with the steamers, it being a practice in many ports for powered vessels to take precedence over sailing ships. The addition of an engine was usually accompanied by the removal of the square topsails, so leading to the engines being dubbed the 'iron topsail'. Working the square sails was most demanding in manpower and their loss meant that crew numbers could be reduced. Two-masted schooners that had once sailed with five men often carried only three when an engine had been installed.

The *J.& M. Garratt* became an auxiliary in 1923, losing her upper yards but retaining a single yard to set a squaresail [PLATE 11A]. She sailed first under the command of Capt. Richard Hutton and then successively two of his sons, David and Robert. She returned to the Coppack agency in the 1930's, where she joined the *Isabella* under Capt. Fellows and the *Useful* under Capt. Wynne. In 1934 the *J.& M. Garratt* had two 50 h.p. diesel engines, a considerable amount of power for a relatively small schooner. It allowed her to make the passage along the narrow channel into Connah's Quay in one tide, the only Dee River schooner capable of this.

The *J.& M. Garratt* continued to trade thoughout the 1930's. She seems to have had a fairly undramatic career, which ended in spectacular fashion at Drogheda in October, 1940. The

106

auxiliary engines that had contributed to her long trading career were also the eventual cause of her loss. Under the command of Capt. Robert Hutton she had sailed for Drogheda with a cargo of 160 tons of firebricks and tiles, destined for use at the local cement factory. As she crossed the bar at the mouth of the River Boyne her engines began to give her trouble, and shortly afterwards one caught alight. The fire quickly spread to engulf the engine room and within forty five minutes was out of control. The schooner crew opened the taps of their oil tanks, to release the 500 gallons of oil that they carried, and then abandoned the blazing ship in their small boat. They reached the shore safely but their ship drifted slowly in towards the quays, " on a pitch dark night, the flames from the oil and paraffin tanks shooting up into the sky and illuminating the countryside for miles around".[183] The harbourmaster, fearing that the main river channel would be blocked by the wreck, organised some dock workers to bravely go aboard the ship and fix a line to her. She was pulled in towards a wharf, where she sank to the bottom and the remaining fires were extinguished with water. Though her cargo was later salvaged, the *J. & M. Garratt* was irretrievably damaged, the stern third of her hull gutted to the beams and frames.

The Isabella

After the Connah's Quay auction in 1909 Thomas and Richard Ashburner retained shares in only three schooners, namely Fishers' *British Queen*, William Hurford's *Christiana Davis* and their own *Isabella*. Trade was continuing to decline for the schooners and some of the smaller ports that they served were going out of use. The tiny natural harbour at Ravenglass on the Cumberland coast had been used by sailing ships since Roman times, but its days as a port ended with the visit of the *Isabella* in March 1913. The cargo was guano for the local farmers, but a few bottles of smuggled brandy ensured that at least this minor historical event did not go uncelebrated.[184]

By 1917 there was still sufficient trade to keep the Connah's Quay schooners regularly employed, but the highest profits were to be found on the South Coast. The war in France meant that there was a vastly increased quantity of cargo to be carried, and the predations of German submarines meant that there were ever fewer ships to carry it. Freights were progressively increased to attract shipping to the cross-Channel trade and to compensate for some of the risks involved. Huge profits were there to be made, and the prices being paid for ships soared. In October the owners of the *Isabella* decided to take some of these profits for themselves, and she was sold to Davis & Stephens (Ship, Steamship & Insurance Brokers) of Plymouth. The price they paid for her, £2340, was four times higher than that which she had achieved at auction eight years earlier.[185]

The *Isabella* survived the hazards of the Channel trade, and she served her new owners for many years after the end of the War. In 1930 she returned to the Dee River, and to the management of the Coppack agency, when she was bought by Capt. Joseph Fellows of Shotton. The once large fleet of Dee sailing ships was by this time reduced to only seven schooners, two of them being auxiliaries. Three were Ashburner schooners – the *Useful*, like the *Isabella* herself, was still unpowered, but the *J. & M. Garratt* had by this time had her auxiliary engines installed. These ships were the last sailing ships owned and operating from a Welsh port.

However, despite being brought home to her old port, the *Isabella* found it difficult to survive in her old trade, even though she was given the benefit of a four-cylinder Ruston & Hornsby oil engine. Together with another Dee-owned schooner, the Fleetwood-built three-master *Emily Warbrick*, she was laid up on the mudbank at Par harbour in 1934 [Plate 11B]. By the end of the following year her long, hard fight against the adverse economics of her trade was over, and she was sold for use as a yacht. Her new owner was an RAF officer based at an

---

183. *Drogheda Independant*, 12th Oct.1940, p6.
184. Henry Peck's Notes on Barrow Sailing Ships, CRO BDX/44.
185. Sale price from Richard Ashburner's Cash Book, *op. cit.*

PLATE 11B: Isabella *laid-up at Par in 1935.*

airfield near Woodbridge in Suffolk. He had a cabin built over the after hatch but otherwise her appearance was not changed. The *Isabella* carried her topmasts and all three yards to her dying days. After spending the war years in Suffolk she was still in use as a houseboat in 1946. Her ultimate fate is uncertain, but it seems that after a career of seventy years she was broken-up at Southampton in 1948.

The Useful

In her early years at Connah's Quay the *Useful* was employed by the Vickers agency, but in 1935 her owner and master, Capt. John Wynne, changed to Coppacks. By this time his ship was an auxiliary schooner, powered by a Widdop engine [Plate 11C]. The *Useful* was a Connah's Quay schooner for nearly all her life, and by 1946 was not only the last of the Dee River schooners, but was also the last schooner owned in Wales. That winter was particularly

PLATE 11C: Useful *at Ellesmere Port, 1937.*

severe in the Irish Sea. In January 1947, loaded with bricks and tiles, she set sail from an anchorage at Mostyn, bound for Belfast. Her crew consisted of only two men, the captain-owner John Wynne and his son, who acted as mate. The ship was enveloped by dense fog almost as soon as she left her anchorage, and the bad visibility continued throughout the voyage. Her crew failed to sight the Langness and Chicken Rock lights off the Isle of Man and, with a heavy sea running, the *Useful* sailed broadside on to jagged rocks at Santon Head. With their ship holed and very soon dismasted, the crew fired distress rockets and then set fire to the galley in a bid to attract attention. With the ship hidden from sight of land by the cliffs these signals went unseen, and soon the heavy seas began to break up the old schooner. The weather worsened into a blizzard and the crew made the desperate decision to jump from their ship, onto rocks at the base of the cliffs. Surviving this first obstacle they then had to climb the icy rock face in pitch darkness and driving sleet. Frozen and exhausted when they eventually reached the cliff top, they collapsed into the deep snow. They were saved by the whimpering of the ship's dog, that had been carried to safety by the mate. It was heard by a shepherd searching the snowdrifts for his stock. He found the two unconscious men and, after summoning help, carried them to the shelter of his farm, where they were soon revived. By the following night Capt. Wynne and his son had returned home. At the base of the cliffs the *Useful* had been smashed to pieces.[186]

After the wreck of the *Useful* only the small ketch *Sarah Latham* still sailed from Connah's Quay, and she was lost in the following year, also off the Isle of Man. Some of the surviving Irish schooners still visited, but as the railways and deeper harbours took away the dwindling trade the port itself began to decline. Connah's Quay continued to receive small steamships right up until the 1960's, but the dock has since been closed and is now completely derelict.

---

186. Loss of the *Useful* reported by Capt. Richard England in *Schoonerman* (1971) p177 from a verbal account received from the mate, John Wynne. Also reported with photograph in *Sea Breezes*, March 1947, p196 & p217.

12 THE IRISH AUXILIARIES

After the Connah's Quay auction in 1909 four of the Ashburner schooners sailed across the Irish Sea to Arklow in the hands of Irish owners. This port to the south of Dublin had a large fleet of sailing vessels, mainly owned by two families, the Kearons and Tyrrells. They had bought many of the larger British schooners that had left the deepwater trades that were then dying. They operated these ships in the general coasting trades around Britain and Ireland and to Europe. As these trades themselves declined the ships were moved into trades from the Irish ports and mostly in the Irish Sea. They relied heavily on the import of coal and bricks from Britain, and were therefore closely associated with the Dee and Mersey ports. Their exports were primarily timber and agricultural produce.

The *James & Agnes* was lost after only a few months in Irish ownership and the *Useful* was fairly quickly sold back to Connah's Quay. The two three-masted schooners, *M.E. Johnson* and *James Postlethwaite*, were destined for long lives and sailed from the Irish port to the end of their days. They were both fully-rigged and without engines when they arrived at Arklow. After being converted to auxiliaries their rigs were gradually reduced over the years to adapt to the changing circumstances of their trades.

The Loss of the *James & Agnes*

The *James & Agnes* operated for nearly a year from her new home, under the management and captaincy of James Horan. In October 1909 she was in Swansea to load 220.8 tons of anthracite, nearly a full cargo, for Cowes, Isle of Wight. After loading she was kept weatherbound in dock for eleven days, but early on the morning of the 19th October she was finally towed from Swansea docks by the tug *Fawn*. In moderate weather she proceeded under her fore-and-aft canvas on the starboard tack, heading down the Bristol Channel towards Land's End. As she passed to the East of Lundy Island she was recognised by the master of another Arklow-owned vessel, the Portmadoc-built barquentine *Venedocian*. She had left Cardiff the same morning, and by the early evening was passing to the West of Lundy, bound for Guernsey. The weather had worsened and a gale was blowing up. After the master of the *Venedocian* lost sight of the old Ashburner schooner at 9 p.m. that evening she was never seen again. She was listed as "Missing", with the presumed loss of Capt. Horan and the other four crewmen. As with many schooner losses, that of the *James & Agnes* brought great tragedy to a small community. All the crew were from Arklow and three of them were brothers.

The reason for the ship's loss was a mystery that was never satisfactorily resolved, even by an Inquiry that was held at Swansea in the following year. A coal gas explosion was considered but then discounted because her anthracite cargo was known to be free of this danger. The ship was certainly seaworthy when she had left Swansea, having only recently passed her Board of Trade survey, and she had not been overloaded. Although the weather around Lundy had deteriorated into a full gale after she was last sighted, it was considered that she was sound enough to have withstood such conditions. Since no identifiable wreckage was found on the island, the Inquiry concluded that the *James & Agnes* must have been sunk by collision with an unknown steamer somewhere to the East of Lundy.[187]

In Arklow between the Wars

Until Irish independance in 1921 all the Arklow schooners were British-registered and sailed under the Red Ensign. In the First World War they therefore faced the same hazards as the ships sailing from the mainland British ports. The *James Postlethwaite* had the misfortune to be one of the first vessels to suffer from the War. In August 1914 she was berthed at Hamburg and she met the same fate as other British ships in German ports. Capt. Ned Hall and his crew

PLATE 12A: *By 1931 the* James Postlethwaite *had been reduced in rig. Here she is seen off Seven Heads, Co. Cork, under what was then probably her full complement of sail.*

were interned as British subjects and the ship herself was put to work by her captors. The Allied blockade prevented them from sending her outside the Elbe estuary, so they removed her masts and employed her as a barge. The Elbe river was one of the major transport routes for munitions and other war materials and the ship spent four years in this arduous work. The strength that the Ashburners had given her was enough to ensure that she survived this mistreatment and she was still in a serviceable condition when peace arrived. Her owners, Kearon & Hall, had her towed to South Shields by the tug *Simson* in January 1919. Refitted with three new masts, and carrying her original rig (see Cover) she eventually resumed her career in April of that year, sailing from the Shields to St. Valery, again under the command of Capt. Hall.[188]

The *James Postlethwaite* resumed her trade around Britain and Ireland, and it seems that the shipwrights at Shields had made an excellent job of her refit, for she was still a fast sailer. In 1921 she circumnavigated Britain, the first part of her journey being from Ireland to Newcastle-upon-Tyne with potatoes. She made a fast passage around the North of Scotland, and loaded a cargo of coal for Falmouth. When she left Newcastle the Fowey-owned barquentine *Waterwitch* was close on her heels. Then noted for her fast passages up and down the East coast, the *Waterwitch* was later to become the last British square-rigger to carry cargo in the Home trade. The *James Postlethwaite* covered the 570 miles to Falmouth in 80 hours, an average speed of more than seven knots. The *Waterwitch* kept pace with her for the whole trip but was never able to pass her smaller rival.[189]

Six years later, in 1926, the *James Postlethwaite* was bought outright by Capt. Hall and had her first auxiliary motor fitted. Her rigging was also altered to fit her new circumstances. Her topmasts were all shortened and the two uppermost yards were removed, leaving only a single yard to carry a squaresail [PLATE 12A]. Capt. William Hagan replaced Capt. Hall as master

---

187. *Report of Inquiries into Wrecks 1909/10*, Inquiry No.7328 (*James & Agnes*), at D.o.T. Marine Division Library, Holborn. The crew were Capt. Horan, Patrick Chatham (mate) and Thomas, Paul & Michael Burn.
188. *Lloyd's List*, 3rd Dec. 1914 & 15th Jan. 1919.
189. "The schooner that starred in films", an article in *The Evening Herald* by Dr. J.E. de Courcy, 16th Nov. 1961.

PLATE 12B: M.E. Johnson *at Newlyn, April 1936. Although she has lost her topsail yards, her topmasts have all been retained and she is very close to her original appearance.*

and in May 1929 he nearly lost his ship when she was run into by a collier whilst anchored in Carlingford Lough. Although she sank, her crew all managed to save themselves, and the ship herself was salvaged and repaired within a few months.[190] Capt. Hagan continued in command until his death in 1935, after which Capt. James Counsell took his place.

Though the *M.E. Johnson* had had a less torrid time than her sister ship up to this point, the next few years were going to see her involved in a series of incidents that she was lucky to survive. She had been fitted with an auxiliary motor much earlier, in 1920. This was an 80 h.p. engine and as usual her two upper yards were removed, though her masts were not shortened [PLATE 12B]. Capt. Jack Kinch became part-owner of her in 1934 and his first six months in command were largely occupied by trips between Garston and Arklow. The *M.E. Johnson* was laid-up at Plymouth for two months late in 1937 whilst she was refitted with a new and more powerful engine. The topmasts were removed to leave her with only three pole masts, and she retained a short yard on the foremast for a small squaresail [PLATE 12C].

The following year had a series of dramas involving both the Ashburner three-masters. Early in the year the *M.E. Johnson* was bound for Runcorn from Cornwall when she ran into a severe gale and was completely dismasted. Her crew abandoned her, but the following day rejoined their ship and sailed her into port with a jury rig and her hold waterlogged. The *James Postlethwaite* ran into trouble at Holyhead, where she grounded after losing her mainsail. She was again salvaged and resumed her work. On 20th December 1938 the *M.E. Johnson* was bound from Plymouth to Runcorn. On board was the captain's bride of only three months Mrs. Winnie Kinch. When the schooner was off Fishguard one of the propellers was lost. With

---

190. Capt. Frank Forde, *The Long Watch* (1981) p14.

PLATE 12C: M.E. Johnson *at Narrow Quay, Bristol Docks, Sept. 1947. Her masts have been poled off but she seems to be in fine condition.*

a gale blowing, and in freezing conditions, the crew fought to control their ship for three days. Eventually she grounded at Carnsore Point on the south Wexford coast. In a very rough sea and with a severe blizzard blowing, the Rosslare lifeboat was launched to give her assistance. They took off the master's wife, but Capt. Kinch and his exhausted crew remained on board. After three days aground the weather abated and the ship was recovered by an Arklow fishing boat and was towed safely back to her home port. Despite the severity of her ordeal, the ship was able to continue with her cargo to Runcorn, where repairs were carried out at Stubbs' shipyard. This dramatic incident attracted the attention of a Daily Mirror reporter and was subsequently described in his newspaper. However, it seems that the story was not quite dramatic enough to escape from some embellishment – Mrs. Kinch supposedly returned to the ship at the height of the storm to retrieve her wedding presents.[191]

In March 1942, the *M.E. Johnson* was reported sunk, after running ashore near the Skerries. The crew of four were taken off by breeches buoy. However, she was re-floated after a few days and was taken to Arklow for repairs. She thus survived to see the end of the War, as indeed did the *James Postlethwaite*, and both played their own small part in the celebrations. Capt. Jack Kinch had commanded the *M.E. Johnson* throughout the War. With his ship in port at Connah's Quay on V.E. Day, Capt. Kinch was asked to ring the bells of the local church to celebrate the peace.[192] Meanwhile the *James Postlethwaite* was taking more practical steps to sustain British morale. From Rosslare she carried 125 tons of blackberries to Preston. These had been picked in Wexford by hundreds of Irish women and children for five shillings per stone.

The Coasting Career of the *William Ashburner*

The *William Ashburner* had joined the Arklow fleet, after being sold by the Bennett family in 1920. She was owned there for over twenty years, sailing under the command of Capt. George Kearon. Her deep draught made her unsuitable for the general coasting trade, so she was

PLATE 12D: William Ashburner *at Dover in the 1920's.*

PLATE 12E: William Ashburner *wrecked at Beachley, March 1950.*

given regular employment in the China clay trade from Fowey to London, returning with cement to Penzance. In 1925 she had an engine installed and her topyards removed, but she still carried a great deal of canvas [PLATE 12D]. At one time she carried a triangular squaresail above her solitary yard. She also briefly acquired a figurehead, salvaged from the wreck of the Portmadoc schooner *Cadwalader Jones*.

In 1943 the *William Ashburner* had been sold from Arklow and had become the last sailing vessel operating from the port of Limerick, on the West coast of Ireland. Her new owner was Capt. Nicholas Sinnott, who had recently retired from a career with the steamships of the Blue Star Line and had returned to his home town. There was a severe fuel shortage in Ireland in those War years and there was a local trade in turf, carried into Limerick from Kilrush at the mouth of the Shannon. Capt. Sinnott had opened a distribution depot near the docks, but he closed this after only a few years, it being impossible to adequately supervise it whilst engaged in sailing his new ship. The *William Ashburner* traded briefly between Cork and Workington with burnt ore and coal cargoes. She also carried grain to the Rank flour mill at Limerick. This same company had many more mills in the Bristol Channel area and Mr. J.V. Rank persuaded Capt. Sinnott to move his ship into those waters.[193] In those years before the construction of the Severn Bridge the transport of grain still supported a substantial fleet of coasters. The *William Ashburner* was still beautifully maintained but now rarely used her sails. Her masts had been poled off and she no longer carried a boom on the mizzen.

---

191. Jim Rees & Liam Charlton, *Arklow – Last Stronghold of Sail* (2nd ed.1986) pp89–91 (*M.E. Johnson*) & pp55–57 (*James Postlethwaite*).
192. Tom Coppack, *A Lifetime with Ships* (1973) p186.
193. Information provided by Harry Sinnott of Limerick, son of Capt. Sinnott.

On 1st February 1950 the *William Ashburner* was travelling light from Swansea to Sharpness to pick up a cargo of grain. Despite having a pilot on board she grounded in dense fog on the Chapel Rock. The crew were safely taken off, but with a strong wind blowing the unmanned ship carried away her moorings on the following day. She drifted with the tide for several hours during the night. Eventually two motor barges managed to get lines aboard, and towed her to Beachley Bay, at the mouth of the River Wye. There she was beached and the damage to her hull could be examined [PLATES 5B, 12E]. Although she had not been holed, there was still considerable damage below the waterline. Repairs could not be justified, and she was declared a constructive total loss.[194] She was left where she lay and eventually the hulk was used by members of Chepstow Sailing Club – perhaps a fate of which the yachtsmen in the Ashburner family would have approved. Until a few years ago the remains of her hull could still be seen upstream from the Severn Bridge.

The Last Years of the Ashburner Schooners

Although the schooners had made high profits during the war years, their owners could not replace them with newer ships since the shipyards were full to capacity, replacing the larger tonnage ships that had been lost in the War. Therefore the money was reinvested in the schooners, and in 1945 the *James Postlethwaite* was given a new 120 h.p. diesel engine, started by compressed air. The ship also suffered a drastic reduction in her rigging. The mizzen mast was removed to allow the new engine to be installed. Since the engine's greater power did away with the need for a squaresail, or for so many headsails, her yard was removed, her bowsprit sawn off close to the bow and her two remaining masts were poled off. To complete the change in appearance, the surplus timber was used to build a wheelhouse [PLATE 12F].

In 1946 there had been twenty six schooners trading from British and Irish ports.[195] The loss of the *Useful* in 1947 left only three of the schooners built by the Ashburners in service, as well as the *Result*. With the loss of the *William Ashburner* and, soon after, the old Millom three-master *Happy Harry*,[196] the Irish sailing fleet was reduced to twelve in number, there being a further four schooners still working for British owners. The *James Postlethwaite* and *M.E. Johnson* continued to operate from Arklow. Their staple trade was in timber from Wicklow to England, and coal from Garston on the return journey. They also carried the occasional cargo of malt to Dublin, bricks from Bridgwater and salt from the Isle of Man. Having survived the years of the Second World War under the command of Capt. Counsell, the *James Postlethwaite* was commanded in 1949 by Capt. James Nolan. She sailed with two deckhands. The *M.E. Johnson* also acquired a new Arklow master, Capt. Jack Rezin, upon the death of Capt. Kinch in 1951.

By 1951 the British had imposed limitations on the quantity of coal that was allowed for export, due to the need to supply the growing demands of their own post-war economy. Ireland began importing coal from Poland and the U.S.A., and one of the staple trades of the Arklow schooners declined. Foreign motor vessels also began to compete for other traditional cargoes, such as the transport of malt. The schooners continued to make trips across the Irish Sea, but increasingly began to sail between British ports. In 1952 the *James Postlethwaite* appeared at Barrow for the last time, and soon after she was seen in Whitehaven harbour. She little resembled the fine three-masted schooner that had sailed between these ports seventy years previously. From astern, it could be seen that one mast veered drunkenly to port and the other to starboard.

The *M.E. Johnson* had recently undergone a refit and was in much better condition than her sister ship, though by now her rig had been reduced just as drastically. She could still manage about six knots in favourable conditions, and was manned by a crew of four. On the 11th November 1953 she made her own last visit to Barrow, arriving from Dublin via Holyhead. It

---

194. "Stranding of the *William Ashburner*", *Sea Breezes*, April 1950, p304.
195. John Anderson, *Coastwise Sail* (1948) describes most of the surviving schooners.
196. "Loss of the *Happy Harry*" in *Sea Breezes* 1950, p381 & p446.

PLATE 12F: James Postlethwaite *at Bridgwater, Sept. 1948. Her rig has been severely cut down and she can be considered little more than a sail-assisted motorship.*

was a less than magnificent return, for she grounded on a sandbank off Piel whilst entering the harbour and had to be pulled clear by a tug before she could berth. The great strength of her hull again served her well, and five days later she sailed from Barrow to the Clyde in a single day. Her return to Arklow early in December was not to be so fortunate. A heavy sea pushed her to the wrong side of the South pier at the harbour entrance. Grounded and pinned to the pier wall by the wind and waves, the old ship began to break up. For the last time the crew abandoned her, being taken off by the Arklow lifeboat. Within a day, in sight of the safe anchorage of her home port, the *M.E. Johnson* had disintegrated under the force of the gale.[197] She was in her 74th year, as had been the *William Ashburner* upon her loss three years earlier. Their owners could not have expected to get much more useful service from them, for the schooner trade was now virtually defunct. Their surviving sister ship was getting beyond the stage where adequate maintenance or repair were an economic proposition. She was laid up at Arklow and it appeared that the *James Postlethwaite* too had ended her career.

There was however one unusual demand for the schooners which were, after all, the last surviving sailing ships. Famous maritime books were being made into films, and whether the book featured a clipper, a whaler, a sloop or a privateer, the only sailing ships available to represent them in films were the old schooners. The *Result* had lead the way, and then the Duddon schooner *Nellie Bywater* had been used in "The Elusive Pimpernel". The *Ryelands*, a three-masted schooner built at Simpson's Lancaster shipyard in 1887, had been used for the part of the *Hispaniola* in the film of "Treasure Island". So when director John Huston selected the port of Youghal, Co. Cork, for the filming of "Moby Dick", he also chartered three of the remaining Irish schooners. The leading role of the whaler *Pequod* went to the *Ryelands*, but the *James Postlethwaite* and the Runcorn-built *Harvest King* were chartered for use as quayside props. By this time the *James Postlethwaite* was in too poor a condition to sail, so in June 1954 she was towed to Youghal from Arklow, on what was to be her last voyage. For filming she was fitted with square yards in imitation of a whaler and, renamed the *Devil Dam*, was moored in Youghal docks. Her appearance in the finished film is so brief that all this effort hardly seems worthwhile. After completion of the film she remained moored at Youghal whilst her owners awaited a tow back to Arklow. She was never able to make this journey, for in November a gale tore her from her moorings and smashed her stern against the quay. Perhaps there is some truth to the sailor's superstition that renaming a ship is unlucky, for this time she was irreparably damaged. She was sold to a local man who beached her nearby for breaking-up. She was the last survivor of the Ashburner schooners built at Barrow, and with her loss there remained only six other Irish schooners, all owned in Arklow. The *Kathleen & May*, built at Connah's Quay, and the *Result* were still trading from British ports.

The *James Postlethwaite* was not yet quite dead and her hull remained on the beach for three years. Those old oak timbers that had endured the hardships of a seagoing career of 73 years were so tough that they defied all attempts at demolition. After protracted disputes between her owner and the port commissioners, who were concerned that she was a hazard to other vessels using the port, her remains were finally set alight on the 7th October 1957.[198]

---

197. Rees & Charlton, *op.cit.* Also *Wicklow People*, 4th Dec. & 11th Dec. 1954. Also *Sea Breezes*, 1955, p144.
198. de Courcy, *op.cit.*

13 FIGHTING AND SURVIVING

Connah's Quay and Arklow were the last schooner ports in Wales and Ireland, and in England the same accolade would be given to the North Devon port of Braunton. This port too had its own schooner from the Ashburner fleet, the steel-hulled *Result*, brought there by Capt. Henry Clarke in 1909. And though Braunton had a large fleet of coastal sailing vessels, this new arrival from the Irish Sea was soon granted the admiration of the local seamen; in the words of one of her crew, "She was the biggest ship we had in Braunton, and the finest. She was a fast and good sailer".[199] The *Result* was to spend the rest of her career sailing from Braunton, interrupted only by a spell with the Royal Navy during the First World War, and outlived all the Ashburners' other schooners.

Soon after the *Result* had arrived at Braunton, Capt. Clarke had quickly sold some of his shares to four of his relatives, and also to Capt. Incledon, who became her new master. From her new home in North Devon the steel schooner continued to sail in the Home trade, at first as a sailing ship. Despite her acknowledged sailing speed, in March 1914 her square topsails and yards were removed and she was fitted with a 45 b.h.p. single cylinder Kromhaut engine. The men of Braunton and the neighbouring port of Appledore had been amongst the first to adopt auxiliary engines, and even the *Result* was vulnerable to the increasing competition from steamships and Dutch-owned motor schooners. The conversion into an auxiliary certainly improved her prospects, for sailing on her engine alone she could still achieve five knots with a full cargo.[200] Soon after this alteration her registration was transferred from Barrow to Barnstaple.

Q-23 – The *Result* at War

The onset of the First World War was to have dramatic consequences for the schooner fleet. More than two hundred British schooners and small sailing ships were lost to enemy action. Though mines were a danger, it was the German submarines that caused most of the losses. Since torpedoes were too expensive to use on small sailing ships, the attacks were usually made by surfacing the submarine and then either shelling the targetted ship or sending a boarding party to place explosives on board. Several Furness schooners were lost in this way, one of the first being George Postlethwaite's *Edith*. In June 1915 she was sunk ten miles S.E. of Capel Island, on a voyage from Silloth to Cork. The *Ellen Harrison*, the last vessel built at Ulverston, was sunk near Cherbourg in April 1917, carrying coal from Cardiff. Fishers' *Louie Bell* was lost in the same place, nine months later, whilst waiting to join the safety of a cross-Channel convoy. The only War loss amongst the Ashburner schooners was the *Tom Roper*. She had also moved into the hazardous Channel trade, after being sold by her Liverpool owner to J.H. Sharpe, a Glasgow coal merchant. He only briefly profited from his gamble. Travelling light from Guernsey, his new ship safely crossed the Channel to Weymouth. After leaving this port bound for Cardiff she was sunk by a submarine twenty miles S.E. of Start Point on the 21st October 1917.[201]

To try and combat the German success, some of the schooners were armed for defensive purposes. This probably saved two of the best Furness schooners, the *Mary Sinclair* and the *Mary Ann Mandall*, when they were attacked by gunfire off Littlehampton in March 1918. Only the *Mary Ann Mandall* was hit, losing a topmast. Both schooners had been armed, and they returned fire at the submarine. They did not succeed in hitting her, but she dived as an armed trawler sped to their assistance. Submarines on the surface were vulnerable, and with this in

---

199. Michael Bouquet, *The Times*, 1st June 1968 p22.
200. *Mer.Sch.*, p259.
201. GLL *Lloyd's War Losses – The First World War: Casualties to Shipping through Enemy Causes 1914–18*.

mind the Royal Navy conceived the idea of the Q-ship. A few inoffensive-looking merchant ships were requisitioned and armed. This armament was camouflaged, so that submarines would be lured to the surface where they themselves could be attacked. Amongst the schooners used as Q-ships were two from Paul Rodgers' shipyard, the *Mary B. Mitchell* and, possibly because she already had an engine, the *Result*. Renamed *Q-23*, she was fitted out by the Admiralty at Lowestoft in January 1917. She was ready for her first trials on the 3rd February, leaving on her first patrol, off the Dutch coast, a week later.

Q-23 was armed with two 18 cwt. 12 pdr. guns, one forward and one aft of the mainmast, in gun-wells sunk into what had been the cargo hatches. She also had a 6 pdr. gun on the port side for'd, and two fixed 14″ torpedo tubes aft, one on each quarter. These pointed astern at an angle of 30 degrees to the line of the keel. To make way for this armament her galley was removed. The crew totalled 23 men. All were volunteers, as was usually the case with the crowded and uncomfortable small ships employed in such hazardous duties. Her captain was Lieut. P.J. Mack and the Second-in-Command was Lieut. George Muhlhauser, a Naval Reservist who subsequently published an account of his War service.

The aim of a Q-ship was to lure a more powerfully armed enemy close enough to be itself destroyed. To aid the deception, only five men would appear on deck at any one time, to represent the usual crew compliment of a trading schooner. During an attack these men, the "panic party", would abandon their vessel, leaving the remaining crew to fight the ship when the enemy approached. Sometimes one of the men would dress in womens' clothing. This was not done because women were commonly seen on schooners, but originated from the theory that, to use Lieut. Muhlhauser's words, "the Hun was a boastful creature" and would therefore be encouraged to come closer than otherwise during the action. To further aid the deception, *Q-23* was flying the flag of Holland, a neutral country, on her first patrol.

Q-23 had her baptism of fire in the North Sea on the 15th March 1917. At the Outer Silver Pit, at the South end of the Dogger Bank, a German submarine was sighted about two miles astern. She approached on the surface and when she had closed to 2000 yards she began firing at the schooner. Belying the theory of the boastful Hun, this particular captain maintained that distance and continued a steady but inaccurate barrage at the schooner. The "panic party", one in a pink frock and bonnet, took to the small boat and stood a short distance from their ship, rowing in circles and doing their best impression of a terror-stricken merchant crew. The eighteen remaining crew hid themselves and endured the continued barrage. Possibly the German captain had been warned about the Q-ships, because he closed no nearer than 1000 yards during the next 45 minutes. The schooner suffered no serious damage. Lieut. Mack eventually decided that the deception was not going to work. He gave the order to open fire on the submarine. The British gunnery was considerably more skilful than that of their enemy. The aft twelve-pounder scored a hit with the first shot, at the base of the conning tower. The next shot, from the six-pounder, scored a hit slightly above the first. The second shot from the aft twelve-pounder missed and by this time, 30 seconds after the first shot from *Q-23*, the German submarine was diving. Though damage had been inflicted, and also probably some casualties, there was no indication that she had been sunk. The submarine's captain certainly survived because the Royal Navy somehow obtained his report of the action a few months later. The submarine involved had been *U.C.45*.

After the action *Q-23* headed for the coast but was unfortunate enough to encounter another, smaller, German submarine the very same night. A torpedo was fired by the submarine, but missed. Both vessels then opened fire, without success on either part, and the submarine dived and made her escape. The schooner eventually arrived safely in port, where two days were spent repairing the damage, which was mainly to the sails and rigging – the foresail alone had thirteen holes in it. Lieut. Mack and the sailing master, J. Reid, who had commanded the "panic party", were mentioned in despatches for their part in the action.

For her next patrol *Q-23* was re-named *Dag* and was adorned with the colours of yet another neutral country, Sweden. She encountered her third submarine on the surface at 4 a.m. on the 5th April near the North Hinder Light. The submarine dived quickly and then proceeded to circle her potential target from beneath the surface. The bemused schooner crew could see her

PLATE 13A: In 1950 the Result *was re-rigged as a topsail schooner for her appearance in the film "Outcast of the Islands". Apart from the white-painted hull, this is close to how she would have appeared in her early days in the Ashburner fleet.*

unusual-looking periscope, but were unaware that she was in fact photographing their ship. Once satisfied with his photographic efforts, the submarine's commander proceeded to a more violent course of actions. He surfaced his ship about 6000 yards off the schooner, under the rising sun where he could hardly be seen by the British crew. He was better armed than the other submarines, having a 4.1″ semi-automatic gun. His barrage was rapid and accurate, and the eleventh shell hit *Q-23* amidships on the waterline, setting fire to the magazine and injuring two men of the ammunition party. The British returned fire immediately, the submarine then diving without taking any hits. The wounded men on the schooner were cared for and the hole in the hull was patched. Presumably the submarine's commander was hoping that the schooner would sink, for he placed his ship astern of her and surveyed her by periscope. *Q-23* could not turn fast enough to bring her torpedoes to bear on the submarine and Lieut. Mack feared that she would sail away to a position for torpedoing his ship. So a depth charge was released, but the resulting explosion probably caused more damage to the schooner than to the submarine. It did however have the desired effect of scaring off her attacker. The submarine departed as several small naval craft approached the scene of the battle.

Months later the photographing of *Q-23* by the submarine was discovered by the Royal Navy. In this time the ship had not had any success in attracting further attacks from German submarines, which would have been forewarned of her attempted subterfuge. In July the crew of *Q-23* was transferred to a steamer, also to be used as a Q-ship, and the schooner herself went for service in the English Channel. She was soon declared unfit for use as a Q-ship because of her limited field of fire and lack of reserve bouyancy (her ballast was merely sand). She was rejected by several bases and in August 1917 *Q-23* became again the *Result* and was returned to her owners.[202] Though she spent the rest of the War in the less dramatic role of a cargo carrier, the severe shortage of merchant tonnage at this time meant that she was no less vital to her country's fortunes.

The Last Survivor

Once back at Braunton the *Result* was rerigged, losing the square yards that had been temporarily restored to her by the Royal Navy. Over the next fifty years the ship's masts and yards were to be frequently altered as her owners adapted her to whatever trade they could find, balancing the advantages of the sails in fuel economy against the costs of maintenance and extra crew. In 1921 the schooner was operating in the slate trade from Portmadoc to Antwerp and other continental ports, and for this she was re-equipped with a single square topsail. However, this brief post-War boom in trade soon subsided, and in 1924 the square yards were sent down for the penultimate time. Rigged as an auxiliary fore-and-aft schooner, the *Result* operated in the short sea trade along the South coast. She was still commanded by Capt. Incledon, though she was now owned jointly by Capt. Clarke and another Braunton seaman, Capt. Tom Welch. For several years their ship was regularly employed in trade between Newhaven and Southampton, in friendly rivalry with a Dutch auxiliary schooner, the *Jacoba*. Shortly before the Second World War her ownership passed in its entirety to Capt. Welch. There was to be no repeat of her previous fighting career, for the *Result* spent the War in the Bristol Channel trade, carrying coal from South Wales ports.

In 1946 the schooner was completely refitted, the first engine being replaced by a more powerful one of 120 h.p. Even so, she retained her full sail plan and was the last coasting schooner to keep her gaff topsails. Her new commander was the owner's son, Capt. Peter Welch, and under him the *Result* was nearly lost. She had arrived at Cardiff to load fertiliser for Falmouth. Capt. Welch and the mate retired to a local pub whilst the cargo was put aboard, and when they returned they found that their ship had been greatly overloaded, and was awash amidships. Nevertheless they decided to sail, and the hatches were battened down

---

202. G.H.P. Muhlhauser, *Small Craft* (1920). Further information in E.K. Chatterton, *Q-Ships and their story* (1972).

PLATE 13B: The Result *ended her days as a ketch-rigged motorship. Here she is seen laid-up at Exeter in 1967, shortly after the death of her master/owner, Capt. Peter Welch.*

PLATE 13C: The bow deck of the Result, *as it appeared in the 1960's. The windlass, pumps and the roller-reefing gear on the foremast-boom are all original fittings.*

with the ship warped between two barges. When they put to sea the amidships were still awash, and when a fresh wind struck the ship in the Bristol Channel she was soon in difficulties. Capt. Welch decided to run for the safety of Barry harbour, but only arrived when it was at low tide. Attempting to enter the harbour, the overloaded ship struck heavily on the bottom. Her stern post split and water flooded into the engine room, stopping the engine. The ship was turned round into the storm, but was now in a desperate position and could not hope to weather the gale. The weight of water in the engine room pulled her down until her stern was below water, and the mate had to be lashed to the wheel in order to prevent him from being washed out of the wheelhouse. Capt. Welch decided to resort to a traditional method of saving a distressed vessel. He headed for Ilfracombe, where he hoped to be able to run her up onto the sandy beach. When she arrived the entire vessel apart from the bows was semi-submerged, and it was impossible to reach the masts to reduce sail. Despite this her master was able run her right up onto the beach, a feat requiring great skill and judgement with a vessel in such an uncontrollable state. This was the last known time that this method of saving a sailing coaster was used. The ship emptied herself of water as the tide retreated, and with the damaged stern temporarily repaired and several tons of cargo shovelled overboard she was refloated at the next tide.

In 1948 the *Result* was in the coal trade across the Bristol Channel. At this time work was becoming scarcer for the coasting fleet, and the schooner was occasionally laid up without work. Late in 1950 her owner found a more glamourous way for her to earn a living. A film was being made of Joseph Conrad's book "Outcast of the Islands", and a sailing ship was required to play the part of the schooner *Flash*. The *Result* was fully re-rigged at Appledore, with her topmasts being restored to their original height. Once again fitted with a square

---

203. *Sea Breezes*, 1950, p381 & p446.
204. Michael McCaughan, "*Result* goes Home", *Ships Monthly*, March 1980 pp20–23.

topsail, and with her bulwarks painted white, the *Result* sailed for the Scilly Isles, where the film was shot [PLATE 13A]. Once filming was completed, however, the full rigging could not be retained and the *Result* returned to Appledore to have her square yards sent down.[203] By January 1951 she had left Appledore for Swansea to resume her more mundane work in the coasting trade. The film was released by London Films in 1951. Amongst the actors who had walked her deck were Ralph Richardson and Trevor Howard.

Capt. Welch continued to trade with her, mainly along the South coast and to the Channel Islands and the French Channel ports. Eventually, to ease cargo loading, the mainmast was removed and she became a ketch-rigged motorship. By 1967 however there was little cargo available to keep the ship in work, and Capt. Welch decided to convert her hold into passenger accommodation, in the hope of gaining charter work. The refit was still incomplete when he died aboard his ship at Jersey in the same year. The *Result* was sailed to Exeter and was laid up in the city basin, a forlorn sight with the traditional blue band of mourning painted around her hull [PLATE 13B]. Her working life had ended after seventy four years, but the Exeter Maritime Museum continued to care for her and three years later she was sold by Mrs. Welch to the Ulster Folk and Transport Museum. The schooner sailed from Exeter on the 4th October 1970 for Brixham, where she was surveyed, and then sailed, on her final voyage, for Belfast. The Museum commissioned the Harland & Wolff shipyard to carry out some restoration work. In 1979 the hull was lifted from the water and transported to a dry-land site at the Museum at Cultra, Co. Down.[204] The Museum's intention was to restore her to her original form as a three-masted schooner, but in the succeeding ten years little if any further work has been done, the cost being too great for the Museum's resources. Today the rusted hull stands without masts in a car park and it can only be hoped that one day the *Result* will be restored to her former majesty.

14 MEMORIES OF THE LAST DAYS OF SAIL

The days of the working sailing ships are now long gone, and with them has disappeared a way of life that was familiar to generations of seamen. The best insight into this way of life is given by the experiences of the schoonermen themselves, and is best told in their own words. A fortunate consequence of the longevity of the Ashburner schooners is that there are still men alive today who sailed in them and who can describe the conditions in which they lived and worked.

The work of the schooner crews was laborious and uncomfortable, and was financially unrewarding. They not only sailed the ships, but were often required to work cargoes, and had to cope with the never-ending maintenance and repairs needed to keep their wooden vessels seaworthy. In their later days the schooners were reduced in rig and had motors fitted, taking much of the toil out of sail setting, pumping and anchor-raising. However the work had still more in common with that of the crews of a century earlier than with that of seamen today. Jim Brauders was on the *William Ashburner* when she was a cut-down fore-and-after motor schooner. Alan Maunder started his seafaring career in the same ship at a later date, when she was a motor coaster in the Bristol Channel trade. Their accounts of their time aboard her tell of the discomfort of their living conditions and the work they were required to do, but also reveal something of the pride that the schoonermen had in their ships and their profession.

JIM BRAUDERS[205]

I joined the *William Ashburner* for the first time in Youghal between 1942 and 1943, when we went from Youghal to Cardiff and back. Capt. Pat Conway of Wicklow was in her then, but I left her, and when I returned to her at the end of 1943 she had been bought by Capt. Sinnott of Limerick. He had been an extra-master in one of the Cunard boats, and when he had left them at the end of his career he came home and bought the *William Ashburner*. She was still registered in England and by that time was the only Irish-owned vessel still to carry the Red Ensign. I joined her in Cork, together with Billy Wolohan, who was the sail-master. Our first run with Capt. Sinnott was from Cork to Workington with burnt ore, and we were on this same run all the time we were in her. We loaded the ore in Cork city itself, just at the bridge before you go up to Patrick's Bridge, where there's a little bit of a tongue. The run to Workington would take about fifty six hours with constant going, if you got a good sail of wind and everything going well. Sometimes we'd have to lay up at Waterford, windbound. At Workington the cargo was discharged and then we'd load coal to take back to Cork. Later Capt. Jack Byrne was in her and we ran turf from the Shannon to Dublin and Cork.[206]

There were five crew on the *William Ashburner*. Capt. Sinnott's brother-in-law was the cook, and there was the engineer and myself. After the skipper there was Bill Wolohan, the sail-master. Billy was sail-master because Capt. Sinnott knew nothing about schooners. He was really a deep-water captain, and had only ever passed by schooners and was hopeless with them. He'd always be there, but Billy Wolohan would take over at sea. If there was a difference of opinion between him and the captain it was the sail-master who had the last say, because he was the man with the education of the sails. If you gybed an oul' schooner, then you were likely to take all the masts out. I'll never forget one day when we were coming down off the Coningbeg and running into the Barrells buoy. The oul' fellow, Capt. Sinnott himself, was on the wheel. She gave a gybe and away goes the mainmast and all, over the side. We were quick to take up the slack rigging, getting it around the belaying pins, but we had to put

---

205. Mr. Brauders was interviewed at Arklow by Jim Rees in December 1989.
206. George Byrne, his brother was mate. Another master of the *William Ashburner* at about this time was Capt. Crienan, later to own and command the *Brooklands*, the last schooner to trade without an engine.

PLATE 14A: William Ashburner *at Penzance Dock in August, 1935. Only her mizzen mast had been reduced from its original height and she still carried a single yard on her foremast for a squaresail, a rig she retained until the end of the War. She was still very much a sailing ship during Jim Brauders' time as a crewman.*

into Rosslare to get a new mast.

The *William Ashburner* [PLATE 14A] was a fine, big, laboursome oul' vessel, heavy in the water but a good sea vessel all the same. Although she was in her seventies then, that wasn't anything to do with her age. It was the way she was built – a big, heavy vessel, and laboursome under sail. She needed half a gale of wind on her masts before she got any way on her at all. She still carried a good bit of sail then. She had a boom jib, a standing jib and a stay-foresail, and three fore-and-afters, and a big squaresail on her foremast. At that time they used to say that the squaresail was the money maker. You'd get the squaresail on her and away she went. She had only a 100 h.p. engine, but it was used all the time, unless you got too much wind, and then the engine was no good to her. Going with the engine, and with her fore-and-afters on her, she could manage about six or seven knots. The big squaresail was on her all the time whenever the wind was after her. We could trim the square sail, as long as there was a point abaft the beam, but we could get more trim on the foresail. With a good gale of wind we could sail her goose-necked as well – that's when the foresail is out on the starboard side and the mainsail is out on the portside.

The routine in port was that we stood-by while she was loading, and then we'd square her up and get her ready for sea. When we were at sea, we would just turn in for an hour or two for wind changes. We had to haul in or reef the sails, or something like that. If we were discharging, breakfast would be at half-seven, ready for an eight o'clock start, if we were going to be working the oul' dolly winch. This was a motor winch that was used for heaving out the cargo, and also for raising the sails. We were lucky because we didn't have any heaving at all to do. After finishing with a cargo of coal we had to bathe ourselves from two big buckets.

There weren't any bathrooms in the schooners in those days, so we would set ourselves up in the sail locker, or in the galley if there was no one in there. We had to heat the water in a kettle, and then wash our hair first, then bathe and finally someone would throw the water down our backs.

The food wasn't up to the mark. For breakfast there might have been a little bit of a cat's ear of a rasher, with no eggs, but maybe some spuds that had been boiled the day before and then sliced and put in the frying pan. Sometimes we got a bowl of porridge. That would do you to twelve o'clock, half twelve or whatever time we could, and then there would be a bit of corned beef and cabbage. All we got at tea-time was bread-and-jam, and maybe an odd time we would get a bit of cheese. When the ship was in port we could go off and get a cup of tea at night time. That would be the end then, until breakfast time the next day.

There was a good oul' crowd on the *William Ashburner*. We knocked about together and were as happy as Larry. The skipper's brother-in-law was there, but he was joking and allegating the same as ourselves. Everyone was happy and there were never any arguments. Sometimes, when we were windbound, the fo'c'stle was scrubbed as white as a hound's tooth. All hands would be there, to see who could tell the tallest story. There'd be all kinds of rawmin'[207] and sea shanties and everything, and the crowd would be happy. And we were very comfortable when we were in out of bad weather.

I was in several of the Arklow schooners, including the *Cymric*, the *Mary B. Mitchell* and the *Venturer*. I was in the *Sarah Latham*, a little vessel of only 180 tons belonging to Connah's Quay. The *Useful* was owned by Capt. Johnny Wynne, also of Connah's Quay. His son, also called Johnny, used to be in her as well. If the two of them met on the port side they used to box one another, and when one went to the fo'c'stle the other would go aft to the cabin. They wouldn't meet one another on the deck and they were like that ashore as well. A funny thing about the *Useful* was that she had been registered in Barrow, and written on her stern was "the Useful Barrow". I was always joking Johnny about it, and it used to have him going up the walls. He was a comical oul' fellow, and I liked him because he was always going on about the oul' schooners. In the *Useful* he was able to sail up to the wind and a point abaft of the beam – he was able to go anywhere in her.

In the oul' schooners we had a kind of pride in ourselves and we would try to keep them as clean as we could. We hadn't much money so an hour here or there didn't make much matter. But the only thing I did hate was scraping down the mast. I remember in the *Venturer* one time, we were scraping down the mast in March. I had an overcoat on, but it sickened me altogether. But apart from that, you took everything else in your stride.

ALAN D. MAUNDER[208]

I joined the *William Ashburner* in Barry Dock on a sunny September day in 1946 and to me she looked beautiful. She was a three-masted schooner with a deadweight of about 300 tons. Although flying the Red Ensign, she was really an Irish ship, being owned by Capt. Nicholas Sinnott of Ennistymon, Co. Clare, who had been a master with the Blue Star Line. The mate, John Healy, and two AB's Barney Shiel and Mick O'Dowd, were also Irish. My lofty position was cook and deck boy.

Alongside the dock, I turned to at 6.30 am to get breakfast for the crew at 7.30. Deckwork started at eight o'clock. Since those days I have seen many dog kennels bigger than the galley of the *William Ashburner*. It was situated abaft the main mast and was more like a rectangular box, about six feet square, bolted to the deck. Against the after bulkhead there was the coal-burning range with the coal bunker alongside it, and against the forward one was a small work bench with the spud locker alongside it, which was also the seat. Washing up was done in a wooden bucket outside on the hatch cover. The bucket was similar to the one each of us had for our own personal use for washing, laundry etc. The only wash-basins aboard were aft in

---

207. Rawmin' = one-upmanship in storytelling.
208. Based on Mr. Maunder's account of his seafaring career which appeared in *Ships Monthly*, Nov.1989 pp20–23, augmented by information provided in subsequent correspondence.

PLATE 14B: William Ashburner *as Alan Maunder knew her, a motor coaster in the Bristol Channel grain trade. All her masts have been poled off and there is no boom on the mizzen. Avonmouth Dock, March 1948.*

the cabins. During heavy weather or rainstorms, when it was necessary to have both sliding doors closed on the galley, it gave one an idea of what lay ahead in the next life if you fell by the wayside – the heat and the gloom were almost unbearable.

The ship had a Widdop semi-diesel 'hot bulb' engine of 100 horsepower which we always used. The day I joined it was in pieces, being worked on by dockyard mechanics. A few days passed and the engine was fixed and we left Barry for Cardiff to go on the grid iron. Then came three days of misery. The grid iron is similar to a dry-dock except it is tidal with keel blocks on a concrete slab and heavy dolphins on the shore side against which the ship lays. We had the boat over the side at daylight and proceeded to scrub and scrape the side as the tide ebbed. I think she drew about 13 feet loaded so this gives an idea of the area to be cleaned. When the water was low enough we got out of the boat and worked from the muddy bottom of the grid iron. As the tide flooded we worked up to our waists and then got back in the boat. In three days we had scraped and painted the hull with Stockholm tar. I remember how it burned our faces and wherever else it touched on us in the hot sun.

We proceeded from there to Sharpness where we loaded grain for Cardiff. While loading I learned another less than enjoyable aspect of my new life, trimming grain. The *William Ashburner* had been built in 1876, an immensely strong vessel with massive frames and planking. She had, I was told, quite a few deep sea voyages to her credit. Consequently, her hatches were very small and the grain had to be trimmed out to the sides and fore and aft quite a bit. This was back-breaking work while lying on one's side. With loading almost completed the hatches would be filled to the top of the coamings while we lay on our sides in the stifling space under the deck in the darkness, shovelling our way to the hatch and praying we (or, at least, I) hadn't been forgotten there. For all this I received 30 shillings cargo bonus on top of my £7 10s 0d a month. My pay was rarely over £11 a month. On top of this I had to cook three meals a day and keep the captain's and mate's accommodation clean and polished.

The captain and mate lived aft in mahogany and brass splendour. The captain had a room to starboard off the saloon, and the mate's room was to port. Both cabins led forward with the companion way between them. All the panelling was beautiful mahogany, as was the curved handrail of the stairs. There was a table in the middle of the saloon, and this had a large brass lamp hanging over it. All the lights aboard burnt paraffin oil, as we had no electricity. The captain had a small wash basin in his cabin which folded up and drained into a bucket. The rest of us lived forward down in the fo'c'stle where, if the hatch was closed, it was so gloomy that it was almost impossible to read, the only light coming from a few prismatic thick glass skylights let into the deck overhead.

Our passages were all within the Bristol Channel, to or from the ports of Sharpness, Avonmouth, Cardiff, Barry and Swansea. We never used the sails while I was in the *William Ashburner* [PLATE 14B]. The trips from Avonmouth to Barry or Cardiff were too short and we only did the longest passages, from Avonmouth to Swansea, three or four times while I was in her, and then the wind was either too much or too little or in the wrong direction. The fore and mainsails were in place but the boom had been removed from the mizzen mast, so she did not have a sail there. The jibs and the staysail were kept down in the forepeak. The old Widdop engine was used all the time, and was adequate for most of our work. It was very economical and gave us a speed of about six knots.

The hours were mostly long and hard, sixteen hours or more not being uncommon, depending on destination and tides. Anchoring was a special nightmare as the chain, which was very heavy, had to be pulled manually up out of the chain locker as much as three shackles, which is 270 feet. This had to be flaked out along the deck. To hoist the anchor we had the windlass, which was coupled by a chain to a little engine in the forward deckhouse – unfortunately it never worked while I was in the ship so it all came in by hand cranking. Thank goodness we did not anchor very often.

The captain's only navigational aid was a little domestic radio on which he listened to an occasional weather forecast. For the crew's entertainment there was one pack of playing cards and Barney's fiddle and little melodeon. We never felt deprived and were generally quite content.

GLOSSARY

Barque	A sailing vessel with three or more masts, all square-rigged except the aftermost, which is fore-and-aft rigged.
Barquentine	A sailing vessel with three or more masts, the foremast being square-rigged and the others fore-and-aft rigged.
Bilges	The part of a hull curving in towards the keel, upon which the ship rests when grounded.
Boom	A fore-and-aft spar at the bottom of a mast, to which usually a sail is furled.
Brig	A two-masted sailing vessel with square rig on both masts and a fore-and-aft sail added to the aftermost mast.
Brigantine	A two-masted sailing vessel with a square-rigged foremast and a fore-and-aft rigged mainmast.
Bulwarks	The parts of a vessel's sides above deck level.
Close-hauled	A vessel sailing to windward (towards the wind), thus having its sails pulled in so that the fore-and-afters lie close to the midline.
Counter	A vessel's stern that extends beyond the sternpost.
Cutter	A single-masted fore-and-aft rigged sailing vessel equipped with a bowsprit and two or more headsails.
Flat	A flat-bottomed, sloop-rigged vessel used in the short sea trade along the Lancashire coast.
Fo'c'stle	The forecastle is the below-deck space in the bows of a vessel, used as the crew's living quarters.
Fore-and-aft rig	Sails set lengthwise along the vessel, from booms and gaffs rather than yards.
Gaff	A spar secured at one end to a mast, and hauled up the mast into position with sail(s) attached.
Galvanising	Deposition of a zinc film onto the surface of iron or steel, to protect against corrosion.
Gunwale	Also **gunnel** or **wales**. The upper parts of a vessel's hull, between the waterline and deck level.
Gybe	A sailing manouevre in which a vessel sailing with the wind behind it moves across the line of the wind. Fore-and-aft rig is swung across the vessel so that it lies at ninety degrees to the hull on the opposite side to its original position. If the manouevre is uncontrolled then the sails are swung across by the power of the wind.
Headsails	The sails at a vessel's stem, bowsprit and jibboom. In the schooners they were the fore-staysail and the jibs.
Hogging	A naval architect's term to describe the result of stress on a hull, causing the ends to drop and the middle to arch.
Jibboom	A spar extending beyond the bowsprit.
Ketch	A two-masted fore-and-aft rigged vessel in which the boom-foresail is the largest sail.
Mainmast	The aftermost mast in a two-masted schooner, brig or brigantine. The middle mast in a three-masted schooner, barque or barquentine.
Mizzen	The aftermost mast in a three-master.
Rigging	Standing rigging is the wire and rope used for the staying of masts and spars. Running rigging is that used for positioning and controlling the spars and sails.
Scantlings	The dimensions of timbers used in a vessel's construction.

Schooner	A fore-and-aft rigged vessel with two or more masts, the boom-foresail of which is smaller than the boom sail on the second mast.
Sheer	The upward slope of a vessel's hull at bows and stern.
Sloop	A single-masted fore-and-aft rigged vessel, differing from a cutter by having only one headsail.
Square rig	Sails set from yards.
Stem	The upright structural timber at the bow end of a vessel's keel.
Sternpost	The upright structural timber at the stern end of a vessel's keel.
Tack	A sailing manouevre to bring a vessel's bows through the line of the wind when sailing towards it. Close-hauled sails are moved to the opposite side of the vessel's midline.
Tonnage	A measurement of a vessel's internal capacity. Unless otherwise specified, tonnages given in this book are gross tons measured under the Lloyd's rules applying at the date of launch. Deadweight tonnage is a measurement of a vessel's cargo capacity and was commonly noted as **tons burthen**. It does not correspond to gross tonnage.
Topgallant	A square sail set from yards on the foretopmast.
Treenail	Wooden fastening used for securing planking.
Yard	A spar crossing a mast, to carry the sails of a square rig.

GENERAL INDEX

A.B. Gowan & Son   29, 90
Arklow   76, 92, 103, 104, 110–8, 128
Ashburner, Capt. Robert   14, 20, 24, 32, 61, 64, 80
Ashburner family   14, 95
Ashburner, Richard jun.   15, 32, 35, 49, 51, 52, 61, 82, 96, 97–100, 103, 104, 105, 107
Ashburner, Richard sen.   14, 15–18, 20, 24, 26, 61, 95
Ashburner, Thomas   15, 30, 32, 51, 61, 73, 78, 80, 97–100, 103, 105, 107
Ashburner, William jun.   15, 32, 95, 105
Ashburner, William sen.   14–15, 18, 20, 24, 27, 30, 55, 58, 61
Ashcroft, James   40, 59, 82, 86–7

Ballina   84
Banister, Capt. Thomas   70
Barrow – iron industry   19, 27–8, 65
– port & docks   28–30, 95 [Plate: 29]
– shipowners   86–90
Barrow Haematite Iron & Steel Co.   27, 88
Barrow Mutual Ship Insurance Co.   79
Barrow Sailmaking Co.   32, 55
Barrow Shipbuilding Co.   37, 57
Barrow Steel Co.   27
Bennet, Capt. James   84
Blundell, Capt. J.   87
Bond, Capt. Henry sen.   22, 61, 80
Bond, Capt. Henry jun.   26, 35
Brauders, Jim   126
Bristol Channel   84, 90, 115, 122, 124, 130
Brockbank, Capt. James   26, 60, 61, 80

Caird & Purdie Ltd.   40
Campbell, Peter   57
Carrickfergus   69, 82, 90
Chamley, William   39, 50, 81, 86
Charnley, Capt. Edmondson   55, 60, 90
Charnley, Capt. Robert   22, 36, 59–60, 61, 64, 65–7, 78
Charnley family   60, 96
Connah's Quay   40, 57, 70, 82, 84, 93, 101–9, 114, 128
Cornish clay ports   74, 84, 105

Dalbeattie   69–70
David Noble & Co.   40
Dee River & ports   68, 71–2, 81, 101–9 [Plate: 102]
Dee Shipowners Mutual Insurance Assn.   79
Douglas, I.o.M.   14–15, 100, 102
Duddon   67, 71–2, 91

Duddon – shipowners   91–3
Duddon Shipbuilding Co.   57, 93–4
Duddon Shipping Assn.   50, 91, 92–4
Duke of Devonshire (Earl of Burlington)   19, 28–30

Fisher fleet   38, 82, 87, 88–91
Fisher, James   29, 30, 39, 49, 55, 63, 77, 88
Foulkes, Capt. John   81
Furness Iron & Steel Co.   86
Furness Railway Co.   19, 26, 27, 28, 30, 37, 40, 96
Furness Ship Building Co.   39, 57, 96

Geldart, Capt. James   87
Graving Dock Shipbuilding Co.   40
Griffiths, Capt. Charles   68

Harrison & Ainslie & Co.   19, 20–4, 61, 81, 97
Henry Stuart's Ropeworks   55, 59
Hindpool   19, 27, 30 [Plates: 30, 38]
Hindpool – shipyards   23, 30–2, 37–40 [Plate: 33]
Hodbarrow Mining Co.   51, 67, 91, 92, 94
Horan, Capt. James   104, 110
Hughes, Capt. John   70, 103, 105
Hurford, William   32, 80, 87, 107

Iddon, Capt. William   84
Isle of Arran   69
Isle of Man   14, 40, 70, 71, 91, 92, 109

James Fisher & Son   88–91
James Little & Co.   86
Jervis, Samuel   39, 64, 80, 86
Johnson, Capt. Robert   55
Jones, Hugh & Micaiah   31, 93–4

Kirkby, Isaac   86

Latham, Capt. James   50
Latham, Capt. John (of *Alice Latham*)   26, 58
Latham, Capt. John (of *Mary Bell*)   25, 31, 35, 48, 59, 78, 80
Latham, Capt. Robert   49, 70–2, 76, 77–80
Latham, Capt. Thomas   31
Lavery, Capt. Bailey   69
Liverpool   15, 48, 64, 70, 71–2, 77, 85, 87, 105

Maunder, Alan D.   128
Milford Haven   35, 70
Millom   91

Morecambe Bay ports   12–14

Newland Co.   11–12, 19

Peet, John   39, 87
Pernie, Capt. James   25, 80, 82, 89
Petty & Postlethwaite   14, 92, 93
Porter, Capt. George   39, 59, 86
Portugese ore ports   35, 63–4, 80
Postlethwaite, William   40, 91–2, 93

Ramsden, James   27, 28–30, 31, 96, 97
Rawlinson, Joseph   24, 30, 37, 39
Rawlinson & Reay   37–9, 90
Reay, Robert   20, 24, 37
Red Bay, Co. Antrim   71, 88
Rodgers, Paul   82, 90, 120
Roper, Thomas   21, 22, 26, 59, 87
Roskell, Capt. Robert   55
Runcorn & Weston   68, 71–2, 73, 80, 90, 114

Schneider, H.W.   19, 27, 29, 30, 88, 97
Simpson, Matthew   12, 49, 57, 90, 97
Sinnott, Capt. Nicholas   115, 126, 128
South American ports   49, 60, 65–7, 86, 90
South Wales ports   24, 36, 48, 49, 64, 74–5, 77, 110
Spanish ore ports   63–4

Stones, Capt. Isaac   16, 22
Stones, Capt. Robert   22, 23
Sumner, Capt. James   70

Tarleton   25, 26, 58–9, 71, 82
Thomas Ashburner & Co.   77–85
Thomas, Capt. John   24
Thomas, William   92, 93, 103, 105
Tinsley, Capt. James   68
Todd, Matthew   22, 23, 24

Ulster coast   68
Ulverston   11, 12, 20, 71
Ulverston – shipbuilders   14, 50, 60, 87, 92–3

Walton & Co.   40, 86, 87, 90
War losses   110, 119
Welch, Capt. Peter   122–5
White, William & John   92
William Thomas & Co.   93, 103
Wilson, John & Margaret   90
Windermere Steam Packet Co.   16–18
Wrecks   16, 35, 60, 68–9, 70, 80, 81, 82, 84–5, 86, 87, 90, 92, 93, 105, 107, 109, 110, 116, 118, 119
Wright, Capt. Robert   55, 82, 102, 104
Wynne, Capt. John   106, 108, 128

Youghal   103, 118, 126

INDEX OF SHIPS

Ada 87
Alice Latham 26, 45, 58, 67, 68, 70, 80, 85, 91, 101
Ann Crewdson 93
Ann Rennison 16
Annie Brocklebank 93
Annie Crossfield 90
Annie McLester 93
Annie Ripley 88, 89, 90, 93
Argo 14
Argus 60, 96

Baron Hill 92
Beatrice 39, 89
Becca and Mary 94
Bella Tumulty 88
Bessie Whinneray 93
Betty Russell 39, 89
Bidsie & Bell 88, 89
Bridget Annie 40, 87
British Queen 87, 107
Burns & Bessie 92

Caroline 29
Carrie Bell 64, 86
Catherine Latham 31, 45, 49, 50, 67, 80, 84, 101, 102, [Plate: 69]
Charles & Ellen 40, 92
Christiana Davis 80, 86, 87, 107
Commercial Traveller 62
Coniston 92
Countess of Lonsdale 93
Cumberland Lassie 92

Donald & Doris 92
Duke of Buccleuch 39

Earl of Glasgow 21
Edith 92, 119
Edith Crossfield 90
Edward and Margaret 18
Eleanor 37
Eleventh Lancashire 88, 89
Elizabeth 60
Elizabeth Anne 38
Elizabeth Barrow 24, 31, 45, 48, 60, 62, 64, 74, 80, 81
Elizabeth Latham 35, 44, 45, 49, 50, 67, 71, 75, 81, 84 [Plate: 46]
Elizabeth Peers 92
Elizabeth Worthington 92
Ella Mary 93
Ellen Clifford 29
Ellen Harrison 57, 92, 119

Ellie Park 39, 57, 90
Emily Barratt 94
Eugenie 86

Fanny Crossfield 90
Fanny Slater 64, 86
Florence Petherick 50, 92, 94
Ford Fisher 90
Francis (Fisher) 38, 80, 89, 90
Francis (Jervis) 86
Frank M. Fisher 88, 89, 90
Furness Maid 25, 35, 45, 59, 67, 69, 71

Gauntlet 49, 64, 89, 90
George 4th 92
George B. Balfour 90
Gilbrow 87
Greyhound 93
Gummershow 24, 37, 60

Hannah Croasdell 92, 93
Happy Harry 50, 94, 116
Harry Russell 39, 89
Helvellyn 30
Hematite 89
Henry & Mary 35, 45, 67, 68, 71, 80
Hodbarow Miner 92
Holly How 89
Hope 14

Isaac & M. Kirkby 86
Isabella 45, 55, 71, 74, 76, 80, 95, 101, 104, 106, 107–108 [Plates: 42, 54, 108]
Isabella Fisher 24

J. & M. Garratt 45, 57, 101, 106–7 [Plate: 106]
J.E. Fisher 88, 89, 90
J.H. Barrow 60, 86
James & Agnes 25, 35, 44, 45, 60, 63, 64, 65, 73, 79, 80, 101, 103, 104
James Postlethwaite 45, 55, 73, 75, 76, 79, 80, 101, 104, 110–4, 116–8 [Plates: 56, 111, 117]
James W. Fisher 88, 89
Jane 16
Jane Roper 22, 26, 45, 64, 74, 87
Joseph 38, 80, 89
Julia 89, 90

Kate 92
Kate Rousfield 88
Kitty 14

Lady Lilford 86
Lady of the Lake 17 [Plates: 16, 17]
Lancashire Witch 64, 88, 89
Lily Baynes 39, 89
Lindal Moor 87
Lord Muncaster 21, 24, 35, 45, 49, 59, 60, 64, 87 [Plate: 25]
Lord of the Isles 18 [Plates: 17]
Louie Bell 90, 119

M.E. Johnson 44, 45, 49, 55, 73, 74, 79, 80, 101, 104, 112–4, 116–8, [Plates: 56, 112, 113]
Mabel 92
Maggie Brocklebank 93
Maggie Townson 40
Maggie Williams 92
Maid of Irvine 88, 89
Maid of Mostyn 37
Manx Queen 40
Margaret 16, 21
Margaret Ann 35, 45, 60, 67, 69–70, 81, 82, 101 [Plate: 34]
Margaret Banister 35, 45, 67, 70–2, 77–80, 81, 84
Margaret Porter 49
Maria McMillan 87
Mary & May 24, 35, 44, 45, 64
Mary Ann Mandall 93, 119
Mary Armstead 90
Mary Ashburner 44, 45, 51–5, 60, 71, 73, 74, 75, 78, 90, 95, 103, 105 [Plate: 53]
Mary Atkinson 87, 92
Mary Bell 35, 44, 45, 48, 50, 63, 71, 78, 95
Mary Goldsworthy 92
Mary Jane 24, 45, 60, 61, 64, 73, 80, 103, 105
Mary Miller 90
Mary Sinclair 49, 60, 90, 119
Mary Watkinson 80, 89, 90
Millom Castle 80, 92
Mineral 37
Morecambe Belle 89
Morris's 80, 89

Nanny Latham 31, 45, 61, 67, 68, 80, 91
Nellie Bywater 50, 91, 93, 118

Nelly Schneider 88
Newland 59

Q–23 120–2

R. & M.J. Charnley 32, 35, 45, 59, 60, 63, 64, 73, 80, 82
R.E.A. Parkinson 90
R.F. Bell 39, 86
Result 80, 82–4, 102, 104, 118, 119–125, [Plates: 83, 121, 123, 124]
Richard Roper 60
Robert & Elizabeth 93
Rose 98–9 [Plates: 96, 97, 98, 99]
Rose Schneider 88
Rusko Castle 89
Ryelands 118

S. & E.A. Charnley 60
Sarah Jane 59
Sarah Latham 109, 128
Sea King 88–9
Seven Sisters 39, 89

T. & E.F. 92
Tom Roper 21, 22, 45, 64, 87, 119 [Plate: 23]
Twin Brothers 71, 73, 80, 86 [Plate: 81]
Twin Sisters 86

Ulverstone 14
Useful 45, 55, 74, 82, 95, 104, 106, 108–9, 116 [Plate: 109]

W. & M.J. 29
Warsash 87
White Rose 99–100
Whitriggs 87
William 16
William Ashburner 32, 36, 44, 45, 48, 49, 51, 55, 60, 63, 65–7, 76, 80, 95, 104, 114–6, 126–130 [Plates: Frontisp., 43, 47, 114, 115, 127, 129]
William Brocklebank 93
William Rawcliffe 93
William Stonard 64